Nooks and Corners of English Life, Past and Present

John Timbs

I. Early English Life.

DWELLING-PLACES OF THE EARLY BRITONS.

t has been well observed that the structure of a house reveals much of the mode of life adopted by its inhabitants. The representations of the dwellings of the people of the less cultivated parts of Europe, contrasted with those of the more cultivated countries, should afford us the means of comparing their different degrees of civilization. In the same manner we may measure the growth of improvement in any one country by an attentive consideration of the structure and arrangement of the homes of the people at different periods.

The aboriginal Britons are described as dwelling in slight cabins of reeds and wattles, and in some instances in *caverns of the earth*, many sets of which, arranged with some degree of symmetry, antiquaries have recognised; but Cæsar tells us that the maritime tribes had buildings in[Pg 2] the fashion of the Gauls—that is, of wood, of a circular figure, and thatched. Such towns as they had were clusters of huts erected on a cleared portion of the forest, which covered the greater part of the island; and they were invariably surrounded by a rampart, constructed of felled trees strongly interlaced and wattled, and a deep fosse, which together formed a fortification. The site of the modern city of London, with the river Thames in front, the river Fleet on the west, and an almost inpenetrable forest in the rear, may be taken as a fair specimen of the locality usually selected for the residence of the British Chief.[1]

That our ancestors lived in caves is attested by the existence of a group of these abodes near Penzance, the most remarkable of all ancient British Caves hitherto discovered in Cornwall, and thus described by Mr. J. Edwards, to the Royal Institution of that county:—"Half of a mile W.S.W. of Caër Bran, and four and a half miles W. by S. of Penzance, there is, in the village of Chapel Euny, a cave, consisting for the most part of a deep trench, walled with stones, and roofed with huge slabs. It extends 30 feet from N.N.W. to S.S.E., and then branches eastward, and probably also to the S. or S.W. So far it accords with the description of an ordinary British cave. But its floor (as I was informed by the miner who opened it about three years ago) was well paved with large granite blocks, beneath which, in the centre, ran a narrow gutter or bolt, made, I imagine, for admitting the external air into the innermost part of the building; from whence, after flowing back through the cave, it escaped by the cave's mouth—a mode of ventilation practised immemorially by the miners in this neighbourhood, when driving[Pg 3] adits or horizontal galleries under ground.

"Another peculiarity is still more remarkable. Its higher or northern end consisted of a circular floor, 12 feet in diameter, covered with a dome of granite, two-thirds of which are still exposed to view; and my informant had observed a still greater portion of the dome-roofed chamber. Every successive layer of the stones forming the dome overhangs considerably the layer immediately beneath it; so that the stones gradually approach each other as they rise, until the top stones must originally have completed the dome; not, however, like the key-stones of an arch, but by resting horizontally on the immediately subjacent circular layer. The miner found no pottery, or anything else, in the cave. The height of the present wall of the dome is about 6 feet above the lowest part I could see; how much lower the original floor might have been, I could not ascertain.

"Another British cave, not even referred to in any publication, is to be seen at Chyoster, nearly three miles north of Penzance, the walls of which, instead of being perpendicular, are constructed on the same principle as the inmost part of the cave at Chapel Euny; so that the tops of these walls which support the huge slabs forming the roof, are much nearer each other than their bases. Each cave formed part of a British village, that of old Chyoster being decidedly in the best state of preservation of all the British villages in this neighbourhood."[2]

Both caves are built of uncemented stones unmarked by any tool. The cave at Chyoster extended originally, as appears from its remains and the rubbish left by its recent spoilers, fifty feet or more in a straight[Pg 4] line up the sloping side of the hill. It is 6 feet high, 4 feet wide on the top, and 8 feet wide at the bottom, and is thought to have been originally a storehouse. It appears to have been built on the natural surface of the hillside, and then covered over with stones and earth, and planted with the evergreens which still abound there.

A few years subsequently to the above investigations, in one of those intellectual excursions by means of which our acquaintance with the early history of our island is so greatly extended, the following results were arrived at:—In the autumn of 1865, in an excursion made jointly by the Royal Institution of Cornwall and the Penzance Natural History Society, they inspected on the north coast of the county, Gurnard's Head, a rocky promontory, jutting some distance into the sea, and bearing very distinct traces of having been fortified by the early Britons against an enemy attacking from the sea, this being the only specimen of an ancient British fortification where traces of sea defences have been found. In all other cases they seem to have been erected as a protection from an attack by the land side, and to have been evidently the last retreat of the natives.

Next was visited the Bosphrennis Bee-hive Hut, first brought to light by the Cambrian Archæological Society: it was seen in clusters or villages by Cæsar. And, on an eminence near the village of Porthemear, was found a large inclosed circle, now hidden by briars and thorns, which, on examination, showed the remains of several circular huts, leaving no doubt that here a considerable ancient British village had once existed.

Of the homes of the Picts, the most distinguished among the barbarous[Pg 5] tribes inhabiting the woods and marshes of North Britain, there remain some specimens in the Orkneys: they are rude and miserable dwellings underground, but they are supposed to be calculated for the requirements of a more advanced state of society than that of the dwellers in Picts' houses. A complete drawing of one of the Orkney specimens has been made, and was exhibited to the British Archæological Association in 1866.

PICTS' HOUSE.

About the year 1853, there was discovered in Aberdeenshire a Pict's house, in the parish of Tarland. It is a subterranean vault, nearly semicircular, and from five to six feet in height; the sides built with stones, and roofed with large stones, six or seven feet wide, and a kind of granite. These excavations have been found in various parishes of Aberdeenshire, as well as in several of the neighbouring counties. In the parish of Old Deer, some sixty years back, a whole village was met with; and, about the same time, in a glen at the back of Stirlinghill, in the parish of Peterhead, one was discovered which contained some fragments of bones and several flint arrow-heads and battle-axes, in various stages of manufacture. Such buildings underground as those described as Picts' houses were not uncommon on the borders of the Tweed. A number of them, apparently constructed as above, were discovered in a field in Berwickshire about fifty years ago. They were supposed to have been made for the detention of prisoners taken in the frays during the border feuds; and afterwards they were employed to conceal spirits, smuggled either across the border or from abroad.

Professor Phillips, in his very able volume on Yorkshire, describes the houses of the Brigantes (highlanders), inhabitants of the hilly country towards the north of Britain, and extending from the German Ocean to the [Pg 6] Irish Sea. Of these huts there appear to be three varieties, of which we have only the foundations. The first occurs in north-eastern and south-eastern Yorkshire; the ground is excavated in a circular shape, so as to make a pit from six to eight feet, or even sixteen or eighteen feet in diameter, with a raised border, and three to five feet in depth. Over this cavity we must suppose the branches of trees placed to form a conical roof, which, perhaps, might be made weather-proof by wattling, a covering of rushes, or turf. The opening we may believe to have been placed on the side removed from the prevalent wind: fire in the centre of the hut thus constructed, has left traces in many of the houses examined. The pits in Westerdale are called "ref-holes," *i.e.* roof-holes, for our Saxon word *roof* has the meaning of the Icelandic *raf* and Swedish *ref*. In several places these pits are associated in such considerable numbers as to give the idea of a village, or even town. On Danby Moor, the pits are divided in two parallel lines, bounded externally by banks, and divided internally by an open space like a street; a stream divides the settlement into two parts; there are no walls at the end of the streets; in the most westerly part is a circular walled space, thirty-five feet in diameter.

"A second type of these foundations of huts has been observed south of the village of Skipwith, near Riccall, south-east of York. These were oval or circular rings slightly excavated in the heathy surface, on the drier parts of the common. On digging into this area, marks of fire were found: they were concluded to be the foundation-lines of huts, mostly enclosed by single or double mounds or ditches.

"The third form of hut foundation, an incomplete ring of stone walls,[Pg 7] has only yet been observed in Yorkshire, on the summit of Ingleborough. How strange to find at this commanding height," says Professor Phillips, "encircled by a thick and strong wall, and within this wall the unmistakeable foundations of ancient habitations! The Rev. Robert Cooke, in 1851, concluded Ingleborough to be a great hill-fort of the Britons, defended by a wall like others known in Wales, and furnished with houses like the 'Cittian,' of Gwynedd. The area inclosed is about 15 acres, in which space are nineteen horse-shoe-shaped low foundations, evidently the foundations of ancient huts, the antecedent of the cottages of England,—a low wall foundation, a roof formed by inclined rafters, and covered by boughs, heath, rushes, grass, straw, or sods. The relative dates, surely, admit of no doubt. The huts and walls of Ingleborough exhibit principles of construction which remove them from the catalogue of barbarian works."[3]

The Britons, before the first Roman invasion, slept on skins spread on the floor of their rude dwellings. Rushes and heath were afterwards substituted by the Romans for skins; and on the introduction of agriculture they slept upon straw, which, indeed, was used as a couch in the royal chambers of England at the close of the 14th century.

BRITAIN BEFORE THE ROMAN COLONIZATION.

itherto we have but glanced at the dwelling-places of our ancestors, chiefly from existing evidences. Of the general condition of the people before the Roman Conquest, we find this picturesque account in Lappenberg's able work on the Anglo-Saxon Kings. The earliest inhabitants of Britain, as far as we know, were probably of that great family, the main branches of which, distinguished by the designation of Celts, spread themselves so widely over middle and western Europe. They crossed over from the neighbouring country of Gaul. At a later period, the Belgæ, actuated by martial restlessness or the love of plunder, assailed the southern and western coasts of the island, and settled there, driving the Celts into the inland country. Lappenberg's life-like picture of the condition of these people is as follows:—

"In the southern parts of England, which had become more civilized through commerce, the cultivation of grain, to which the mildness of the climate was favourable, had been greatly improved by the art of marling. The daily consumption was taken from the unthrashed corn, preserved in caves, which they prepared for food, but did not bake as bread. Horticulture was not in use among them, nor the art of making cheese; yet the great number of buildings, of people, and of cattle, appeared striking to the Romans. Copper and bits of iron, according to weight,[Pg 9] served as money. Their custom of painting themselves with blue and green, for the purpose of terrifying their enemies, as well as that of tattooing, was retained till a later period by the Picts of the North. At certain sacrifices, even the women, painted in a similar manner, resembling Ethiopians, went about without clothing. Long locks and mustachios were general. Like the Gauls, they decorated the middle finger with a ring. Their round simple huts of reeds or wood resembled those of that people; and the Gaulish chequered coloured mantles are still in common use in the Scottish Highlands. Their clothing, more especially that of the Belgic tribes of the south, enveloped the whole body; a girdle encircled the waist, and chains of metal hung about the breast. The hilts of their huge pointless swords were adorned with the teeth of marine animals; their shields were small. The custom of fighting in chariots, on the axles of which scythes were fastened, and in the management of which they showed great skill, was peculiar to this and some other of the Celtic nations, in a generally level country, and where the horses were not sufficiently powerful to be used for cavalry. The charioteer was the superior person; the servant bore the weapons. They began their attacks with taunting songs and deafening howls. Their fortresses or towns consisted in the natural defence of impenetrable forests. In the interior of the country were found only the more rugged characteristics of a people engaged in the rearing of cattle; which, together with the chase, supplied skins for clothing, and milk and flesh for food. The northern part of the country seems in great measure to have been abandoned to the shaft and javelin of the roving hunter, as skilful as he was bold. Simplicity, integrity, temperance, with a[Pg 10] proneness to dissension, are mentioned as the leading characteristics of the nation. The reputation of bravery was more especially ascribed to the Norman races."

The only persons in Britain who possessed any knowledge before the Roman invasion, and even for some considerable time after it, were the Druids: the real extent of their attainments is, however, doubtful and superficial, from the fact that, though they were acquainted with the Greek letters, they taught almost entirely by memory, and committed little or nothing to writing. A summary of what is known concerning Druidical knowledge is contained in the following particulars:—Concerning the universe, they believed that it should never be entirely destroyed or annihilated, though it was expected to suffer a succession of violent changes and revolutions, by the predominating powers of fire and water. They professed to have great knowledge of the movements of the heavens and stars; indeed, their religion required some attention to astronomy, since they paid considerable regard to the changes of the moon. Their time was computed by nights, according to very ancient practice, by moons or months; and by years, when the planet had gone the revolutions of the seasons. That at least they knew the reversion of the seasons, as adapted to agricultural purposes, is evident from the fact, that Cæsar landed in Britain on the 26th day of August, when he states that the harvest was all completed, excepting one field, which was more backward than the rest of the country.

The sacred animal of the Druids' religion was the milk-white bull; the sacred bird, the wren; the sacred tree, the oak; the sacred plant, the mistletoe; the sacred herbs, the trefoil and the vervain; the sacred[Pg 11] form, that of three divine letters or rays, in the shape of a cross, symbolizing the triple aspect of God. The sacred herbs and plant, with another plant, hyssop, the emblem of fortitude in adversity, were gathered on the sixth day of the moon. The great festivals of Druidism were three: the solstitial festivals of the rise and fall of the year, and the winter festival. At the spring festival, the bâltân, or sacred fire, was brought down by means of a burning-glass from the sun. No hearth in the island was held sacred till the fire on it had been relit from the bâltân. The bâltân became the Easter festival of Christianity, as the mid-winter festival, in which the mistletoe was cut with the golden sickle from the sacred oak, became Christmas. The mistletoe, with its three berries, was the symbol of the Deity in his triple aspect—its growth on the oak, of the incarnation of the Deity in man.

The canonicals of the Arch-Druid were extremely gorgeous. On his head he wore a tiara of gold, in his girdle the gem of augury, on his breast the *ior morain*, or breastplate of judgment; below it, the *glan neidr*, or draconic egg: on the forefinger of the right hand, the signet ring of the order; on the forefinger of the left, the gem of inspiration. Before him were borne the volume of esoteric mysteries, and the golden implement with which the mistletoe was gathered. His robe was of a white linen, with a broad purple border.

The sickle with which the mistletoe was cut could not have been of gold, though so described. Stukeley maintains that the Druids cut the mistletoe with their upright hatchets of brass, called celts, put at the end of their staffs. The kind of mistletoe found to this day in Greece is the same with that found in England; and Sir James Smith, the[Pg 12] distinguished botanist, contends that when the superstitions of the East travelled westward, our Druids adopted the Greek mistletoe as being more holy or efficacious than any other. The Druids, doubtless, dispensed the plant at a high price: "as late as the seventeenth century peculiar efficacy was attached to it, and a piece hung round the neck was considered a safeguard against witches." (*W. Sandys, F.S.A.*)

It is concluded that the Druids possessed some knowledge of arithmetic, using the Greek characters as figures, in the public and private computations mentioned by Cæsar; they were not unacquainted with mensuration, geometry, and geography, because, as judges, they decided disputes about the limits of fields, and are even said to have been engaged in determining the measure of the world. Their mechanical skill, and particularly their acquaintance with the lever, is generally argued from the enormous blocks of Stonehenge, and the numerous other massive erections of rude stone which are yet remaining in many parts of the kingdom, and which are commonly attributed to these times.

The remains of the mystic monument of Stonehenge, which stands in the midst of Salisbury Plain, have been variously explained, as to the purpose for which Stonehenge was reared. When perfect, it consisted of two circles and two ellipses of upright stones, concentric, and environed by a bank and ditch; and outside this boundary, of a single upright stone, and a sacred way, *via sacra*, or cursus. One writer has beheld in Stonehenge a work of antediluvians, and another, a sanctuary of the Danes; and Inigo Jones, a temple of the Romans. By the Saxons it was termed *Stonhengist*, the hanging stones; and thence came Stonehenge, of which we have this terrible historic legend:—

Ebusa, brother of Hengist, with his brother Octa, landed on the Frith of[Pg 13] Forth with an armament of five hundred vessels. The Britons flew to arms. A conference was proposed by Hengist, and accepted by Vortigern. It was held at Stonehenge (Hengist's Stones), and attended by most of the nobility of Britain. On the sixth day, at the high feast, when the sun was declining, was perpetrated the "Massacre of the Long

Knives," the blackest crime, with the exception of that of St. Bartholomew, in the annals of any nation. The signal for the Saxons to prepare to plunge their knives, concealed in their boots and under their military cloaks, into the breasts of their gallant, unsuspicious conquerors was, "Let us now speak of friendship and love." The signal for action were the words, "Nemet your Saxas," ("Out with your knives,") and the raising of the banner of Hengist—a white horse on a red field—over the head of Vortigern. Four hundred and eighty of the Christian chivalry of Britain fell before sunset by the hand of the pagan assassins; three only of name—Eidol Count of Gloucester, and the Princes of Vendotia and Cambria—escaping, the first by almost superhuman courage and presence of mind. Priests, ambassadors, bards, and the boyish scions of many noble families, were piled together in one appalling spectacle on the site of the banquet, "Moel Œore"—the Mound of Carnage, about three hundred yards north of the great Temple.

A learned band of inquirers are induced to consider Stonehenge as a Druidic temple, reared on the solitary plain long before Roman, Dane, or Saxon had set foot within the country. Still, Stonehenge was the work of two distinct eras: the smaller circles are attributed to the Celtic Britons, and the other to the Belgæ. There is a common notion that the[Pg 14]stones cannot be counted twice alike; but when Charles II. visited Stonehenge in 1651, he counted and re-counted the stones, and proved to his satisfaction the fallacy of this notion.[4]

A few months since, Professor Nielson, in a paper read to the Ethnological Society, considered that Stonehenge was a temple of early fire-worshippers, and of pre-Druidical origin, and belonging to the "Bronze Period" of the northern archæologists. The remains of Stonehenge, he remarked, are placed, not on the summit, but on the declivity of a hill surrounded by numerous barrows, from which bronze articles have been exhumed, with others of flint, but never any of iron. He considers that fire-worshippers preceded Druids in Britain and Gaul, and gives what he regards as numerous proofs of the building of such stone open temples by colonies of Phœnicians. Circles of large stones, exactly identical in description with those called Celtic or Druidical, he continued, are found in countries where neither Celts nor Druids ever existed; but who knows at what time the ancient religion of this country may be truly said to have been pre-Druidical or pre-Celtic in its principles? From various considerations the author of the paper thinks there may be sufficient reason to regard the remains of[Pg 15] Stonehenge as Phœnician, and connected with the rites of Baal, or the early worship of fire.

Mr. Fergusson and others say that to the Buddhists rather than to the Druids we owe Stonehenge. It is also thought to have been an assemblage of burial-places.

A popular poet has thus apostrophised this mysterious circle and its historical associations:

"Thou noblest monument of Albion's isle!
Whether by Merlin's aid from Scythia's shore
To Amber's fatal plain Pendragon bore,
Huge frame of giant hands, the mighty pile,
To entomb his Britons slain by Hengist's guile:
Or Druid priests, sprinkled with human gore,
Taught 'mid thy mighty maze their mystic lore:
Or Danish chiefs, enrich'd with savage spoil,
To Victory's idol vast, an unhewn shrine,
Rear'd the rude heap: or in thy hallow'd round,
Repose the kings of Brutus' genuine line:
Or here those kings in solemn state were crown'd:
Studious to trace thy wondrous origin,
We muse on many an ancient tale renown'd."
WARTON.

The Druids were suspected of magic, which, Pliny remarks, derived its origin from medicine. They highly esteemed a kind of stone, or fossil, called *Anginum Ovum*, or Serpents' Egg, which should make the possessor superior in all disputes, and procure the favour of great persons. It was in the form of a ring of glass, either plain or streaked, and was asserted to be produced by the united salivas of a cluster of serpents, raised up in the air by their hissing; when, to be perfectly efficacious, it was to be caught in a clean white cloth before it fell to the ground, the person who received it instantly mounting a swift horse, and riding away at full speed from the rage of the serpents, who[Pg 16] pursued him with like rapidity, until they arrived at a river. It has been supposed that these charms were no other than rings of painted glass; and, as it is allowed that the British had home manufactures of glass, it seems that there were imitations of them sold at an equally high price with the real amulet. Their genuineness was to be tried by their setting them in gold, and observing if they swam against the stream when cast into the water; they were, in fact, beads of glass, and the notion of their rare virtues exactly accords with the African exposition in the present day of the Aggry beads. Sir Richard Colt Hoare found one of the Druidic beads in a barrow in Wiltshire, in material resembling little figures found with the mummies in Egypt, and to be seen in the British Museum. "This curious bead," says Sir Richard Hoare, "has two circular lines, of opaque sky-blue and white, and seems to represent a serpent entwined round a centre, which is perforated. This was certainly one of the Glain Neidyr of the Britons; derived from *Glain*, which is pure and holy, and *Neidyr*, a snake."[5]

The accounts we have of the Druidical orations and discourses afford some notion of their admitted eloquence, which was of a lofty, impassioned, and mysterious character. Their counsel was equally solicited and regarded; and those orators who succeeded the Druids in the Western Islands seem to have possessed no less power, since, if one of them asked anything even of the greatest inhabitant, as his dress, horse, or arms, it was immediately given up to him—sometimes from respect, and sometimes from fear of being satirized, which was considered a great dishonour. The British chieftains, also, appear to have been gifted with considerable oratorical powers when they addressed[Pg 17] their soldiers before a battle; as Tacitus translates the British names of such by "incentives to war."

The Druids were the only physicians and surgeons to the Britons; in which professions they blended some knowledge of natural medicines, with the general superstitions by which they were characterised. The practice of the healing art has ever commanded the esteem of the rudest nations; hence it was the obvious policy of the priests or Druids to study the properties of plants. Their famous Mistletoe, or *All-heal*, we have seen, was a cure in many diseases, an antidote to poisons, and a sure remedy against infection. We have in the present day a popular remedy for cuts and other wounds, sold under the name of *Heal-all*. Another plant, called Samulus, or Marsh-wort, which grew chiefly in damp places, was believed to be of excellent effect in preserving the health of swine or oxen, when it had been bruised and put into their water-troughs. But it was required to be gathered fasting and with the left hand, without looking back when it was being plucked. A kind of hedge hyssop, called *Selago*, was esteemed to be a general charm and preservative from sudden accidents and misfortunes; and it was to be gathered with nearly the same ceremony as the mistletoe. To these may be added Vervain, the herb *Britannica*, which was either the great Water-dock, or scurvy-grass; besides several other plants, the virtues of which, however, were greatly augmented by the rites in plucking them; superstitions not entirely out of use, while the old herbals were regarded as books of medicine. We gather from Pliny's *Natural History* some hints on the preparation of these materials, showing that sometimes the juices were extracted by bruising and steeping them in cold water, and sometimes by boiling them; that they were occasionally infused in a[Pg 18] liquor which he calls wine; that they were administered in fumigations; and that the dried leaves, stalks, and roots of plants, were also used to impart a virtue to various liquids. The almost solitary shop of the herbalist in our great market in Covent Garden, will thus carry the mind's eye back through many centuries.

It appears that the Druids prepared ointments and salves from vegetables. Of their surgery nothing is certainly known, though much has been conjectured of their acquaintance with anatomy, from the barbarity of their human sacrifices; but it is probable that their practice extended only to the plainer branches of the art, as healing of wounds, setting of fractured bones, reducing dislocations, &c.; all which were perhaps conducted with great rudeness, though with considerable ceremony. It has been asserted that one of the Druid doctors, called Hierophilus, read lectures on the bodies of upwards of 700 living men, to display the wonders and secrets of the human fabric.

The Greek letters were used by the Druids for keeping the public or private records, the only matters which they reduced to writing. The Druid schools and seminaries were held in the caves such as we have already described, or in the recesses of the sacred groves and forests of Britain. The most eminent academy is said to have been in the Isle of Anglesey, near the residence of the Arch-Druid; and there are still two spots there called "the Place of Studies," and "the Astronomer's Circle." The British youth, separated from their parents, were under Druidical instruction until they were fourteen, and no one was capable of a public employment who had not been educated by a Druid. The Roman invasion, however, greatly improved the Druidical plan of instruction; since Julius Agricola was careful that the sons of the principal Britons[Pg 19] should be taught the liberal sciences. His endeavours were considerably assisted by the expulsion of the Druids, which took place about this period; and also by the ability of the British youth, whom he declared to excel the Roman. The ranks of the priests were recruited from the noblest families of the early Britons: their education, which often extended over a period of twenty years, comprehended the whole sciences of the age; and beside their sacred calling, they were invested with power to decide civil disputes. Their dwellings and temples were situated in the thickest oak groves, which were sacred to the Supreme Deity.

No sculptured stones or storied bricks have ever been found of this period; nothing but weapons of stone, of bronze, and lastly, of iron, remain to attest the slow progress of a rude people towards a higher stage of civilization, in the arts relating to the chase and to war. As the Gauls used to ornament their shields and helmets with brass images of animals and horns, it is not improbable that some rude endeavour decorated the armour of the Britons. Whatever their skill might be, it was, doubtless, greatly improved by the Romans, since their bas-reliefs and effigies have been found in different parts of the kingdom; and as early as A.D. 61, not twenty years after the invasion of Claudius Cæsar, a statue of Liberty was erected at Camulodunum, or Colchester.

The early custom of painting the body has been incidentally mentioned. The Southern Britons stained their bodies with woad, deep blue, or a general tint; the Northern Britons added something of design by tracing upon their limbs figures of herbs, flowers, and trees, and all kinds of animals. It is doubtful whether in these arts they were improved by the Romans; since the delineation of deities, which Gildas mentions, on the[Pg 20] walls of the British houses, are said by him only to resemble demons.

Although Cæsar describes the natives of Britain as a hardy race of shepherds, whose simple wants were provided for in their own country, even then the commerce of Britain was of considerable importance; since the tin of Cornwall, and the hides of the vast flocks of cattle, had already induced the merchants of Phœnicia to visit and settle on our southern shores. They are believed to have supplied the Eastern world with Cornish tin, of such important use in the manufacture of bronze tools, weapons, and helmets of antiquity.[6]

The principal and most ancient exports from Britain were, besides its[Pg 21] famous tin, lead and copper; but lime and chalk, salt, corn, cattle, skins, earthenware, horses, staves, and native dogs, which appear always to have been held in great estimation, were also carried thence. The largest and finest pearls, too, are said to have been found on the British coasts; and the wicker baskets of Britain are celebrated by Martial and Juvenal as luxuries in Rome. And from Rome, the Britons received ivory, bridles, gold chains, amber cups, and drinking glasses.

There are few remains of the ornaments in use amongst the Britons at a very early period: there are many relics, however, of that just preceding the Roman Conquest. We find torques or chains for the neck and wrists coarsely manufactured, like curb-chains. Beads were also in use. Many of the most ancient ornaments were cruciform. With the Roman Conquest came in the Roman ornamentation. This does not seem to have been modified by its introduction into Britain. The Romans imported Rome bodily into Britain, as was their custom in all the conquered countries, and the Britons were too uncivilized to make improvements on what was presented to them. For this reason it is that there is the greatest difficulty to distinguish between pure Roman and Anglo-Roman ornaments.

That the Britons both understood and practised the art of working in[Pg 22] metals, is ascertained from the relics of their weapons, as axes, spear and arrow heads, swords, &c. which are yet extant; and it is supposed that tin was the first ore which they discovered and refined. Lead they found in great abundance, very near the surface. The British iron was of uncommon occurrence, and was much prized, since it was used in personal ornaments, and was even formed into rings and tallies for money. This then precious metal has contributed more than any other to the greatness of England in those mighty works of our own times, her railways and vast ships of passage and war.

All the Britons, except the Druids, were trained early to war. Their most ancient weapons were bows, reed-arrows with flint or bone heads, quivers of basket-work, oaken spears; and flint battle-axes, which are now considered to have been called *celts*, though there is no connexion between this word and the name of the nation, Celtæ. The British forces included infantry, cavalry, and such as fought from war-chariots. The southern foot soldiers wore a coarse woollen tunic, and over it a cloak reaching below the middle, the legs and thighs being covered with close garments. They had brass helmets, breastplates full of hooks, and long swords suspended from an iron or brazen girdle. They also carried large darts, with iron shafts eighteen inches long; and shields of wicker or wood. The inland foot soldiers were more lightly armed, with spears and small shields, and dressed in skins of oxen. The Caledonians and other northerns usually fought naked, with only a light target; their weapons pointless swords and short spears. The British cavalry were mounted upon small but strong horses, without saddles, and their arms were mostly the[Pg 23] same as those of the infantry. The soldiers of the war-chariots were mostly the chiefs of the nation, and the flower of the British youth. Their chariots were of wicker, upon wooden wheels, with hooks and scythe blades of bronze attached to the axles, with which the charioteer mowed down the enemy. Other chariots contained several persons, who darted lances; both machines broke the hostile ranks, and threw an army into confusion. Their number must have been very great; since Cassibellaunus, after he had disbanded his army, had still 4,000 remaining.

Primitive British vessels have occasionally been found embedded in morasses. In 1866, there was discovered at Warningcamp, about a mile from South Stoke, in Sussex, a canoe, in widening a ditch, or sewer, which empties itself into the river Arun: although now narrow, it appears to have been, until recently, of much greater extent, and at one time must have formed an important estuary of the river, for in the soil are now seen several thousands of shells of fresh-water fish. About four feet beneath the surface the end of the canoe was found. It proved to be 13½ feet long, and consisted of the hollowed trunk of an oak tree; but bears evidence of design, for having insertions cut on the edge, in which it is evident three seats had been secured for the boatmen. It is perhaps not so interesting as the canoe discovered at Stoke about twenty years ago, and now in the British Museum, because it is not so perfect. Still, it would appear of the greatest antiquity, from its extremely rude form. The canoe is the general vessel of New Zealand, the present state and people of which country are thought to exhibit more nearly than any other land the condition of Britain when the Romans entered it nearly eighteen centuries since.

[Pg 24]

THE ROMANS IN ENGLAND.

"The Romans in England they once did sway."

OLD SONG.

rchæological information obtained of late years shows that at the time of the Roman invasion, there was a larger amount of civilization in Ancient Britain than had been generally supposed: that in addition to the knowledge of the old inhabitants in agriculture, in the training and rearing of horses, cows, and other domestic animals, they were able to work in mines, had skill in the construction of war-chariots and other carriages, and in the manufacture of metals; and there is evidence that British manufactures and materials were exported to certain parts of the Continent, probably in British vessels. The ancient coinage of this period is also well worthy of attention.

In connexion with the Ancient British period, it would seem that probably 2,000 years before the Roman times there had been in Great Britain a certain degree of civilization, which from various causes declined in extent. If Stonehenge may be considered as of the same antiquity as similar remains in various parts of the East—which are reckoned by good authorities to be 4,000 years old—we had in this country a degree of civilization which was contemporary with the prosperous period of the Egyptian empire; and, in times more immediately[Pg 25] preceding the Roman occupation, we know that Britain was the grand source of Druidical illumination (whatever relation that may have had to a true civilization) to the whole of Continental Europe.

That the Ancient Britons, even after they were conquered by the Romans, had still a strength considered dangerous, is shown by the fact that upwards of forty barbarian legions which had followed the Roman standards were settled chiefly upon the northern and eastern coasts; and it is shown that a force of about 19,200 Roman foot and 1,700 horse was required to secure peace, and the carrying out of certain laws in the island.

The encampments, Roman and British, are thus described. In the Roman camp, the plan is invariably the same—a rectangular area, surrounded by a ditch, the earth thrown inwards, forming a high mound, defended on the top with wooden palisades, but of these all vestiges have disappeared: in the middle of each side the entrance, from which a way led to the opposite gate; and at or near the outer action of the two ways, was the Prætorium, the remains of which may frequently be traced. These camps are not usually found on very high hills. The Britons, on the other hand, always occupied the highest ground, frequently an isolated hill, which they surrounded with deep trenches and a series of low terraces scooped out of the side of the hill, rising one above another, not in an unbroken line, but forming, in some places, a network of flat forms, commanding every approach to the entrances, with advantageous positions for the sling, in the use of which the Britons peculiarly excelled. Every inequality of the ground was taken advantage of: the entrances sometimes opened into one of the trenches, through which the approach to[Pg 26] the interior leads, so as to expose an enemy to an overwhelming storm of darts and stones from the heights above.

Our early historians mention four great roads by which South Britain was traversed, and these usually have been considered as the work of its conquerors; but recent researches have led to the conclusion that the Romans only kept in repair, and perhaps improved, the roads which they found in use on their settlement in the island. Along the course of the great roads, or in their immediate vicinity, are found the principal cities, which, in pursuance of their usual policy, the Romans either founded or re-edified; and to which, according to the privilege bestowed, the various names were given of colonies, municipalities, stipendiary, and Latian cities. Many other Roman roads exist.

"The old British roads, or trackways, were not paved or gravelled, but had a basis of turf, and wound along the tops or sides of the chains of hills which lay in their way. Surrey furnishes a remarkable example of such an appropriation of one of its chalk ridges; and it may be inferred that the agger called the Hog's Back presented to the earliest inhabitants of Britain a natural causeway of solid chalk, covered with a soft verdant turf, peculiarly suited to the traffic of the British chariots, and connecting the western Belgæ with the Cantii, and affording through them an access towards the continent at all seasons of the year. These advantageous peculiarities, no doubt, rendered it the grand strategic route by which an invading army would have penetrated to the westward; and Vespasian may be supposed, with great reason, to have marched along it."[7]

To return to the Roman Roads. Although inferior to the Britons of the[Pg 27] nineteenth century in the art of spending money, if judged by the present state of science, the Roman road-makers could not be despicable engineers: their levels were chosen on different principles, but their lines of roads passed through the same counties, and generally in the same direction as our railways. A diagram in the *Quarterly Review*, exhibiting a general view of the direction of the principal Roman roads in England, shows that, on comparing one or two of our principal lines, we shall find, that the Great Western supplies the place, with a little deviation near Reading, of the Roman *iter* from London to Bath and Bristol; the Liverpool and Manchester, and on to Leeds and York, replaces the northern Watling-street; the Great Eastern follows a Roman way, and so of the rest.[8]

Professor Phillips has thus strikingly illustrated this comparison to be made in the North of England. "As now two railways, so a little earlier two mail-roads, and far earlier two British tracks, conducted the traveller from South Britain through the sterner country of the North. This is the inevitable result of the great anticlinal ridge of stratified rocks—our Pennine Alps—thrown up from Derbyshire to the Scottish Border. This is the 'heaven water' boundary of the river drainages: on the west of it ran the line of road northward from Mancunium; on the east of it the line from Eburacum; the former nearly in the course of the North-eastern, the latter not lately deviating from the North-eastern rail. Along these routes Agricola divided his troops: these were the routes followed alike by the Pict and Scot, Plantagenet and Tudor, Cavalier and Roundhead. Wade lay on the east of these[Pg 28]mountains, while the Stuart overran their western slopes: and Rupert swept up the western tract to surprise the besiegers of York."[9] On the whole it appears that the lines of the earlier British roads were indicated by the great features of nature; and that, for the most part, the Roman ways followed and straightened the old tracks.

"It is equally remarkable and significant that the Roman municipia and coloniæ became the centres of Saxon and Anglican strength; and if in this day of the steam-engine their relative importance is less conspicuous, it is still a matter of English history. From the top of the Brigantian mountain we may reanimate the busy world which has long passed away from life: the jealous boundaries of propriety disappear; the chimneys vanish; the thundering hammer is silent. From the midst of boundless forests of oak and pine, rise many peaks or bare summits of heaths crowned with monumental stones or burial mounds. The rivers gliding through the deepest shade, bear at intervals the light wicker boat, still frequent in Dyfed, loaded with fish, or game, or fruit. On dry banks above are the conical huts of the rude hunters, and near them the not narrower houses of the dead,—perhaps not far off the cave of the wolf. Lower down the dale, the richest of pastures is covered with the fairest of cattle and the most active of horses. Still lower, the storehouse of the tribe, the water station to which large canoes, hollowed from the mighty oaks of Hatfield Chase, have brought from the Humber the highly-prized beads and amulets, perhaps the precious bronze which is to replace the arrow, spear, and axe of stone.

"Both north and south of the Humber very different scenes appear on the[Pg 29] high and open Wold: within the memory of man, many parts of these wild regions were untouched by plough, traversed by bustard, and covered with innumerable flocks. The more we reflect on the remains which crowd this region—the numerous tracks, the countless tumuli, the frequent dykes—the clearer grows the resemblance between the Yorkshire Wolds and the Downs of Wilts and Dorset. On opening the tumuli we discover similar ornaments, and from whatever cause, consanguinity of race, or analogy of employments and way of life, the earliest people must be allowed to have been very much the same along the dry chalk hills from the vicinity of Bridlington to the country of Dorchester. This is the region of the tumuli: on its surface are not unfrequent foundations of the British huts."

The main population did not reside on these hills, since they are for miles naturally dry. But, from below their edge rise innumerable bright streams, by which, "no doubt, were the settled habitations, the Cyttian of the early Britons, followed by the Saxon *tun* and the Danish *by*; on the hills above were long boundary fences, and within these the raths and tumuli, the monumental stones and idols. In situations where nature gave peculiar advantages, one of the grand manufactures of the tribes was established. The fabrication of pottery, from the Kimmeridge clay about Malton, was undoubtedly very extensive in British days, and characteristic both as to substance and fashion; that of bricks and tiles at York was equally considerable in Roman days, and it is curious to walk now into the large brick-yards and potteries which are successfully conducted at these same places, on the very sites which furnished the funeral urn, and the perforated tube which distributed air from the hypocaust."

We may acquire some idea of Roman road-making from the following[Pg 30] details:—"From the wall of Antoninus to Rome, and from thence to Jerusalem, that is, from the north-west to the south-east point of the empire, was measured a distance of 3,740 English miles; of this distance 85 miles only were sea-passages, the rest was the *road of polished silex*. Posts were established along these lines of high road, so that 100 miles a day might be with ease accomplished. A fact related by Pliny affords an example of the quickest travelling in a carriage in ancient times. Tiberius Nero, with three carriages, accomplished a journey of 200 miles in twenty-four hours, when he went to see his brother Drusus, who was sick in Germany." (*Burgess.*)

The towns, and forts, and roads are, however, very far from being the only traces of Roman occupation that remain in our country. Camps, occupying well-chosen positions, occur in numbers, which testify the difficulty with which the subjugation of the island was accomplished; while the remains of stately buildings, with ornamented baths, mosaic pavements, fresco paintings and statuary, and articles of personal ornament, which are discovered almost every time that the earth is uncovered to any considerable depth, prove the eventual wide diffusion of the elegant and luxurious mode of life which it was the aim of the conquerors to introduce. Roman glass and pottery, in great variety, and frequently of the most elegant shape, abound; but the most valuable are the sepulchral urns, which betoken the neighbourhood of towns, of which perhaps no other traces now remain.

At Aldborough, in Yorkshire (the Roman Isurium), and in some of the small towns on the line of Hadrian's wall, in Northumberland, masses of[Pg 31] the small houses have been uncovered, and their appearance leads us to believe that the houses of a Roman town in Britain were grouped thickly together; that they were mostly separated by narrow alleys, and that there were in general few streets of any magnitude; most ancient towns, even in the present day, abound with alleys.

It is maintained by some antiquaries that London is almost of Roman origin. In the "Conquest of Britain," by Claudius, A.D. 44, "the first care of the Romans was, to make good military communication across the north of Essex, and the tenure of

London was then a matter of minor importance. It is remarkable that, though the bridge over the Thames is mentioned, there is no allusion to a city. It is not improbable that the Romans, perceiving the advantage of the position at the head of the estuary and at the mouth of a large river, and having the power (after the occupation of both banks of the Thames) of giving it better military protection than the native tribes, continually in conflict, could ever give it, promoted the commercial growth of the city by all means in their power. Thus it would seem that London, almost from its origin, is a Roman city."

In the revolt of the Britons, A.D. 61, Londinium (London), already, according to Tacitus, "famed for the vast conflux of traders, and her abundant commerce and plenty," was destroyed by the Britons.

London has hitherto yielded up many traces of the manners and indications of our Roman ancestors, but few of our earliest antiquities. Our Roman London has been buried beneath the foundations of the modern city, or rather beneath the ruins of a city several times destroyed, and as often rebuilt. It is only at rare intervals that excavators strike[Pg 32] down upon the venerable remains of the earliest occupation; and huge masses of genuine Roman fortifications have been seen in our day, but by few persons in comparison with the busy multitudes which daily throng our streets.

When the Roman legions were finally withdrawn, Britain possessed more than fifty walled towns, united by roads with stations upon them; there were also numerous military walled stations. These towns and stations possessed public buildings, baths, and temples, and edifices of considerable grandeur and architectural importance, and their public places were often embellished with statues: one bronze equestrian statue, at least, decorated Lincoln; a bronze statue stood in a temple at Bath; one of the temples at Colchester bore an inscription in large letters of bronze; and Verulam possessed a theatre for dramatic representations, capable of holding some 2,000 or 3,000 spectators. Verulam now presents nothing to the eye but some fields, a church, and a dwelling-house, surrounded by walls overgrown with trees. Colchester, Lincoln, and Bath exhibit few indications of their Roman times; but Chester is richer in these characteristics. The spacious villas which once spread over Roman Britain, are now known to us as from time to time their splendid pavements are laid open under cornfields and meadows. In a nook of the busy Strand is a Roman bath, of accredited antiquity, its bricks and stucco corresponding with those in the City wall: this bath can be traced to have belonged to the villa of a Leicestershire family, which stood upon this spot,—the north bank of the Thames.

In the year 1864, there was discovered on the site of the portico of the East India-house, in Leadenhall-street, the remains of a Roman room, *in situ* 19 ft. 6 in. below the present surface of the street, and 6 ft.[Pg 33] below the lowest foundations of the India-house. The room was about 16 ft. square; the walls built of Roman bricks and rubble; the floor paved with good red tesseræ, but without any ornamental pattern; the walls plastered and coloured in fresco of an agreeable tint, and decorated with red lines and bands. This was a small room, attached to the *atrium* of a large house, of which near the same spot a large and highly ornamented pavement was found in 1804; the central portion of this pavement is now preserved in the Indian Museum at Whitehall. This was the most magnificent Roman tesselated pavement yet found in London. It lay at only 9½ ft. below the street, and appeared to have been the floor of a room 20 ft. square. In the centre was a Bacchus upon a tiger, encircled with three borders (inflections of serpents, cornucopiæ, and squares diagonally concave), and drinking-cups and plants at the angles. Surrounding the whole was a square border of a bandeau of oak, and lozenge figures, and true lovers' knots, and a 5 ft. outer margin of plain red tiles.

Mr. Roach Smith has shown, in his admirable *Illustrations of Roman London* (the originals now in the British Museum), that the area and dimensions of the Roman city may be mapped out from the masses of masonry forming portions of its boundaries, many of which have come to light in the progress of recent City improvements. The course of the Roman Wall is ascertainable from the position of the gates (taken down in 1760-62), from authenticated discoveries and from remains yet extant. Recent excavations have also proved that within the area thus inclosed, most of the streets of the present day run upon the remains of Roman[Pg 34] houses; and it is confidently believed that the Romans had here a bridge across the Thames, probably a wooden roadway upon stone piers, like those of Hadrian at Newcastle, and of Trajan across the Danube. It seems to be ascertained that there was a suburb also on the southern side of the Thames (Southwark), not inclosed in walls; and that the houses constructed upon this swampy spot were built upon wooden piles, of which some remains are still in existence.

The Roman inscriptions and sculptures which have been discovered in London are very numerous. Sir Christopher Wren brought to light a monument to a soldier of the Second Legion, now among the Arundelian Marbles at Oxford. At Ludgate, behind the London Coffee-house, a monumental inscription, a female head in stone (life-size), and the trunk and thighs of a statue of Hercules, were dug up in 1806. In 1842 was found at Battle Bridge a Roman inscription, attesting the great battle between the Britons under Boadicea and the Romans under Suetonius Paulinus, to have been fought on this spot. Stamped tiles have been found in various parts of the city. A group of the *Deæ Matres* was discovered in excavating a sewer in Hart-street, Crutched-friars, at a considerable depth, amongst the ruins of Roman buildings, and is now in the Guildhall Library. A fine sarcophagus was dug up in Haydon-square, Tower Hill; a statue of a youth in Bevis Marks; and an altar, apparently to Diana, was found under Goldsmiths' Hall. Fragments of wall-paintings have been carried away by cart-loads. Bronzes of a very high class of art have been found: a head of Hadrian, of superior workmanship, has been dredged up from the bed of the Thames; a colossal bronze head found in Thames-street; an exquisite bronze Apollo, in the Thames, in 1837; a[Pg 35] Mercury, worthy to be its companion; the Priest of Cybele; and the Jupiter of the same date, are most important figures, and the first two worthy of any metropolis in any age. A bronze figure of Atys was also found at Barnes among gravel taken from the spot where the preceding bronzes were discovered. A bronze figure of an archer, also a beautiful work of art, was discovered in Queen-street, in 1842. An extraordinary bronze forceps, adorned with representations of the chief deities of Olympus, was also found in the Thames, whence again, in 1825, came the small silver Harpocrates, now in the British Museum.

Nowhere has the pottery of antiquity been so abundantly discovered as at London. Roman kilns were brought to light in digging the foundations of St. Paul's, in 1677; specimens of the Castor pottery have been found here; Samian ware is abundant, as have been potters' stamps which present 300 varieties, fragments of clay statuettes, terra-cotta lamps, tiles, and glass; and among the Roman glass discovered in London are several fragments of a flat and semi-transparent kind, which have every appearance of having been used as window-glass. And still more curious it is to find that specimens of a glass manufacture termed pillar-moulding, and for which Mr. James Green took out a patent, have also turned up among the *débris* of the Roman city. Mr. Green's patent had been worked for some years under the full belief that it was a modern invention, until Mr. Apsley Pellatt recognised in the fragments evidence of the antiquity of the supposed discovery.[10] Among the personal ornaments and implements of the toilet are the gold armillæ dug up in Cheapside in 1837; the tweezers, nail-cleaners, mirrors, and[Pg 36] strigils of the city dames of Londinium; the worn-out sandals thrown upon the dust-heaps; the sporls, spindles, fishhooks, bucket-handles, bells, balances, cocks, millstones, mortars, and other utensils which show the resources of an opulent city in the enjoyment of ancient luxury, and of the choicest appliances of ancient civilization. Of Roman coins found in London, in the bed of the Thames, Mr. Roach Smith enumerates 2,000; from gravel dredged from the Thames, 600 were picked out; a hoard of denarii of the Higher Empire was found in the city; and vast quantities were found in removing the piers of old London Bridge. In excavating for the foundations of the new Royal Exchange, in 1841, was discovered a gravel pit, supposed by Mr. Tite, the architect, to have been dug during the earliest Roman occupation of London; and then to have been a pond, gradually filled with rubbish. In it were found Roman work, stuccoed and painted; fragments of elegant Samian ware; an amphora, and terra-cotta lamps, seventeen feet below the surface; also pine-wood table-books and metal styles, sandals and soldiers' shoes, a Roman strigil, coins of Vespasian, Domitian, &c.; and almost the very footmarks of the Roman soldier.

More recently, the investigation of the ruins of the Roman city of Uriconium, at Wroxeter, near Shrewsbury, has presented us with a scene for our special wonder. The earliest antiquarian report of this interesting spot will be found in the *Philosophical Transactions* for the year 1701, where Lyster has described a Roman sudatory, or hypocaustum, discovered in Wroxeter in that year. It is strange that so important a locality should have remained unexplored during a century and a half of archæological research. The present is the first instance in which there has been in this country the chance of penetrating into a[Pg 37] city of more than fourteen centuries ago, on so large a scale, and with such extensive remains of its former condition; where the visitor may walk over the floors which had been trodden last, before they were thus uncovered, by the Roman inhabitants of this island.

Giants are frequently associated with ruins and ancient relics in the legends of Shropshire.[111] In the history of the Fitzwarines we are given to understand that the ruined Roman city of Uriconium, which we are now exploring at Wroxeter, had been taken possession of by the giants. The city is mentioned by the geographer Ptolemy to have been standing here as early as the beginning of the second century, when it was called Viroconium, a name which appears to have been changed in the later Romano-British period to Uriconium. The line of the ancient town-wall forms an irregular oval more than three miles in circumference, on the Watling-street road, which occupies the line of one of the principal streets of the old city. The only portion of the buildings above ground is upwards of twenty feet high, seventy-two feet long, and three feet thick, and is a solid mass presenting those unmistakeable characteristics of Roman work—the long string courses of large flat red bricks. This "Old Wall" stands nearly in the centre of the ancient city, which occupied the highest ground within the walls—a commanding position, with the bold isolated form of the Wrekin in the rear, and in front a panorama of mountains formed by the Wenlock and Stretton Hills, Caer Caradoc, the Longwynd, the Breidden, and the still[Pg 38] more distant mountains of Wales. With the exception of this wall, all the remains of the Roman city had long been buried beneath the soil, when, in February 1859, the excavation of the remains was commenced by public subscription. In one of the plundering invasions by the Picts and Scots, Uriconium is thought to have perished, towards the middle of the fifth century, by fire, and such of the inhabitants as were not massacred were dragged away into captivity. Thus the town was left an extensive mass of blackened walls; and such was the condition in which the ruined Roman towns remained during several centuries. The ruins would in time be overgrown with plants and trees, and would become the haunt of wild beasts, which were then abundant. Thus Uriconium stood ruined and deserted from the middle of the fifth century to the middle of the twelfth; the level of the ground was raised by decaying floors and roofs, and vegetation; for at this time England was covered with the *débris* of Roman ruined towns and villages standing above ground. Such ruins were frequently pillaged for building materials; and Uriconium was probably one of the great quarries from which the builders of Haughmond Abbey, and other monastic houses in this part of the country, were supplied.

The ruins were explored for treasure, and the damaged state of the floors of the Roman houses is attributed to this cause. In the excavations at Wroxeter, we see the floor sometimes perfect, and sometimes broken up; the walls of the remaining houses, to the height of two or three feet, as they were left by the mediæval builders, when they carried away the upper part of the walls for materials; the original level of the Roman town on which its inhabitants trod, strewed with[Pg 39] roof-tiles and slates and other material which had fallen in during the conflagration under which the town sank; and the upper part of the soil mixed up with fragments of plaster and cement, bricks and mortar, which had been scattered about when the walls were broken up.

In the early excavations at Uriconium, the bottom of the Old Wall was found at fourteen feet deep; it must have been a public building; portions of the capitals, bases, and shafts of columns were found scattered about, and among other objects were a fragment of strong iron chain, the head of an axe, and pavements of fine mosaic; the building is concluded to have formed the corner of two principal streets of the Roman city. A hypocaust, of great size, was found, with a quantity of unburnt coal; and from the end wall of this hypocaust we learn the interesting fact, that the Roman houses were plastered and painted externally as well as internally; the exterior wall was painted red, with stripes of yellow. A sort of dust-bin was found filled with coins, hair-pins, fibulæ, broken pottery and glass, bones of birds and animals which had been eaten. In another hypocaust were the remains of three persons who had crept in there for concealment; near one lay a little heap of Roman coins, 132 in number, and a decomposed box or coffer. This, Mr. Wright believes, "is the first instance which has occurred in this country, in which we have had the opportunity of ascertaining what particular coins, as being then in daily circulation, an inhabitant of a Roman town in Britain, at the moment of the Roman dominion, carried about with him. The majority of these coins point to the very latest period previous to the establishment of the Anglo-Saxons as the date at which Uriconium must have been destroyed."

Three fine wide streets, paved with small round stones in the roadway,[Pg 40] have been found in Uriconium. The Roman houses in Britain had no upper stories, and all the rooms were on the ground-floor; no traces of a staircase have ever been found; the roofing in Uriconium was slates or flags, fixed with an iron nail to the wooden framework; they lapped over each other, in lozenges or diamonds; some of the walls were tesselated in ornamental patterns; few doorways were discovered; window-glass was found one-eighth of an inch thick, though until recently it was thought that the Romans, especially in this distant province, did not use window-glass. The rooms were sometimes heated by hot air circulated in the walls, from hypocausts, and flue-tiles with holes in the sides for the escape of the air; though the hot air merely under the floor was more used, the ashes, wood and coal, and the soot of the fires were found in the hypocausts at Uriconium just as they were left when the city was overthrown and ruined by the barbarians. A large hypocaust is described with 120 columns of bricks, and is thought to have belonged to the public baths. A wide space is pointed out as the forum of Uriconium, and the basilica here holds exactly the same place as at Pompeii.

We have thus glanced at the houses of Uriconium; we now turn to their domestic articles. First is the pottery, of which the most striking is the ware of the colour of bright red sealing-wax, commonly known as Samian ware; several of the pieces found at Wroxeter have been mended, chiefly by metal rivets. There were also found specimens of the Upchurch ware, of simple ornamentation; and of the pottery from Castor, ornamented with hunting-scenes laid on a white substance after the pottery had been baked: the colour of both wares is blue, or[Pg 41] slate-colour. Two classes of Roman pottery, both evidently made in Shropshire, were also found: the first, a white ware, consisted of elegantly formed jugs, mortaria or vessels for rubbing or pounding objects in cookery; and bowls painted red and yellow. The other Romano-Salopian pottery is a red ware, and included bowls pierced all over with small holes so as to have served for colanders. Fragments of glass vessels were found, with a ladle, several knives, a stone knife-handle, and several whetstones. Hair-pins of bone, bronze, and wood were found, with bronze fibulæ, buttons, finger-rings, bracelets, combs, bone needles, and bronze tweezers for eradicating superfluous hairs. The most curious of the miscellaneous objects is a medicine-stamp for salves or washes for the eyes, inscribed with, probably, the name of a physician resident in Uriconium. The stones with Roman inscriptions, chiefly sepulchral, are numerous. The church, a Norman edifice, at Wroxeter contains amongst other architectural and sepulchral fragments two capitals, richly ornamented, of the late period of Roman architecture which became the model of the mediæval Byzantine and Romanesque; also, a Roman *miliarium*, or mile-stone. The general result of these discoveries, is that they show the manner in which this country was inhabited and governed during nearly four centuries; we also learn, from the condition of the ruins of Uriconium, and especially from the remains of human beings which are found scattered over its long-deserted floors, the sad fate under which it finally sank into ruins; and thus we are made vividly acquainted with the character and events of a period of history which has hitherto been but dimly seen through vague tradition.[12]

Many of our Roman cities have become entirely wasted and desolate.[Pg 42] Silchester is one of these, where corn-fields and pasture cover the spot once adorned with public and private buildings, all of which are now totally destroyed. Like the busy crowds who inhabited them, the edifices have sunk beneath the fresh and silent greensward: but the flinty wall which surrounded the city is yet firm, and the direction of the streets may be discerned by the difference of tint in the herbage; and the ploughshare turns up the medals of the Cæsars, so long dead and forgotten, who were once masters of the world.[13]

Silchester, thirty-eight acres in extent, is now being excavated, at the cost of the Duke of Wellington. Unlike other Roman sites, Silchester has never been built upon by Britons or Saxons; many beautiful mosaics have been found here, as well as more than 1,000 coins; and in July, 1866, a portion of a wall, hitherto undetected, was brought to light; and here have been found shells of the white snail, which was most extensively imported as food for the Roman soldiers.

We now approach the close of the Roman Era, when, in the words of the *Saxon Chronicle*, A.D. 418, the conquerors "collected all the treasures that were in Britain, and some they hid in the earth, so that no one has since been able to find them; and some they carried with them into Gaul." With this passage the authentic history of Britain ceases for a period of nearly sixty years. The Roman power being finally withdrawn, a[Pg 43] state of society prevailed in the island, much the same as had existed at the coming of Cæsar. The British cities formed themselves into a varying number of independent states, usually at war among themselves, but occasionally united by some common danger into a confederacy under an elective chieftain. Such was Vortigern, who bears the reproach of calling in the aid of the Saxons against both his foreign and domestic foes. Recent researches have rendered it probable that the well-known names of Hengist and Horsa, ascribed to their leaders, are not proper names, but rather titles of honour, signifying war-horse and mare, bestowed on many daring leaders of bands. Meanwhile, the mighty empire of Rome, of which Britain had so long formed a part, was falling into utter ruin. The Britons made several applications to the Romans for aid: one, couched in the most abject terms, is known in history as "The Groans of the Britons;" but the succour they received had no permanent effect on the contest.

In a retrospect of the Roman Era, the conquest of Cæsar is commonly referred to as the starting point in our social progress; and it has been thus felicitously illustrated by a leading writer of our time:—"If," he says, "we compare the present situation of the people of England with that of their predecessors at the time of Cæsar's invasion; if we contrast the warm and dry cottage of the present labourer, its chimney and glass windows (luxuries not enjoyed by Cæsar himself), the linen and woollen clothing of himself and his family, the steel and glass and earthenware with which his table is furnished, the Asiatic and American ingredients of his food, and, above all, his safety from personal injury, and his calm security that to-morrow will bring with it the comforts that have been enjoyed to-day; if we contrast all these[Pg 44] sources of enjoyment with the dark and smoky burrows of the Brigantes or the Cantii, their clothing of skins, the food confined to milk and flesh, and their constant exposure to famine and to violence, we shall be inclined to think those who are lowest in modern society richer than the chiefs of their rude predecessors. And if we consider that the same space of ground which afforded an uncertain subsistence to a hundred, or probably fewer, savages, now supports with ease more than a thousand labourers, and, perhaps, a hundred individuals beside, each consuming more commodities than the labour of a whole tribe of ancient Britons could have produced or purchased, we may at first be led to doubt whether our ancestors enjoyed the same natural advantages as ourselves; whether their sun was as warm, their soil as fertile, or their bodies as strong, as our own.

"But let us substitute distance of space for distance of time; and, instead of comparing situations of the same country at different periods, compare different countries at the same period, and we shall find a still more striking discrepancy. The inhabitant of South America enjoys a soil and a climate, not superior merely to our own, but combining all the advantages of every climate and soil possessed by the remainder of the world. His valleys have all the exuberance of the tropics, and his mountain-plains unite the temperature of Europe to a fertility of which Europe offers no example. Nature collects for him, within the space of a morning's walk, the fruits and vegetables which she has elsewhere separated by thousands of miles. She has given him inexhaustible forests, has covered his plains with wild cattle and horses, filled his mountains with mineral treasures, and intersected all the eastern face of his country with rivers, to which our Rhine and[Pg 45] Danube are merely brooks. But the possessor of these riches is poor and miserable. With all the materials of clothing offered to him almost spontaneously, he is ill-clad; with the most productive of soils, he is ill-fed; though we are told that the labour of a week will there procure subsistence for a year, famines are of frequent occurrence; the hut of the Indian, and the residence of the landed proprietor, are alike destitute of furniture and convenience; and South America, helpless and indigent with all her natural advantages, seems to rely for support and improvement on a very small portion of the surplus wealth of England."[14]

At length, the connexion between Britain and Rome was entirely severed. The Saxons joined the Picts and the Scots in their great invasion, and continuing their predatory warfare reduced the country to the greatest misery. Any degree of union amongst the Britons might have enabled them to repel their enemies; the walls of the principal cities, fortified by the Romans, were yet strong and firm. The tactics of the legions were not forgotten. Bright armour was piled in the storehouses, and the serried line of spears might have been presented to the half-naked Scots and Picts, who could never have prevailed against their opponents. But the Britons had no inclination to use the sword, except against each other.

DOMESTIC LIFE OF THE SAXONS.

he infant state of our Saxon ancestors when the Romans first observed them, exhibited nothing from which human sagacity could have predicted greatness. A territory on the neck of the Cimbric Chersonesus, and three small islands, contained those whose descendants occupy the circle of Westphalia, the Electorate of Saxony, the British Islands, the United States of North America, and the British Colonies in the two Indies. Such is the course of Providence, that empires, the most extended and the most formidable, are found to vanish as the morning mist; while tribes, scarcely visible, or contemptuously overlooked, like the springs of a mighty river, often glide on gradually to greatness and veneration.

Our inquiry, however, must be confined to the arts of these people. Concerning their architecture, it is supposed that the most ancient buildings were of wood; since the Saxon verb *Getymbrian*, to build, signifies literally to make of timber. The early English churches were built of logs of wood; and the erection of buildings of reeds and trunks of trees seems to have existed in some parts of England to a late period; since, in 940, Hoel Dha, King of North Wales, erected his White House, where his famous laws were made, of twisted branches, with the bark stripped and left white, whence it derived its name. Even in the days of Henry I. also, Pembroke Castle was built of twigs and turf. Bricks were made in England by the Saxons; but they were thin, and were[Pg 47] called wall-tiles. It has been supposed that the Saxons and Normans adopted the masonry which the Romans introduced into England, altering it as architecture improved. The principal peculiarities of the Saxon style are the want of uniformity in all its parts, massive columns, semicircular arches, and diagonal mouldings. The first two are common to the barbaric architecture of Europe; the round arches are believed to have been taken from the Romans; and the zig-zag mouldings have been thought to allude to the stringing of the teeth of fishes. According to the best authorities, there are very few specimens of architecture now in existence in this country which can properly be called Saxon,—that is, of date anterior to the Conquest, and not of Roman origin; and these few are of the rudest and most inferior description. Saxon, therefore, as far as the architecture of this country is concerned, is an improper term.[15]

The ordinary Saxon homes were of clay, held together by wooden frames; bricks being uncommon, and only used as ornaments: the houses were generally low and mean, or as we should call them, cottages. In a Saxon house of larger proportions, the upper rooms only are lighted by windows; there is no appearance of chimneys; the doorway is in one of the gables, and reaches more than half-way to the top of the house; and above it are some small square windows, which indicate an upper room or rooms. On one side is a low shed, or wing, apparently constructed with square stones, or large bricks, covered, like the house, with semicircular tiles, probably shingles, such as we to this day see on church-spires.

[Pg 48]

From the Mead-hall and the other Saxon houses of the period, we also get the type of the modern English mansion, with its *enceinte* and its lodge-gate, as distinguished from its hall-door. The early Saxon house was the whole inclosure, at the gate of which beggars assembled, for alms, and the porter received the alms of strangers. The whole mass inclosed within this wall constituted the burgh, or tun; and the hall, with its *duru*, or door, was the chief of its edifices. Around it were grouped the sleeping-chambers, or *bowers*, as they were designated till a late age, with the subordinate offices. Mr. Wright (in his able work on the *Domestic Life of the Middle Ages*) draws many of his inferences from the description of the Mead-hall, or *beer-hall*, of Hrothgar, and adds that he believes Bulwer's description of the Saxonized Roman house inhabited by Hilda, in *The Last of the Barons*, is substantially correct.

We learn from the romance of Beowulf, that "there was for the sons of the Geats (Beowulf and his followers altogether), a bench cleared in the beer-hall; there the bold spirit, free from quarrel, went to sit; the thane observed his office, he that in his hand bare the twisted ale-cup; he poured the bright sweet liquor; meanwhile the poet sang serene in Heorot (the name of Hrothgar's palace); there was joy of heroes." Although our conceptions of this scene are faint and vague, the antiquary is enabled to represent certain items as "the twisted ale-cup," a favourite fashion of our forefathers, many of whose ale-cups, as discovered in their barrows or graves, are incapable of standing upright, implying that their proprietors were thirsty souls.

The lamps of the Romans were certainly used by the Saxons, and were indispensable in the winter-time. Their beds were simply sacks filled[Pg 49] out of the chest with fresh straw, and laid on benches as they were wanted; though the pictures indicate that there were some bedsteads of a more elaborate construction, and that others were placed in recesses and protected by curtains. These bed-rooms were public enough, for they were sitting-rooms as well, and we find Dunstan walking to the king's bedside "as he lay in his bed with the queen," and rating him as freely as if he had audience by appointment. The Saxon ladies were very opt to scourge their domestic servants for very slight offences, and the punishment of servile and other transgressors was in other respects barbarous. They were given much to bathing in the baths which the Romans had left them, and it may be that this resource had some influence in determining the national bias towards personal cleanliness, which is such a distinguishing characteristic of the English among northern nations. We may add that the Saxon knew how to build a gallows, how to bait a bear, drive a chariot, fly a hawk, cultivate roses and lilies, and that he certainly knew the use of an umbrella.

A convivial custom which originated in this rude age is too interesting to be omitted here. It is said by some writers that Vortigern married Rowena, the daughter of Hengist. She was very beautiful; and when introduced by her father at the royal banquet of the British king, she advanced gracefully and modestly towards him, bearing in her hand a golden goblet filled with wine. Young people, even of the highest rank, were accustomed to wait upon their elders, and those unto whom they wished to show respect; therefore, the appearance of Rowena as the cup-bearer of the feast was neither unbecoming nor unseemly. And when the lady came near unto Vortigern, she said in her own Saxon[Pg 50] language—"*Wæs heal plaford Conung;*" which means, "Health to my Lord the King." Vortigern did not understand the salutation of Rowena, but the words were explained to him by an interpreter. "*Drinc heal,*" "Drink thou health," was the accustomed answer, and the memory of the event was preserved in merry old England by the *wassail cup*—a vessel full of spiced wine or good ale, which was handed round from guest to guest, at the banquet and the festival. Well, therefore, might Rowena be recollected on high tides and holidays for the introduction of this concomitant of good cheer.

This story has, however, a pendant. At our great city feasts, to this day—especially at the Mansion House of the Lord Mayor—the Wassail or Loving Cup is passed round the table immediately after dinner, the Lord Mayor having drunk to his visitors a hearty welcome. The more formal practice is for the person who pledges with the loving cup to stand up and bow to his neighbour, who, also standing, removes the cover of the cup with his right hand, and holds it while the other drinks; a custom said to have originated in the precaution to keep the right, or dagger hand employed, that the person who drinks may be assured of no treachery, like that practised by Elfrida on the unsuspecting King Edward the Martyr at Corfe Castle, who was slain while drinking: this was why the cup possessed a cover.

The usages of domestic life, especially at dinner, are copiously illustrated in ancient manuscript illuminations. Mr. Wright quotes the *Boke of Kervyng*, which enjoins the carver to handle the meats with his thumb and two fingers only,—for the Middle Ages, with all their artistic ingenuity, had not attained to the invention of a fork. In none of the pictures have the guests any plates; they seem to have eaten with[Pg 51] their hands and thrown the refuse on the table. We know also that they often threw the fragments on the floor, where they were eaten up by cats and dogs, which were admitted into the hall without restriction.[16] In the *Boke of Curtesye* it is blamed as a mark of bad breeding to play with the cats and dogs while seated at table. The drinking vessels of this period display fine workmanship and ingenious devices. The Anglo-Saxons were unquestionably huge drinkers, and ornamented their drinking vessels with all the skill in working the precious metals for which they were so famous. But the primitive drinking-cup was the simple horn of the bullock, which was retained as an appendage of the Anglo-Saxon dinner-table until after the Conquest. There were also other drinking vessels, suggested by that ornamentation with which the Anglo-Saxon artificers had enriched the simple cup of the Danes. Peg Tankards are of the Saxon period: one is to be seen in the Ashmolean Museum; but a finer specimen, of undoubted Anglo-Saxon work, formerly belonging to the Abbey of Glastonbury, is now in the possession of Lord Arundel, of Wardour: it holds two quarts, and formerly had eight pegs inside, dividing the liquor into half-pints. On the lid is carved the crucifixion, with the Virgin and John, one on each side; and round the cup are carved the twelve apostles.

Drinking-horns are represented on the Bayeux tapestry, and in the magnificent collection of antiquities in the British Museum there is a[Pg 52] capacious specimen of one formed of the small tusk of an elephant, carved with rude figures of that animal, unicorns, lions, and crocodiles. It is mounted with silver; a small tube, ending in a silver cup, issues from the jaws of a pike, whose head and shoulders inclose the mouth of the vessel, on which the following legend is engraved:—

Drink you this and think no scorne
All though the cup be much like horn.

The horn was not long before it had rivals: the commonest of these was the Mazer-bowl, a utensil which, with its cover on, resembled two saucers placed together rim to rim, with a topknot on the upper one. It was usually made of maple wood, from which it is supposed to have derived its name—*maeser* being Dutch for maple. Of this shape was the early and famous wassail-bowl. When these bowls, which in process of time were made of costlier materials than maple, were large, they were lifted to the mouth with both hands; when small, in the palm of one hand. Our ancestors were much attached to their mazers, and incurred considerable expense in embellishing them, in embossing legends admonitory of peace and good fellowship on the metal rim or on the cover, or in engraving on the bottom a cross or the image of a saint. Spenser, in *The Shepherds Calendar*, thus describes a vessel of this kind:—

"A mazer ywrought of the maple warre,
Wherein is enchased many a fayre sight
Of bears and tygers, that maken fiers warre;
And over them spred a goodly wilde vine,
Entrailed with a wanton yvy twine.

"Tell me, such a cup hast thou ever seene?
Well moughte it beseeme any harvest queene."

The Mazer continued in use to the seventeenth century, when it was still[Pg 53] a favourite with the humbler classes. But on the tables of the rich it gave place to new vessels. There was the Hanap, a cup raised on a stem, with or without a cover. Besides the Hanap, a sort of mug or cup, called the Godet, had also come into vogue; then there were the Juste, used in monasteries to measure a prescribed allowance of wine; the Barrel, the Tankard, the "standing-nut," or mounted shell of the cocoa-nut; and the Grype, or Griffin's Egg, probably the egg of the ostrich. These vessels, except of course the nut and the egg, were ordinarily of silver, and sometimes of ivory, but rarely of gold; and still more rarely of glass, which did not obtain for drinking cups until the close of the fifteenth century. They were for the most part embossed or enamelled with the armorial bearings of their owners, parcel-gilt—*i.e.*where part of the work is gilt and part left plain; set with jewels and elaborately designed with dances of men and women, with dogs, hearts, roses, and trefoils.

One of the most esteemed Saxon trades was the smith, including workers in gold, silver, iron, and copper. The English were very expert in these arts; and in the laws of Wales the smith ranked next to the chaplain in the Prince's court. The Saxons produced some very highly-finished specimens of jewellery, goldsmith's work, and even of enamelling. A very beautiful specimen of gold enamelled work is preserved in the Ashmolean collection at Oxford: it is commonly known as *Alfred's Jewel*, as it bears his name, and was found in 1693, in the immediate neighbourhood of his retreat. It is filagree work, inclosing a piece of rock crystal, under which appears a figure in enamel, which has not been satisfactorily explained. The ground is of a rich blue, the face and[Pg 54] arms of the figure white, the dress principally green, the lower portion partly of a reddish-brown. The inscription is "Aelfred mee heht gevrean," (Alfred ordered me to be made,) thus affording the most authentic testimony of its origin. Curious reliquaries, finely carved and set with precious stones, were, for excellence, called "the English work" throughout Europe. The representations of the crowns of the Saxon kings, commencing with Offa, present us with specimens of the ornamentation of the period. The ring was also a most important ornament. It was used not only for display, but also as a charm, or protection against natural or supernatural evil. The gems with which the ring was set, were believed to possess, severally, special qualities, and symbolical meanings. The sapphire indicated purity—the diamond, faith—the ruby, zeal—the amethyst was good against drunkenness—the sapphire was a protection against witchcraft, and the toad-stone against sickness. The accredited properties of decade rings, pontifical rings, alchemy rings, posie rings, and gimel rings are illustrated in various anecdotes and legends. In the medal-room of the British Museum is a gold ring, bearing the name of Ethelwulf, upon blue and black enamel: it was found in a cart-rut, at Laverstock in Hampshire; its weight is 11 dwts. 14 grains.

The crosiers of the bishops of this period were curious specimens of metal-work and gem ornamentation; as were also the shrines of the saints. In 1840 a hoard of about 7,000 coins (beside many silver ornaments) was discovered at Coverdale, near

Preston, in Lancashire; they are considered by the best numismatists indisputably to belong to the chief of the Danish invaders in the ninth century, and their[Pg 55] immediate successors. In the sepulchre of Thyra, ancestress of Canute, in Jutland, have been found the figure of a bird formed of thin plates of gold, as well as a silver cup plated with gold, both being remarkable examples of the state of the decorative arts in the tenth century.

The art of glass-making was introduced to the Saxons in the seventh century, and ordinary window-glass was first used for building purposes at the great monasteries at Monkwearmouth, on the river Wear, and at Jarrow-on-the-Tyne; although we have already seen that window-glass was used in the Roman city of Uriconium. The Venerable Bede, in the seventh century, relates that his contemporary, the Abbot Benedict, sent for artists beyond seas to glaze the Monastery of Wearmouth; and such was the change made in their churches by the use of glass, instead of other and more obscure substances for windows, that the unlettered people avowed a belief, which was handed down as a tradition for many generations, "that it was never dark in old Jarrow Church." By a singular coincidence, the first manufactory of window or crown glass in Great Britain was established at Newcastle-upon-Tyne, within a few miles of these monastic establishments. In the year 1616 Admiral Sir Robert Maunsell erected glassworks at the Ouseburn, Newcastle, which were carried on without interruption till nearly the middle of the present century, when they were closed.

The art of making woollen cloth, which was known to the Britons, was, by this time, brought to perfection in England, especially in the south. This seat of manufacture must have been handy to the fuller's-earth pits of Nutfield, where fuller's-earth has been for centuries dug:—"While Bradford was still the little local centre of a wild hill tract in[Pg 56] pastoral Yorkshire, the 'grey cloths of Kent' kept many a loom at work in the homesteads of Tenterden, and Biddenden, and Cranbrook, and all the other little mediæval towns that dot the Weald with their carved barge-boards and richly-moulded beams." (*Saturday Review*, No. 182.) The distaff and the spindle, which appear to have been anciently the type, and symbol, and the insignia of the softer sex in nearly every age and country, were in the Saxon times still more conspicuous as the distinguishing badge of the female sex. Among our Saxon ancestors the "spear-half" and the "spindle-half" expressed the male and female line; and the spear and the spindle are to this day found in their graves.

The Saxons had the arts of dyeing of purple and various colours; and the Saxon ladies were eminent for their embroidery. There are descriptions extant of a robe of purple embroidered with large peacocks in black circles; and a golden veil worked with the siege of Troy, the latter a king's bequest to Croyland Abbey, where it was to be hung up on his birthday. The standards were also beautifully worked: the Danish standard, called the Raefen, was woven in one night by the three sisters of Ubbo, the Danish leader. The standard of Harold, the last Saxon sovereign of England, was the figure of a warrior richly embroidered with precious stones. In the Anglo-Saxon, and even in late periods, men worked at embroidery, especially in abbeys. At this time the dressing of hides and working in leather was practised to a great extent by the shoewright; and the wood-workman, answering to our modern carpenter, was also in general estimation. Sandals were worn by the early Saxons: there exists a print of one, made of leather, partly gilt, and variously coloured, and for the left foot of the wearer; so that "rights and[Pg 57] lefts" are only a very old fashion revived.

The art of smelting iron was known in England during the Roman occupation; and in many ancient beds of cinders, the refuse of iron-works, Roman coins have been found. Cæsar describes iron as being so rare in Britain, that pieces of it were employed as a medium of exchange; but a century later it had become common, since in Strabo's time it was an article of exportation. There is reason to believe that the Romans worked iron ore in the hills of South Wales, as they undoubtedly did in Dean Forest, where ancient heaps of slag have occasionally been struck upon. Remains of ancient iron furnaces have also been found in Lancashire, Staffordshire, and Yorkshire.[17]

The working in steel was also practised in Britain before the Norman[Pg 58] Conquest; and we are told that not only was the army of Harold well supplied with weapons and defensive armour of steel, but that every officer of rank maintained a smith, who constantly attended his master to the wars, and took charge of his arms and armour, and had to keep them in proper repair.

The inventions attributed to Alfred must be noticed. It will be remembered how he measured time by graduated wax-tapers—the consumption of an inch denoting twenty minutes; but the wind rushing through windows, doors, and crevices of the royal palace, or the tent-coverings, sometimes wasted them, and disordered Alfred's calculations. He then inclosed his tapers in lanterns of horn and wood; but their invention has been attributed to an earlier period, from some Latin verses attributed to Aldhelm, Abbot of Malmesbury, in the seventh century. "Let not," say they, "the glass lantern be despised, or that made of a horn, hide, or thin skin, although a brass lamp may excel it." This passage[Pg 59] has, however, sometimes been referred to the twelfth century.

Travelling, in the Saxon times, was very different from what it is in the present day: coaches were not invented, and the only vehicles which went upon wheels were carts and wagons, and these were very heavy and clumsy. Horseback was the only conveyance, so that the sick and infirm could hardly ever leave their houses. In those times there were very few roads upon which one could travel with safety. The Romans left excellent roads, which, however, were neglected, and they fell into decay. Marshes were perilous to cross: a bridge might be broken down, and when you tried to ford the stream, your horse might get out of his depth, and then he and his rider might be drowned. Sometimes the traveller had to pass through a dark forest, abounding with bears and wolves; and, at the end of his day's journey, instead of putting up at a comfortable inn, he was often compelled to stretch his cloak on the dark earth, in some wretched hut. And what was worst, the kings and princes were almost always at war with each other, and a stranger was constantly liable to be plundered and seized, or put to death by the contending parties.[18]

Stirrups and spurs were known to the Saxons; the Britons had bridles[Pg 60] ornamented with ivory: a bit, presumed to have belonged to a British chief in the Roman service, is a jointed snaffle. The side-pieces, or branches, of curb bits, are of equal antiquity. The Saxons had very superb bridles, ornamented with plates of tin and pewter; and those for women's horses were lily-white. We have seen a bridle of Norman manufacture, said to have been on the horse which William Rufus rode when killed in the New Forest: it has blinkers, is very broad; and cloth, cut by a mould into rich patterns, is glued upon the leather. We read of Athelstan receiving valuable presents of running horses, with their saddles and bridles studded with gold; one of our earliest illustrations of horse-racing.

MEALS—BRITISH, ANGLO-ROMAN, AND SAXON.

[Pg 61]

he Britons, we learn, made their table on the ground, on which they spread the skins of wolves and dogs. The guests sat round, the food was placed before them, and each took his part. They were waited upon by the youth of both sexes. They who had not skins were contented with a little hay, which was laid under them; they ate very little bread, but much meat, boiled, or broiled upon coals, or roasted upon spits, before fires kindled as gipsies do in these days. The best living appears to have been in South Britain, where venison, oxen, sheep, and goats were eaten; and ale or mead was the common drink. The whole family attended upon the visitors, and the master and mistress went round, and did not eat anything till their guests had finished their meal.

The Romans made little use of cattle as food; and the fattening of cattle for this specific purpose was unknown to them. Neither can we find evidence that beef and mutton were eaten by the Roman people generally. Pliny mentions the use of beef, roasted, or in the shape of broth, as a medicine, but not as food. Plautus speaks of beef and mutton as sold in the markets; but, amidst the immense variety of fish, flesh, and fowl, we hear little of the above meats in the Roman larder. Fish and game, poultry, venison, and pork, are often mentioned as elements of[Pg 62] a luxurious banquet; but undoubtedly the common food of all classes was vegetable, flavoured with lard or bacon. Among the Romans the hare was held in great estimation. Alexander Severus had a hare daily served at his table; yet Cæsar says that in his time the Britons did not eat the flesh of hare.

"The Romans, after their colonization of Britain, must have enjoyed its great supplies of fish; with them its fine oysters were celebrities. They were fattened in pits and ponds by the Romans, who obtained the finest oysters from Ruterpiæ, now Sandwich, in Kent. The Roman epicures iced their oysters before eating them; the ladies used the calcined shell as a cosmetic and depilatory. Apicius is said to have supplied Trajan with fresh oysters at all seasons of the year. The Romans, according to Pliny, made *Ostrearii*, or loaves of bread baked with oysters. There is one secret we may well desire to learn from the Romans; namely, the manner of preserving oysters alive in any journey, however long or distant. The possession of this secret is the more extraordinary, as it is well known that a shower of rain will kill oysters subjected to its influence, or the smallest grain of quick-lime destroy their vitality."[19] Pliny records that one gentleman, Asinius Celer, gave 8,000 nummi (between 64*l*. and 65*l*. sterling) for one mullet, such as may now be bought in good seasons in London for sixpence! How the Anglo-Roman epicure must have enjoyed the mullet from our western coast! The lamprey was also with the Romans a pet fish: it is now rare. The celebrated Roman garum must here have been made in perfection. A Roman supper is thus described by the officer of the household of Theodosius:—"For the first course there were[Pg 63] sea-hedgehogs, raw oysters, and asparagus; for the second, a fat fowl, with another plate of oysters and shell-fish; several species of dates, fig-peckers, roebuck, and wild boar, fowls encrusted with paste, and the purple shell-fish, then esteemed so great a delicacy. The third course was composed of a wild-boar's head, of ducks, of a *compôte* of river-birds, of leverets, roast-fowls, Ancona-cakes, called *panes picandi*," which must have somewhat resembled Yorkshire pudding. The old Romans had their fancy bread as well as the moderns, as loaves baked with oysters, cakes like our rolls, and others. A sort, of nearly the same quality as our middle sort of wheaten bread, was sold, according to the calculation of antiquaries, at 3*s*. 2*d*. the peck-loaf, present money.

Before the arrival of the Romans, *mead*, that is, honey diluted with water, and fermented, was probably the only strong liquor known to the Britons; and it continued to be their favourite drink long after they had become acquainted with other liquors. Its manufacture was an important art; for the mead-maker was the eleventh person in dignity in the courts of the ancient princes of Wales, and took precedence of the physician.

Of Saxon living we have many details. The Saxons were noted for their hospitality. On the arrival of a stranger he was welcomed, and water was brought him to wash his hands; his feet were also washed in warm water. A curious law was enforced at this period respecting *host and guest*; if any one entertained a guest in his house three days, and the guest committed any crime during that period, his host was either to bring him to justice, or answer for it himself; and by another law, a guest, after two nights' residence, was considered one of the family, and his[Pg 64] entertainer was to be responsible for all his actions.

The meal now assumed more regularity; the parties sat at large square tables, on long benches, according to rank; and by a subsequent law of Canute, a person sitting out of his proper place, was to be pelted from it with bones, at the discretion of the company, without the privilege of taking offence! The mistress of the house sat at the head of the table, upon a raised platform, beneath a canopy, and helped the provisions to the guests; whence came the modern title of *lady*, being softened from the Saxon *liefdien*, or the server of bread. The tables were covered with fine cloths, some very costly; a cup of horn, silver, silver-gilt, or gold, was presented to each person; other vessels were of wood, inlaid with gold; dishes, bowls, and basins were of silver, gold, and brass, engraven; the benches and seats were carved and covered with embroidery; and some of the tables were of silver. All tables were square at this period; they were displaced by the old oaken table, of long boards upon tressels.

The food of the period consisted of meat and vegetables, and the tables were plentifully but plainly supplied. There were oxen, sheep, fowls, deer, goats, and hares, but hogs yielded a principal part of the provision. On this account, swine were allowed by charter to run and feed in the royal forests. All sorts of fish now taken, were eaten at the above time; herrings were preferred. The porpoise, now no longer eaten, was then preferred. Bread was made of barley; wheaten bread was a delicacy. Baking was understood, as well as cookery; and if a person ate anything half-dressed, ignorantly, he was to fast three days; and four, if he knew it. Roasted meat was a luxury; but boiling was general, and broiling and stewing were in use. Honey was used in most of the meals of[Pg 65] this period, on which account, added to that of sugar not being brought to England until the fifteenth century, the wild honey found in the English woods became an article of importance in the forest charter. Fruit, beans, and herbs were commonly eaten; the only vegetable was kale-wort; peppered broths and soups, and a kind of *bouilli*, were esteemed; buttermilk or whey was used in the monasteries; and salt was employed in great quantities, both for preserving and seasoning all sorts of provisions.

In representations of Anglo-Saxon feasts, the men and women are seated apart at table; a person is cutting a piece of meat off the spit into a plate, held underneath by a servant; and cakes of bread, with oblong, square, and round dishes are on the table. Festivals were given to people on religious accounts; they kept it up the whole day on state occasions, and the feast was accompanied with music. The company sat on forms, the chief visitors seated in the middle, and the next in rank on the right and left. A dish on the table was set apart for alms for the poor; and when our Anglo-Saxon kings dined, the poor sat in the streets, expecting the broken victuals. At private parties, two persons eating out of the same dish was a peculiar mark of friendship. Forks were not invented, and our ancestors made use of their fingers; but, for the sake of cleanliness, each person was provided with a small silver ewer containing water, and two flowered napkins, of the finest linen. The dessert consisted of grapes, figs, nuts, apples, pears, and almonds.

In early baking the use of ovens was unknown; and when the *lady* had kneaded the dough, it was toasted either upon a warm hearth, or bake-stone, as it was called, when later it was made of some metal. In[Pg 66] Wales, bread is, or was, lately baked upon an iron plate, called a griddle. The earliest bakers were probably the monks, since bakehouses were commonly appended to monasteries; and the host, or consecrated bread, was baked by the monks with great ceremony. In a charge to the clergy, date 994, we find:—"And we charge you that the oblation (*i.e.* the bread in the Eucharist), which ye offer to God in that holy mystery, be either baked by yourselves, or your servants in your presence." Bakehouses were also appended to the churches; for, on taking down some part of the church at Crickhowell, county Brecon, a small room with an oven in it was discovered, which had long been shut up. Although the monks were early bakers, they do not appear to have fared much more sumptuously than the people on bread; for the Anglo-Saxon monks of the Abbey of St. Edmund, in the eighth century, ate barley bread, because the income of the establishment would not admit of the feeding twice or thrice a day on wheaten bread.

Elecampane, now known as the sweetmeat of childhood, was esteemed for ages in the domestic herbal. The leaves are aromatic and bitter, but the root is much more so. The former were used by the Romans as pot-herbs; and appear to have been held in no mean repute in after times, from the monkish line,—"*Elena campana reddit præcordia sana.*" When preserved, it is still eaten as a cordial by Eastern nations; and the root is used in England to flavour the small sugar-cakes, which bear its name. It is tonic and stimulant.

Of the manufacture of Ale and Beer we have a record of the fifth century, directing it to be made without hops, instead of which various bitters were used. Ale is next mentioned in the laws of Ina, King of[Pg 67] Wessex, who ascended, the throne about the year 680. It was the favourite drink of the Saxons and Danes; and so attentive were the Saxons to its quality, that in their time it was a custom in the city of Chester to place any person who brewed bad ale in a ducking-chair, to be plunged into a pool of muddy water, or be fined 4*s*. In the Saxon Dialogues, in the Cotton Library, a boy, in answer to the question, what he drank, replies, "Ale, if I have it; or water, if I have it not." He adds, that wine is the drink of the elders and the wise. Ale was sold to the people at this time, in houses of entertainment; but a priest was forbidden by law to eat or drink at places where ale was sold. About the middle of the eleventh century, ale was one of the articles of a royal banquet provided for Edward the Confessor. At this time the best ale could be bought for 8*d*. the gallon. This was spiced, and double the price of common ale, and mead was double the price of spiced ale. One of the vessels out of which ale was drunk was the Saxon *nap*, now the *neap*, or *nip*, out of which we drink Burton ale. The Saxons had also cups of wood, ornamented with gold, besides the peg tankards introduced by King Edgar, to check excessive drinking. In Northamptonshire—a famous ale county—a small public-house is to this day called an *ale-hus*, the original Saxon *hus* being retained.[20]

As the monasteries were in ancient times reputed for ale, which the monks brewed for themselves with such remarkable care, so colleges, which rose upon the Dissolution, became famous for ale, and their celebrity continues to this day. Warton, poet-laureate in 1748, has left[Pg 68] a panegyric on Oxford ale (which he dearly loved), and thus apostrophises:—

"Balm of my cares, sweet solace of my toils,
Hail, juice benignant!

"My sober evening let the tankard bless,
With toast embrown'd, and fragrant nutmeg fraught.
What though me sore ills
Oppress, dire want of chill-dispelling coals
Or cheerful candle, save the make-weight's gleam
Haply remaining, heart-rejoicing ale
Cheers the sad scene, and every want supplies.

"Be mine each morn, with eager appetite
And hunger undissembled, to repair
To friendly buttery; there on smoking crust
And foaming ale to banquet unrestrain'd,
Material breakfast. Thus, in ancient days
Our ancestors, robust with liberal cups
Usher'd the morn, unlike the squeamish sons
Of modern times; nor ever had the might
Of Britons brave decay'd, had thus they fed,
With British ale improving British worth."

They who recollect the ale of Magdalen and Queen's will acknowledge that Oxford well maintains its character for our national drink.

The brewers were formerly women, and those who sold the ale were *ale-wives*, one of whom, "Eleanor Rumming, the famous ale-wife of England," is commemorated by another poet-laureate, Skelton. Of her ale-house, at Leatherhead, there are some remains, and she lives in the rude woodcut portrait (1571), with this inscription:—

"When Skelton wore the laurel crown,
My ale put all the ale-wives down."

The introduction of foreign wines by the Normans did not altogether[Pg 69] supersede the wines of our own country. The vine had been cultivated here long before. Vines are mentioned in the laws of Alfred, and Edgar makes a gift of a vineyard, with the vine-dressers. In a Saxon Calendar, preserved in the British Museum, there is a series of rude drawings representing the different operations of the rural economy of the year; that prefixed to February showing husbandmen pruning what are supposed to be vines. At the time of the Norman Conquest, new plantations appear to have been made in the village of Westminster; at Chenetone, in Middlesex; at Ware, in Hertfordshire, and other places. Of ancient wine-cellars we find some curious particulars, and drinking-glasses have been found in Roman-British barrows.

The Danes, in their visits to this country, added much to the gross hospitalities, against the consequences of which Saxon laws were enacted. They were accustomed to sing and play on the harp in turn; and to be entertained by the gleemen, ale-poets, dancers, harpers, jugglers, and tumblers, who frequented the earliest taverns, called guest-houses, ale-shops, wine-houses, &c. And it may be regarded as indicative of the reckless manners of the times, that the last of the Danish kings of England died suddenly at a marriage-feast; his death being imputed by some to poison, but, with more likelihood of truth, to his being then intoxicated.

We have now reached the period at which the Danes arrived in this country; but they so neglected the arts essential to life as to have little claim upon our respect. Their neglect of husbandry was great. The other arts were abandoned to the women, who spun wool for their clothing. Rude carving with the knife seems to have been the principal and natural talent of the Danes. Their houses were mostly erected near a spring, a wood, or an open field, at a distance from any others. The[Pg 70] best of their dwellings were only thick, heavy pillars, united by boards, and covered with turf; though there sometimes existed a pride in having them of great extent, and with lofty towers.

In a late volume of the *Gentleman's Magazine*, we find this interesting page of research upon the names of provisions, which throw some light upon the mode of living among the higher and lower classes of our population. "Bread, with the common productions of the garden, such as pease, beans, eggs, and some other articles which might be produced in the cottage-garden or yard, retain their Saxon names, and evidently formed the chief nourishment of the Saxon portion of the population. Of meat, though the word is Saxon, they ate probably little; for it is one of the most curious circumstances connected with the English language, that while the living animals are called by Anglo-Saxon names, as oxen, calves, sheep, pigs, deer, the flesh of those animals when prepared for the table is called by names which are all Anglo-Norman—beef, veal, mutton, pork, venison. The butcher who killed them is himself known by an Anglo Norman name. Even fowls when killed receive the Norman name of poultry. This can only be explained by the circumstance that the Saxon population in general was only acquainted with the living animals, while their flesh was carried off to the castle and table of the Norman possessors of the land, who gave it names taken from their own language. Fresh meat, salted, was hoarded up in immense quantities in the Norman castles, and was distributed lavishly to the household and idle followers of the feudal possessors. Almost the only meat obtained by the peasantry, unless, if we believe old popular songs, by stealth, was *bacon*, and that also is still called by an Anglo-Norman name."

II. Castle Life.

ENGLISH CASTLE-BUILDING.

he history of building of Castles in England and Wales may be divided into periods of transition, changing with the exigencies and requirements of the age, and its character of civilization.

The Castles of England consist of those erected by the Romans; of British and Saxon castles erected previous to, and Norman castles erected after, the Norman Conquest; also of the more modern stone and brick castles, erected from about the reign of Edward I. to the time of Henry VII.

The Roman castles in this country are numerous, and some of them still in very perfect condition, such as Burgh Castle and Richborough. More popularly known is Pevensey, once a maritime town of considerable importance, the site of which is now fixed with all but certainty, as that of the strong old city, Anderida, though this distinction has been claimed by no less than seven Sussex towns. Abundance of

Roman bricks have been found here, affording strong presumption of there having been originally a Roman fortress on the spot. But the celebrity of Pevensey (for, though reduced to a village, it has an undying name in our history) rests upon its having been the place of debarkation of William,[Pg 72] Duke of Normandy, on his successful invasion of this land in 1066. It was, therefore, the first scene of the Norman Conquest, the most momentous event in English history, perhaps the most momentous in the Middle Ages. Here William landed from a fleet of 900 ships, with 60,000 men, including cavalry; and having refreshed his troops, and hastily erected a fortress, he marched forward to Hastings, and thence to Battle (then called Epitou), where, on the 14th of October, he obtained a decisive victory over King Harold. Southey, upon the conjoint authorities of Turner, Palgrave, and Thierry, gives such a version of the Normans landing at Pevensey, as to decide its having been a Roman station. "They landed," he says, "without opposition, on the 28th of September, between Pevensey and Hastings, at a place called Bulverhithe. William occupied the *Roman castle* at Pevensey; erected three wooden forts, the materials of which he had brought ready with him for construction; threw up works to protect part of his fleet, and burnt, it is said, the rest, or otherwise rendered them unserviceable."[21]

Upon his accession, the Conqueror gave the town and castle to his half-brother, Robert, Earl of Mortagne in Normandy, whose descendant, William, was deprived of all his possessions, and banished the realm, by Henry I. for rebellion. That monarch granted them to Gilbert de Aquila, in allusion to whose name this district was afterwards styled the Honour of the Eagle.

The outer work of the castle contains many Roman bricks and much herring-bone work. The outer walls, the most ancient part of the fortification, inclose seven acres, and are from twenty to twenty-five[Pg 73] feet high. The moat on the south side is still wide and deep; on the other side it has been filled up. The entrance is on the west or land side, between two round towers, over a drawbrige. Within the walls is another and much more modern fortification, approaching a pentagonal form, with nearly five circular towers, moated on the north and west. It is entered from the outer court by a drawbridge on the west side between two towers. The principal barbican, or watch tower, is not at the entrance, but towards the north-east corner. The walls are nine feet thick, and the towers were two or three stories in height. The castle was of great strength: it withstood the attacks of William Rufus's army for six days, protecting Odo, Bishop of Bayeux, who ultimately yielded only for want of provisions; and it afterwards successfully resisted the siege of King Stephen, who personally superintended the attack, but met with so gallant an opposition from Gilbert, Earl of Clare, that he was obliged to withdraw his force, leaving only a small body to blockade it by sea and land. It once more resisted hostile attacks, when it was fruitlessly assailed in 1265, by Simon de Montfort, son of the renowned Earl of Leicester. Again, when Sir John Pelham was in Yorkshire, in 1339, assisting Henry,

Duke of Lancaster, to gain the crown, the castle, left under the command of Lady Jane Pelham, was attacked by large bodies of the yeomen of Kent, Surrey, and Sussex, who favoured the deposed King Richard, but was bravely and successfully defended by Lady Jane Pelham.

Pevensey castle remained as a fortress till the reign of Elizabeth: two ancient culverins, one of which bears her initials, are yet preserved; after which its history is not traced till the Parliamentary survey of[Pg 74] 1675, when the fortress was in ruins, and the ground within the walls was cultivated as a garden. The demesne and castle are now held by the Cavendish family, under a lease from the Duchy of Lancaster, which was originally granted to the Pelhams by Henry IV., son of the famous John of Gaunt, Duke of Lancaster, to whom the Honour of the Eagle had been given, on his surrender of the great earldom of Richmond.

It is remarkable that no mention is made of Pevensey Castle in the Saxon times; but if not erected by the Romans, it was certainly built from the remains of an older fortress. The Saxons most probably adapted the Roman inclosures to their modes of defence; and it appears that they often raised a mound on one side of the walls, on which they erected a keep or citadel.

We are indebted to the Saxons but for few social improvements; since, in the words of the Wiltshire antiquary, John Aubrey, "They were so far from having arts, that they could not even build with stone. The church at Glaston (bury) was thatched. They lived skittishly in their houses, they ate a great deal of beef and mutton, and drank good ale in a brown mazzard, and their very kings were but a sort of farmers. The Normans then came, and taught them civility and building."

In various parts of England, Scotland, Ireland, and Wales, there are numerous encampments or castles, mostly occupying the summits of hills, which have been ascribed to the aboriginal inhabitants. Amongst the most remarkable are the Hereford Beacon, on the Malvern hills, in Worcestershire; the Caer-Caradock, near Church Stretton, in Shropshire; Moel Arthur, in Flintshire; Chun Castle, in Cornwall; and the[Pg 75] magnificent hill-fort, Maiden Castle, or the Castle of the great Hill, within three miles of Dorchester.

Maiden Castle had four gateways of stone; in excavations have been found round stones, probably sling stones, and pottery, denoting its original occupation by Britons; how the fortress was supplied with water has not been traced. This famous earthwork is considered of a period anterior to that of the Britons and Romans: the extent of the work is one mile, and the ramparts are, in some places, sixty feet high. Another famous earthwork in Dorset is Poundbury, a Roman encampment, though it has been set down as Danish, and an Anglo-Saxon camp of council.[22]

Before we leave the Roman period, we may remark that the manufacture of bricks and tiles must then have been known in England, because it was practised in such perfection by our conquerors during their occupation, as is evident in the numerous remains of their buildings.[23] It has, however, been asserted that up to the reign of Elizabeth, the houses of the gentry throughout England were built entirely of timber; whereas, of[Pg 76] the mansions of earlier date than that reign, which remain entire or in part to this day, three-fourths, at least, are built of stone or brick. The latter material is stated by Bagford and others to have been first introduced in the reign of Henry VII. Yet, Endure Palace, in Oxfordshire, erected by William De la Pole, and Hurstmonceux Castle, in Sussex, both of which are of brick, are attributed to the reign of Henry VI. Oxburgh Hall, in Norfolk, was erected in the reign of Edward IV. Leland mentions the walls of Hungerford, as early as the reign of Richard II., being of that material; and Stow records Ralph Stratford, Bishop of London, inclosing the burial-ground of Charter-house, for those that died of the plague in 1348, with a wall of brick. That roofing-tiles were in use before the time of Richard I. is proved by the order made in the first years of that reign, Henry Fitzalwayne being Mayor of London, that the houses of that city should be covered with "brent tyle," instead of "strawe," or reeds. The ancient name for bricks appears to have been wall-tiles, to distinguish them from floor-tiles, used for paving.

William the Conqueror lost no time in erecting strong castles in all the principal towns in the kingdom, as at Lincoln, Norwich, Rochester, &c. for the double purpose of strengthening the towns, and keeping the citizens in awe. The Conqueror's followers, among whom he parcelled out the lands of the English, imitated their master's example by building castles on their estates; and so rapidly did they increase, that in the reign of Stephen, or within a century after the arrival of the Conqueror, there are said to have been 1115 castles completed in England alone.

One of the earliest was Conisborough Castle, built by William, the first[Pg 77] Earl of Warren, about six miles west of Doncaster: the remains, as far as can be traced, extend about 700 feet in circumference; but the chief object is a noble round tower, strengthened by six massive square buttresses, running from the base to the summit. The extreme thickness of the walls is 15 feet; of each buttress 23 feet; and the entrance is 24 feet from the ground, up a flight of steps. In the centre of the first floor is a round hole, which is the only entrance to a lower apartment, or dungeon. This Castle is chosen by Sir Walter Scott for one of the principal scenes of his romance of *Ivanhoe*.

Many of the castles of this age were of great size. Instead of a single tower, they consisted of several towers, both round and square, united by walls, inclosing a space called a courtyard, the entrance to which was generally between two strong towers. The whole building was surrounded by a moat or ditch, across which a drawbridge led to the massive doors, which were covered with plates of iron, and in front of them, an iron portcullis—like a harrow, such as we see in the arms of the city of Westminster—was let down the rough, deep grooves in the stonework; whilst overhead projected a parapet, resting on corbels, with openings through which melted lead or hot water could be poured, or stones thrown on the heads of the assailants, who should attempt an entrance by forcing, or, as was the usual mode of attack, by setting fire to the door.[24] The gateways of Caerlaverock, Conway, Carisbrooke, and Caernarvon castles, present good specimens of this kind; as do the[Pg 78] Middle Tower, and the Bloody Tower, in the Tower of London: the latter has the most perfect portcullis in the kingdom.

A principal tower or keep rose prominently above the rest, and generally from an artificial mount. It contained the well of water, without which the garrison, when besieged, could not hold out in this their last place of refuge. The keep also had its subterranean prison, and several stories of apartments communicating by a staircase, either in the walls, or built outside the tower.

As the railway traveller journeys along the South Eastern line, he will see close to the Tunbridge station, the towered entrance-gate of the castle built by Richard de Tonbridge, a follower of the Conqueror. The whole building was moated, and the exterior walls inclosed an area of about six acres. There remain only two massive towers flanking an arched gateway, with walls of great thickness, and having no other openings than long narrow slits, called *oilets*, through which, when besieged, archers shot their arrows. In front of this entrance was formerly a drawbridge, thrown across the moat, which, when raised, formed a strong door, closing up the archway. This opening was again guarded by two portcullises and two thick doors. The towers appear to have been divided into four stories, or floors, the lower being dungeons or prisons, and the upper formed into a large and noble hall, extending the whole width[Pg 79] and depth of the two towers. It was lighted by two large windows towards the inner court. The towers are supposed, from their style, to have been built in the reign of King John, or Henry III. The windows were not glazed, but had iron bars; the floor and ceiling were of immense thickness, the latter three feet. Branching from this tower-entrance, are certain walls to the right and left; the first extending up the side of a lofty hill, whereon was the keep-tower, or chief residence of the baron: to this, it is presumed, he retreated when other parts of his castle had been taken by an enemy.

The following account of the siege of Bedford Castle by Henry III., given in Camden's *Britannia*, is interesting, as containing a summary of the principal portions of the building, and the several stages of the attack:—"The castle was taken by four assaults: in the first was taken the barbican; in the second, the outer bail (ballium); at the third attack, the wall by the old tower was thrown down by the miners, where, with great danger, they possessed themselves of the inner bail through a chink; at the fourth assault, the miners set fire to the tower, so that the smoke burst out, and the tower itself was cloven to that degree, as to show visibly some broad chinks; whereupon the enemy surrendered."

The most perfect of our northern castles now existing, is Raby, the stately seat of the Duke of Cleveland, the history of which is traced through eight centuries and a half. Raby, pointing by its name to a Danish origin, is first mentioned in connexion with King Canute, who, after making his celebrated pilgrimage over Garmondsway Moor to the[Pg 80] shrine of St. Cuthbert, there offered it, with other possessions, to the saint. Bishop Flambard wrested the rich gift from the monastics, but restored it again on his death-bed. It continued in the peaceful possession of the monks till 1131. In that year they granted it, for an annual rent of £4, to Dolphin, son of Ughtred, of the blood-royal of Northumberland. Whoever the original founder might have been, Dolphin's descendant, Robert filius Maldred, was Lord of Raby when, early in the thirteenth century, he married Isabel Neville, by the death of her brother the last of that line. From their son Geoffrey, who assumed his mother's surname, the history of the Nevilles may be said to date. To his descendant, John Lord Neville, they owed Raby. Some portion of the older fabric is thoroughly incorporated with the new, so as to present the work and ideas of one period, and a perfect example of a fourteenth-century castle, without any appearance of earlier work or later alteration whatever. Its apparent weakness of site has been pointed out; but though not set on a hill, it had the defence of water, which was drawn off centuries since. But the real defences of Raby lay beyond the mere circuit of its own walls and waters. They are to be found in the warrior spirits of its lords and in the border castles of Roxburgh, Wark, Norham, Berwick, and Bamburgh, which they commanded continuously as warders and governors from the days of Robert Neville, in the thirteenth century, to the time of Queen Elizabeth. Apart from the question of the site, the stately castle itself is of great strength, and skilfully disposed.

Passing through a fine gate-tower, the bailey (immediately within the outer ward) is entered. The castle itself consists of a quadrangular[Pg 81] mass of great dignity and splendour, with an open court in the centre. One side of the court, or the quadrangle, is occupied by two halls, one above the other, of such stupendous proportions that carriages are admitted to drive across the quadrangle *into* the lower hall. The sides of the quadrangle have the kitchen and offices springing from one end of the hall, and the principal chambers of the castle from the other, according to the usual distribution of the age.

Although a view of most of those fortresses which are destined chiefly for the purposes of war or defence, suggests to the imagination dungeons, chains, and a painful assemblage of horrors, yet some of these castles were often the scenes of magnificence and hospitality,

"Where the songs of knights and barons bold
In weeds of peace high triumph hold;"

or where, in the days of chivalry, the wandering knight or distressed princess found honourable reception; the holy palmer repose for his wearied limbs; and the poor and helpless their daily bread.

Leland considered Raby as "the largest castle of logginges in all the north country." At different periods alterations have been made, according to the more modern ideas of comfort and convenience, without materially affecting its external form, so that it recalls to the mind the romantic days of chivalry. The embattled wall with which it is surrounded, occupies about two acres of ground. At irregular distances are two towers, named from their founders, the Clifford Tower and the Bulmer Tower. The halls are large and grand. In the upper, or Baron's hall, ninety feet in length, and thirty-four in breadth, the baronial[Pg 82] feasts were held; and here,

"Seven hundred knights, retainers all
Of Neville, at their master's call,
Together sat in Raby's Hall."

When the British Archæological Association visited Raby in the autumn of 1865, the Duke of Cleveland, as the President of the Association, entertained some 200 guests at a sumptuous dinner, in which venison, venison pasties, and grouse were paramount. The kitchen is on a scale to correspond with the enormous festivals of the seven hundred knights: it is a square of thirty feet, having three chimneys, one for the grate, a second for stoves, and the third (now stopped up) for the great cauldron. The roof is arched, and has a small cupola in the centre; it has likewise five windows, from each of which steps descend, but only in one instance to the floor; and a gallery runs round the whole interior of the building. The ancient oven is said to have allowed a tall person to stand upright in it, its diameter being fifteen feet; according to Pennant, it was one time converted into a wine-cellar, "the arches being divided into ten parts, each holding a hogshead of wine in bottles." "The park and pleasure grounds belonging to this magnificent castle are upon the same extensive scale, with woods that sweep over hill and sink into valley, and command a constant change of beautiful prospects."[25]

Durham Castle is another noble pile of the north. The outer gateway is a Norman arch; traces of Norman work are seen in the courtyard; and we[Pg 83] then reach the hall, which, as left by Bishop Hatfield, was at least a third longer than it is at present. It owes it curtailment to Bishop Fox (1494-1502), who erected a kitchen and other offices at the lower end. This kitchen remains in its original form, with wide-yawning fireplaces still applied to their original purpose; and the buttery hatches in old black oak have the motto of "*Est Deo gracio*," in black-letter, carved upon them. A tapestried gallery, with an elaborate Norman doorway, leads to Bishop Tunstall's chapel; and in another apartment, now the senate-room of the University of Durham, is some curious tapestry of the history of Moses. The keep, now refaced and restored, was rebuilt by Bishop Hatfield. The castle is commonly said to be no older than

William the Conqueror; but a fortress must have existed from a much earlier period, and the mound is artificial. The Norman chapel of the castle, its most ancient portion, is usually assigned to King William I., though of the time of Rufus. The pavement of herring-bone is, no doubt, coeval. The whole of Durham Castle is now in excellent preservation, and the union of the past with the present is well maintained; for the old keep, which commands beautiful views of the Wear and the outlying country, is parcelled out into rooms, which are occupied by the students of the University. The great hall of the castle is hung with old paintings, chiefly the portraits of bishops and ecclesiastics connected with the see. At the lower end of the apartment, about half way between the roof and the ground, are two niches, at opposite sides, built for the minstrels of the period, and from which they regaled the guests.

The legendary histories of our castles would take us too far afield for[Pg 84] our limits. Sometimes, in these legends, the very names of the Teutonic mythic personages are preserved. Thus, a legend in Berkshire has retained the name of the Northern and Teutonic smith-hero, Weland, the representative of the classical Vulcan. The name of Weland's father, Wade, is preserved in the legend of Mulgrave Castle, in Yorkshire, which is pretended to have been built by a giant of that name. A Roman road, which passes by it, is called Wade's Causeway; and a large tumulus, or cairn of stones, in the vicinity is popularly called Wade's Grave. According to the legend, while the giant Wade was building his castle, he and his wife lived upon the milk of an enormous cow, which she was obliged to leave at pasture on the distant moors. Wade made the causeway for her convenience, and she assisted him in building the castle by bringing him quantities of large stones in her apron. One day, as she was carrying a bundle of stones, her apron-string broke, and they all fell to the ground, a great heap of about twenty cart-loads,—and there they still remain as a memorial of her industry. Another castle in Yorkshire, occupying an early site, was said, according to a legend related by Leland in the sixteenth century, to have been built by a giant named Ettin. This is a mere corruption of the name of the *eotenas*, or giants of Teutonic mythology.

One of our most celebrated castles of defence is Corfe Castle, in Dorset, a remarkable specimen of mediæval military architecture. The earliest notice of this fortress is in an Anglo-Saxon charter of the year 948. In 981 Corfe was the scene of the murder of King Edward the Martyr. After the death of his father, Edgar, Elfrida, his widow, headed a faction in opposition to the accession of Edward, and continued her[Pg 85] intrigues until her unscrupulous ambition at last led her to the perpetration of a deed which has covered her name with infamy. This was the murder of her step-son by a hired assassin, as he stopped one day while hunting, at her residence, Corfe Castle; he was stabbed in the back, as he sat on his horse at the gate of the castle, drinking a cup of mead. The 18th of March, 978, is the date assigned to the murder of King Edward, who was only in his seventeenth year when he was thus cut off. He is retained in the calendar of the Anglican Church as a saint and martyr. The castle, which was the strongest fortress in the kingdom, formed an irregular triangle, the apex of which was connected by a narrow isthmus with the high ground, on which the town of Corfe stands. The isthmus had been cut through, and the ditch thus formed was spanned by a stately bridge of arches leading to the principal entrance of the fortress. Only the south side and parts of the east and west sides of the keep are standing, and large masses of prostrate walls lie in confusion around. The keep is Norman, believed to have been built by the Conqueror. King John kept his treasure and regalia here, and used the castle as a state prison. Twenty-four nobles concerned in the insurrection by his nephew, Arthur, Duke of Brittany, were, save two, it was said, there starved to death. King John caused Prince Arthur to be murdered, and sent his sister, the beautiful Princess Eleanor, prisoner to Corfe, where she remained several years.

Edward II., when he fell into the hands of his enemies, was, for a time, imprisoned here. In 1635, the castle and manor came into the possession of Sir John Bankes, Lord Chief Justice of England, and ancestor of the present owner. In the great Civil War, Corfe Castle was strongly[Pg 86] defended for the king, by Lady Bankes, wife of the Lord Chief Justice, with the assistance of her friends and retainers, and of a governor sent from the king's army. The castle was one of the last places in England that held out for Charles I. In the year 1645, it was captured by the Parliamentary forces through treachery, and reduced to the shapeless but picturesque fragments that now remain. Lady Bankes's heroic defence is narrated in the *Story of Corfe Castle*, a volume of stirring interest; and the event is a favourite subject with our historical painters. The ruins of Corfe are extensive, and from their very high situation, form a very striking object. "The vast fragments of the King's Tower," says Hutchins, "the Round Tower, leaning, as if nearly to fall, the broken walls, and vast pieces of them tumbled into the vale below, form such a scene of havoc and desolation, as strikes every spectator with sorrow and concern. The abundance of stone in the neighbourhood, the excellence of the cement, harder to be broken than the stones themselves, have preserved these prodigious ruins from being embezzled and lessened."

In the age of Edward III. the castles differed from those of previous periods. The confined plan of the close fortress expanded into a mixture of the castle and the mansion; comprising spacious and magnificent apartments, the hall, the banqueting-room, the chapel, with galleries of communication, and sleeping chambers. The keep was entirely detached, and independent of these buildings. Such was the royal palace of Windsor, erected by Edward III.; and such were the splendid baronial castles of Warwick, Ludlow, Stafford, Harewood, Alnwick, Kenilworth, Raglan, and many others. The last-mentioned is one of the most perfect[Pg 87] examples we are acquainted with, of the union of vast strength and security, with convenient accommodation and ornamental splendour. The keep is a perfect fortress in itself, and encircled by a range of minor towers and moat. Its masonry is unrivalled.[26]

Of one of these spacious castles we give a descriptive outline, chiefly from the paper read by Mr. J. H. Parker, on the visit of the Archæological Institute to Windsor, in July 1866. Amongst the royal and palatial edifices of Europe, that of Windsor holds a very high rank, and is, in a manner, to England what Versailles is to France and the Escurial to Spain; and while it is infinitely superior to both in point of situation, it far exceeds them, and indeed every other pile or building of its class, in antiquity. From having been the residence of so many of our kings, its history is, to a certain extent, identified with that of the kingdom itself from the time of the Conquest. The castle stands on an outlying promontory of chalk, commanding the winding shores of that part of the Thames, with a rich valley, which seems to have pointed it out as a natural position for a fortress in primitive times, when the natives wished to protect their country from invasion. The wide and deep entrenchments, and the high artificial mounds, indicate an early date. There are also roads at the bottom of the fosses, with a wide bank between them, on which several keeps were erected, first of wood and afterwards of stone. A subterranean passage leading from the bottom of the outer foss, at a depth of thirty feet, to the bottom of the inner foss, at a depth of fifteen feet (the present pantries), cut in a very rude manner through the solid chalk, has a[Pg 88] vault of the time of Henry II. carried on chalk walls, built over a small part of it as far as the Norman buildings extended only: the doorways are of the same period, one of which is quite perfect, and opens into the inner foss. If Windsor Castle had been built in the fifth century by King Arthur, as was believed by Edward III. and the chronicler Froissart, the roads would have been on the level. They are more likely of the time of Caractacus or Julius Cæsar. Edward the Confessor is believed to have resided chiefly at Old Windsor, where some of the ancient earthworks certainly belong to a period before the Norman Conquest. William himself is said to have built a castle at Windsor, but there is no evidence of it. The Domesday Survey rather proves that there was one previously existing, which had been inhabited by Earl Harold in the time of the Confessor. Henry I. is said by Stow, writing in the fifteenth century, to have built New Windsor chiefly of wood; some of the fragments of stone carving found in the castle may be of his time.

Stephen built nothing here, but Windsor is mentioned in the treaty of Wallingford as a fortress of importance. The name "Norman Tower," as given to one part of the pile, is erroneous, as the Norman keep is nothing more than earthworks surmounted by a wooden structure. The earliest date which can be assigned to any stone masonry which has been discovered at Windsor is the reign of Henry II. In the time of Henry II. the first mention of the castle is made in the Pipe Rolls. The outer wall of the south front of the upper ward remains, with the lower part of the king's gate, its hinges, and portcullis groove; the upper part was destroyed, and the whole concealed in other buildings by Wyatville, in the restoration works under George IV. In the reigns of Richard I.[Pg 89] and John only necessary repairs were made.

With Henry III. the history of the existing castle may be said to begin. The whole of the lower ward was then first built of stone, and many portions of the existing walls are found to be of that period. The Clewer Tower—now known as the Curfew Tower—remains almost unaltered, and exhibits in good condition a prison of the above period.

The King's Hall is now the Chapter library, but the chambers of the King and Queen have been destroyed. Plans and drawings of them have been preserved; and the measurements agree with the orders of the kings, as recorded in the public rolls.

Of the primitive chapel the north wall is still preserved; the galilee being now the east end (behind the altar) of St. George's Chapel. The doorways of the galilee are one of Henry III., the other of Edward III.; the west end of the chapel has been rebuilt several times. The arcade in the cloisters was protected by a wooden roof only. This chapel was completed by Edward III. and made into a lady-chapel, when the great St. George's Chapel was built. It was partly rebuilt by Henry VII. for the tomb of Lady Margaret, his mother, and afterwards was proposed for that of Henry VIII. It was much altered by James II. and partly restored by George IV. At the present time it is being made the object of devoted care, under the direction of Mr. Gilbert Scott. The roof has been vaulted in stone, the pattern of that of Henry VII. is being inlaid with mosaic work, and the windows filled with stained glass; and the edifice is to be a sepulchral chapel over the Royal vaults, in memory of the late Prince Consort. Mural paintings of kings' heads have been found of[Pg 90] the date of Henry III. and Edward III., and are preserved in the cloister and galilee.

During the reign of Edward I. the accounts show that the great works begun by Henry III. were carried on and completed; but no new works appear to have been undertaken. In the reign of Edward II. there were considerable sums expended on repairs of the walls, towers, and bridges, chiefly for timber and carpenters' work.

The reign of Edward III. is one of the most important in respect to the history of Windsor, a large part of the existing castle having been built at that period, and its survey has been lately brought to light. Another equally important document is the builder's account for the Round Tower, which was entirely built from the ground in the eighteenth year of this reign, and still remains, though much altered in appearance, from the additional story superposed by Mr. Wyatville, under George IV.

This building is sometimes called the Round Tower, and sometimes the Round Table; and, from other peculiarities in the same accounts, it is evident that the tower was built to hold the table. The galleries on which this round table was placed are still remaining, and the general disposition of the apartment where the knights dined on St. George's day is well seen from the summit of the Round Tower. The tables of those days were seldom more than a few planks in width, and the guests sat round on one side, the other being open for the service of the attendants. The centre of this great round table, then, was designed for the latter purpose, and was open to the air, a passage communicating on a level from this central space to the kitchen on the top of the middle gate, which has thus acquired the title of the "Kitchen Tower." The[Pg 91] tower and table were erected in ten months, the greatest haste being made in order that the new order of knights might dine here on St. George's day following.

Edward III. did not build a chapel at Windsor, but only completed the one which had been begun by Henry III.; adding to it or rebuilding a cloister, a vestry, and other adjuncts.

After the thirteenth year, when William of Wykeham was appointed clerk of the works, with a salary of one shilling a day, an entirely new hall, with a new suite of apartments and offices, was built in the upper bailey, where the royal apartments now are; and the fine series of vaults under these apartments, forming ceilings to the servants' hall and other rooms and offices, still remain in perfect preservation, as built by Wykeham, who remained in this appointment only six years. The summary of his accounts during that time shows an expenditure of 5,658*l.*—equivalent to 120,000*l.* (?) of our money.

From this period, comparatively little was done for a century, when Edward IV. began to re-erect St. George's Chapel, nearly as we now see it; thereby adding, if not immediately to the castle itself, to the buildings within its precincts, one of extraordinary beauty and interest, as being in some respects the very finest specimen of the Perpendicular style and of ecclesiastical architecture in the kingdom. What adds, in some degree, to the interest of this edifice is, that the architects' names are preserved to us, it being known to be the work, first of Richard Beauchamp, Bishop of Salisbury; and, after his death, in 1481, it was completed by Sir Reginald Bray, who was also architect of Henry VII.'s Chapel. This sovereign intended to erect a mausoleum for[Pg 92] himself at Windsor, and had begun to do so on the site of the original chapel built by Henry III.; but he abandoned the idea in favour of that at Westminster. Henry VII., however, added to the castle that building which is still called after him, and which is situated at the western extremity of the north side of the great quadrangle. Fortunately, this has been preserved, owing, perhaps, partly to its situation; for, although a mere "bit," it is a singularly fine one, and a noble specimen of palatial architecture, in that particular style.[27]

The small tower at the south-west angle of the Royal apartments near the library, now called erroneously King John's Tower, is an octagonal building, and the two chambers in it have very good vaults, with the ribs meeting in a central boss, which is in both cases carved into the form of a rose. This enables this rose-tower and the rose-vaults to be identified in a very remarkable manner. The tower was very richly painted, and the quantity of paint and other materials charged on the roll misled the late Mr. Hudson Turner, who had only seen a portion of these accounts, and made him think they belonged to the great Round Tower, and that it was painted on the outside. The dates do not agree with this, and there is no evidence of external painting.

The works which had been carried on during a great part of the long reign of Edward III. were not completed at the time of his death, and were continued under Richard II.; but with the exception of necessary repairs, the accounts for this reign relate chiefly to the offices and dependencies of the cattle, especially the mews for the falcons, which[Pg 93] was evidently a large and important establishment not within the walls.

Geoffrey Chaucer, "the father of English poetry," was appointed, in the fourteenth year of this reign, clerk of the works, but very little was done in his time. The old chapter house, the remains of Henry the VII.'s palace, and the Clewer Tower and prison, are objects of much interest. A flight of about twenty steps leads down into the dungeons, which had been constructed by Henry III. for the confinement of State prisoners: it is a large and finely-arched vault, surrounded by seven small cells, each dismally lighted through a loop-hole in the thick wall.

The reign of Elizabeth forms almost an epoch in the architectural history of the castle, because, though she did not do much to it in the way of building, except annexing the portion erected by Henry VII., that which is distinguished by the name of Queen Elizabeth's Gallery, she first caused the terraces to be formed, thereby adding to the royal abode of Windsor, these truly regal characteristics. Under the Stuarts nothing material was done until the Restoration, when the castle began to be modernised, but in insipid taste. The principal addition made by Charles II. was the Star Building (containing the State Apartments shown to the public). The rooms were spacious and lofty, with large arched windows, commanding enchanting prospects; their only embellishment was derived from the sprawling pencil of Verrio. The first two Georges did nothing for Windsor; George III. on the contrary, much, especially in restoring the interior of St. George's Chapel. In 1796, James Wyatt Gothicised the Star Building, and other portions. Meanwhile, the east and south sides, the portions actually inhabited, were so inconvenient[Pg 94] that it was found indispensable, in 1778-82, to erect a separate building for the actual occupation of the royal family: this was the Queen's Lodge, a large, plain house on the south side of the castle, near the site of the present stables. About 1823, George IV., with a grant of 300,000*l.* from Parliament, began his grand improvements, with Jeffry Wyatt for his architect; commencing with George the Fourth's Gateway, the entrance into the quadrangle on the south side, in a direct line with the Long Walk. We shall not attempt to detail the improvements: among the most effective is the fine architectural vista quite through from the north terrace by George the Fourth's Gateway; the addition of the Waterloo Gallery, lighted from above, and brought into a group with the Throne-room and the Ball-room. St. George's Hall has been greatly improved, and at its western end has been constructed the Chapel. By renovation and remodelling the exterior, greater height has been given to most of the buildings; some of the towers have been carried up higher, and others added: amongst these last are the Lancaster and York, flanking George IV.'s Gateway; and the Brunswick Tower at the north-east angle. But the most striking improvement of the kind was that of carrying up the Round Tower thirty feet higher, exclusive of the Watch Tower on its summit, which makes the height in that part twenty-five feet more; thus rendering the castle much more conspicuous than formerly as a distant object.

The architect's work has been much animadverted on: the details and strange intermixture of the earliest and latest styles of Gothic are very objectionable; and, as to general effect, Canon Bowles objected that the renovated pile looked as if it had been washed with soap and water! Nevertheless, it is a stately pile; the venerable Canon, just[Pg 95] named, says of it: "Windsor Castle loses a great deal of its architectural impression (if I may use that word) by the smooth neatness with which its old towers are now chiselled and mortared. It looks as if it was washed every morning with soap and water, instead of exhibiting here and there a straggling flower, or creeping weather-stains. I believe this circumstance strikes every beholder; but, most imposing indeed is its distant view, when the broad banner floats or sleeps in the sunshine, amidst the intense blue of the summer skies; and its picturesque and ancient architectural vastness harmonizes with the decaying and gnarled oaks, coeval with so many departed monarchs. The stately, long-extended avenue, and the wild sweep of devious forests, connected with the eventful circumstances of English history, and past regal grandeur, bring back the memories of Edwards and Henries, or the gallant and accomplished Surrey." In 1825, Canon Bowles, who had been chaplain to the Prince Regent, and writes himself down as not a Laureate, but "a poet of loyal, old Church of England feelings," sung as follows:—

"Not that thy name, illustrious dome, recalls
The pomp of chivalry in banner'd halls,
The blaze of beauty, and the gorgeous sights
Of heralds, trophies, steeds, and crested knights;
Not that young Surrey here beguiled the hour,
With eyes upturn'd unto the maiden's tower.[28]
Oh! not for these, and pageants pass'd away,
I gaze upon your antique towers, and pray—
But that my SOVEREIGN here, from crowds withdrawn,
May meet calm peace upon the twilight lawn;
That here, among these grey, primeval trees,
He may inhale health's animating breeze;
And when from this proud terrace he surveys
[Pg 96]Slow Thames revolving his majestic maze,
(Now lost on the horizon's verge, now seen
Winding through lawns, and woods, and pastures green,)

May he reflect upon the waves that roll,
Bearing a nation's wealth from pole to pole,
And feel (ambition's proudest boast above)
A KING'S BEST GLORY IS HIS COUNTRY'S LOVE!"

"The range of cresting towers has a double interest, whilst we think of gorgeous dames and barons bold, of Lely and Vandyke's beauties; and gay, and gallant, accomplished cavaliers like Surrey. And who ever sat in the stalls of St. George's Chapel, without feeling the impression, on looking at the illustrious names, that here the royal and ennobled knights, through so many generations, sat each installed, whilst arms, and crests, and banners glittered over the same seat?"[29]

The interior of Windsor Castle, half a century since, mostly presented the decorative taste of the time of Charles the Second. To the seventeen State Apartments the public were admitted, until they were wearied with the mythological ceilings of Thornhill, Rigaud, and Matthew Wyatt; and the crowning genius of Verrio, in St. George's Hall. Throughout the apartments was placed the royal collection of pictures, then including the cartoons of Raphael; and the seven pictures of the glories of Edward III. painted by West for George III., remarkable for their historical accuracy, attributable to the friendly aid of Sir Isaac Heard, Garter King-at-arms, who was constantly at the elbow of the artist. And foremost among the decorative furniture were the State Bed of Queen Anne, silver chandeliers and glass-frames, and a "massive silver table[Pg 97] from Hanover." Most of Gibbons's fine carvings appear to have been removed to Hampton Court. The Keep, or Round Tower, was the residence of the Constable or Governor of the castle, which he defended against all enemies, and he had the charge of all prisoners brought thither: the last was Major Belleisle, who lived in tapestried chambers, and beguiled his captivity with the loves of Hero and Leander and Cupid and Psyche. In the guard-chamber was a small magazine of arms. At the top of the stairs, within the wall, was planted a large piece of cannon, levelled, through an aperture, at the lower gate; there were also seventeen pieces of cannon mounted at the embrasures round the curtain of the towers, which was then the only battery in the castle, though formerly the whole place was strongly fortified with cannon on each of the several towers, besides those on the two platforms in the Lower Ward.

The remodelling of the private apartments of the castle has been effected with due regard to convenience and splendour. Among the more pleasurable memorials of royal visits, are the fittings of the apartments refurnished for the Emperor and Empress of the French, in which satin hangings, bordered with long-stitch needlework, in the natural colours of the flowers portrayed, are much admired, as are also the Brussels lace and white silk toilet-table, &c. There are in the state-rooms some fine Gobelin tapestries, inlaid cabinets, superb clocks, and a malachite vase and doors. In the plate room, among other superb works, is a tall vase of oxydized silver, produced for the Prince Consort, a short time previous to his death, at the cost of 1,000*l.*; besides rock crystal cups and beakers, the gold mounts studded with jewels, and the cups engraved and ornamented with flowers in silver[Pg 98] filigree. Two of the most splendid receptions at the castle in the present reign, were the fêtes at the christening of the Prince of Wales in 1842, and the visits of Louis Philippe and some of his family in 1844: upon the latter occasion, the castle, seen from a distance, in the shades of an autumnal evening, with lights gleaming from nearly every window of the long-extended and stately pile, had a most enchanting effect.

Next to Windsor, deserves to be ranked Warwick Castle, in picturesqueness of site rivalling the royal palace; it is one of the finest specimens in the kingdom of the ancient residences of our feudal nobles. Not only for its architecture, but for its scenic accessories, and the sylvan character of the surrounding grounds, Warwick Castle is of almost matchless beauty. Of its archæology, on reference to the Pipe Rolls, we find it first mentioned in the 19th of Henry II., when it was furnished and garrisoned, at an expense of 10*l.* (equal to 200*l.* now), on behalf of the king against his son, and so it remained in the hands of Henry II. for three years. In the 20th and 21st of Henry II. are records of outlay for the soldiers, and in the latter year 50*l.* was spent in repairs. In the 7th year of King John, the castle, then belonging to the Crown (not the present castle, but a castle on the same site), was defended for 253 days; and in the days of Henry III. the walls were completely thrown down and destroyed. In the 9th of Edward II. (1315) it was returned, on an inquisition, as worth nothing except for the herbage in the courts and ditches, valued at 6*s.* 8*d.* a year. In the reign of Edward III. (1357) a new building was commenced by Thomas Beauchamp, Earl of Warwick, and finished about 1380. Guy's Tower was built in 1394. The next period in the architectural history of the[Pg 99] castle is two or three hundred years later. The castle was then used as a gaol. The next work was the erection of the entrance-hall. Mr. Salvia, the architect, has been called in by the Earl of Warwick, and has made habitable a portion of the castle which before had been unused. The extreme beauty of the two towers is considered as unequalled in the world.

In the valuable collection of pictures in Warwick Castle are a curious portrait of Queen Elizabeth, painted very early in her reign; portrait of Sir Philip Sydney, the intimate friend of Fulke Greville; Charles I. on horseback, probably a copy made by Vandyke from that at Blenheim; and the colossal picture of Charles I. copied from the original in the Vandyke Room at Windsor, a duplicate of which is to be seen at Hampton Court. At Warwick, too, is Holbein's portrait of Henry VIII. noted for the exquisite finish of its details. The collection of ancient and modern armour is very valuable. The great hall of the castle, in its appearance and furniture, retains much of its ancient character. Externally, the form of the building has sustained little alteration; its site is a solid rock, in which the cellars are excavated. Cæsar's Tower is the most ancient; Guy's Tower, of Decorated English character, is la fine preservation. In one of the greenhouses is the celebrated ancient marble vase brought to England by the

Earl of Warwick, to whom it had been given by Sir William Hamilton; it is known as the *Warwick Vase*, and has been copied in various materials.

As you look from the castle windows upon the soft-flowing Avon, with its gentle ripple in your ears, the effect is fascinating, and you are almost carried back to the age of fays and fairies. Henry V. visited Guy's Cliff; and Shakspeare is supposed to have made it a favourite[Pg 100] retirement.

Warwick has its apocryphal antiquities, more especially Guy's curiosities. The story of this famous fellow is said to have been taken from the exploits of Earl Leofric, husband of Lady Godiva; though the legendary Guy is derived by some from a French romance of the twelfth or thirteenth century. Guy, or a prototype, was reputed to be a living personage, and his sword and coat of mail formed the subject of a bequest in 1369. In the reign of Henry VIII. a pension was granted for the preservation of Guy's porridge-pot; but the conflict with the dun cow is not mentioned until in a seventeenth century play, though Dr. Caius, about 1552, saw a bone of a bonassus (cow) at Warwick Castle kept with the arms of Guy. In 1636 the rib of the dun cow was exhibited at Warwick. Guy's armour is a medley: a bassinet of Edward III.; breast-plate, fifteenth and seventeenth century; sword, Henry VIII.; staff, an ancient tilting-lance, very curious; the horse-armour, and "Fair Phillis' slippers" (strap-irons), are fifteenth century. In conclusion, "the renowned Guy" is considered to be a myth.

The first historical Earl of Warwick was so created by the Conqueror. The history of the castle has some strange episodes. In 1468, Edward IV. marching towards Warwick, was met by an embassy from the Earl of Warwick to treat for peace; which the king, too credulously listening to, rested in his camp at Wolvey; but the Earl surprised him by night in his bed, and took him prisoner to his castle at Warwick. In the Civil War, 1642, Warwick Castle, garrisoned for the Parliament, was besieged; and, after the battle of Edge Hill, when Charles left Birmingham, the inhabitants[Pg 101] seized the carriages containing the loyal plato, and conveyed them to Warwick Castle. Then Warwick and Kenilworth were in deadly hate: in 1230 (47th Hen. III.), Maudit, Earl of Warwick, and his Countess, were surprised in Warwick Castle, by a party of rebels from Kenilworth Castle, when the walls were thrown down lest the royalists should use them again; and the Earl and Countess were carried prisoners to Kenilworth Castle.

Kenilworth, five miles from Warwick and Coventry, respectively, had a castle which was demolished in the war of Edmund Ironside and Canute the Dane, early in the eleventh century. In the reign of Henry I. the manor was bestowed by the king on Geoffrey de Clinton, who built a strong castle, and founded a monastery. The castle keep is attributed to the reign of King John; the outer wall to the time of Henry III. The castle was one of the strongholds of Simon de Montfort, Earl of Leicester, in his insurrection against Henry III. and afforded shelter to his son, and others of his adherents, after the fatal battle of Evesham, in 1265; next year, however, it capitulated, after a gallant defence. A tournament of 100 knights was held here in 1278, the Earl of March principal challenger of the tilt-yard: of the ladies, who were splendidly attired, it is recorded, that they wore "silken mantles." The east range of buildings is referred to the middle of the reign of Edward II. who was confined in the castle, shortly before his murder in Berkeley Castle, in 1327. In the following reign, John of Gaunt became owner of the castle, which he much augmented by new and magnificent buildings. Henry IV. son of John of Gaunt, united the castle, which he inherited, to the domains of the Crown, of which it formed a part until the time of Elizabeth, who granted it to Robert Dudley, Earl of[Pg 102] Leicester, who erected "Leicester's Buildings." The magnificent entertainments given here by Leicester to Elizabeth are minutely described by Laneham, an attendant on the court, in a tract, entitled *The Princely Pleasures of Kenilworth*. On her way thither, the Queen was entertained by Leicester under a splendid tent at Long Itchington. Kenilworth has been made familiar to the general reader by Sir Walter Scott's picturesque romance, which has sent thousands to pic-nic among the castle ruins: it was dismantled after the Civil War of Charles I.

Kenilworth ruins remind one of a *puzzle*, a few of the pieces of which have been lost, but are so few as to be readily supplied. The ruins are principally Late Perpendicular, but there are some Norman portions. Cæar's Tower, of which three sides remain, has walls sixteen feet thick. John of Gaunt's large and massive additions are in decay; and the Leicester Buildings, though comparatively modern, present, from the friable nature of the stone, an appearance of great antiquity: they contain the remains of the noble banqueting-hall. The gate-house, also Leicester's, is better preserved, and has in our time been occupied as a farm-house. The ruins are, in many parts, mantled with ivy, which adds to their picturesqueness; and being on an elevated, rocky site, they command extensive views of the country round:

"Grey memory of centuries past,
Proud Kenilworth! How dear
The charm that mellowing time hath cast
Over thy portals drear.
Thy battlements are crumbling now,
And ivy decks thy faded brow.

"Green grows the moss, where banners told
[Pg 103]Ambitions Leicester's hour of pride;
Years their all-changing course have roll'd—
All tenantless the chambers wide.
Bank weeds upon the portals grow;
Noble and knight, where are ye now?"

Traditional tales of the festive joys of Kenilworth linger on the spot; and among other things, it is told that the great clock was stopped during Elizabeth's stay at the castle, as if Time had stood still, waiting on the Queen, and seeing her subjects enjoying themselves!

Arundel Castle, the last baronial home we have to describe, is a seat of great historic interest, derived from the long list of warriors and statesmen, whose names are identified with the place; and whose deeds, during the lapse of eight centuries, have shed lustre on our national history:

"Since William rose, and Harold fell,
There have been Counts of Arundel;
And earls old Arundel shall have
While rivers flow and forests wave."

The castle stands on the river Arun in Sussex, at a short distance from the sea, which is once supposed to have washed the castle-walls, as anchors and other implements have been found near it. The castle is mentioned as early as the time of King Alfred, who bequeathed it to his nephew Adhelm. After the Norman Conquest, it was given by William to his kinsman, Roger de Montgomeri, created Earl of Arundel and Shrewsbury. Robert, one of the successors of this Earl, supported Robert, Duke of Normandy, the eldest son of William I. against Henry, the youngest son of the Conqueror. Afterwards the castle passed into the family of Albini; and at last, by the marriage of that race with Thomas, Duke of[Pg 104]Norfolk (in the reign of Elizabeth), into the family of the Howards. It gives to its possessor (now the Duke of Norfolk) the title of Earl of Arundel, and is an instance of a peerage attached to the tenure of a house, which is now an anomaly. In 11th Henry VI. it was decided that the tenure of the castle of Arundel alone, without any creation, patent, or investiture, constituted its possessor Earl of Arundel. Sir Bernard Burke, however, considers this fact to admit of doubt. (See *Visitation of Seats and Arms*, vol. i. p. 89.) For a place of defence, the castle must have been well calculated, standing, as it does, at the extreme point of an eminence which terminates one of the high and narrow ridges of the South Downs; and in the two immense fosses which still remain, we have evident tokens of the ancient mode of fortification. The entrance gateway, anciently defended by a drawbridge and a portcullis, was built by Richard Fitzalan, in the reign of Edward I. This, with some of the walls and the keep, is all that remains of the ancient castle.

The keep is a circular stone tower, sixty-eight feet in diameter, and the most perfect in England. In the middle of it is a dungeon, a vault about ten feet high, accessible by a flight of steps, and thought to have served as a storehouse for the garrison. The keep has long been tenanted by some owls of large size and beautiful plumage, sent over from America as a present to the then Duke of Norfolk. The barbican was named Bevis's Tower from this legendary story. A giant named Bevis officiated here as warder, in payment for which the Earl of Arundel built this tower for his reception, allowing him two hogsheads of beer every week, a whole ox, and a proportionate quantity of bread and[Pg 105] mustard. So huge was the giant, that he could, without inconvenience, wade the channel of the sea to the Isle of Wight, and frequently did so for his amusement. So, great as that wonder may be, a greater marvel is, how he ever got into his tower, which, upon ordinary calculations, must have been totally inadequate to contain him.

Among the Norman remains is an extensive vault, now used as a cellar, about fifteen feet in height. That it was anciently used as a dungeon is undoubted; and in it were confined not only military captives, but every civil delinquent within the privileges of the honour. This was a considerable source of profit to the Earls, and was, therefore, sturdily maintained by them as a vested right. The ancient hall, with its appendant buildings, was in the style of the reign of Edward III. The north-east wing was last erected. Such was the building as it stood at the commencement of the seventeenth century, inclosing five acres and a half, and resembling in ground-plan Windsor Castle.

Arundel Castle was almost battered to pieces in the Civil War: the hall and other living apartments were rendered untenantable, and the place was abandoned by its noble owner, till about the year 1720, from which period until 1801 only partial restorations were carried out. Then was built the magnificent library for 10,000 volumes, in imitation of the aisle of a Gothic cathedral; with ornamentation from Gloucester Cathedral, and St. George's, Windsor: the ceiling, columns, &c. are of mahogany. In 1806 was begun the Barons' Hall: the roof is of Spanish chestnut, designed from Westminster, Eltham, and Crosby Halls; and it has a large stained end window, of King John signing Magna Charta,[30] and thirteen windows painted with baronial and family portraits; and in[Pg 106] the drawing-room is a stained glass window, by Eginton, representing the Duke and Duchess of Norfolk as King Solomon and the Queen of Sheba at a banquet! The renovation of the castle cost Charles Howard, the eleventh Duke of Norfolk, the large sum of 600,000*l*. Upon the completion of the work in June, 1815, he gave a magnificent fête, which accelerated his death in December following. The appointments of the castle are very superb. The Duke of Norfolk received here, in 1846, a state visit from Queen Victoria and Prince Albert.

The park is extensive and finely wooded, and has much picturesque scenery. Vineyards formerly abounded in this country; so that, in 1763, there were sixty pipes of excellent wine resembling Burgundy, in the cellar of the castle, the produce of one vineyard attached to it. The river Arun, on which the town of Arundel stands, is famous for the grey mullets which, in summer, come up here in large shoals, in quest of a particular weed, the feeding on which renders them a great delicacy.

Among the events in the castle history was the reception of the Empress Maud, in 1139, at Arundel Castle, by Adeliza, a relict of Henry I. King Stephen, apprised of her movements, appeared suddenly before the castle, with a well-appointed army. The Queen Dowager sent him this spirited message:—"She had received the Empress as her friend, not as his enemy; she had no intention of interfering in their quarrels," and therefore[Pg 107] begged the King to allow her royal guest to quit Arundel, and try her fortune in some other part of England. "But," added she, "if you are determined to besiege her here, I will endure the last extremity of war rather than give her up, or suffer the laws of hospitality to be violated." The Queen's request was granted, and the Empress retired to Bristol.

To conclude. No place in England deserves more notice than the Castle of Arundel—a grand pile of buildings, modern for the most part, and not capable of supporting criticism; but the ivy-grown keep, at least as old as the days of Henry I., may challenge comparison with any of the same date in this country. The castle has not withstood sieges as others have; it is but too well known for its surrender to Sir William Waller, who took from it seventeen colours of foot, two of horse, and a thousand prisoners. Nor is it associated with any decisive battles or events; but no residence presents us with such a picture of feudal times; no other baronial home has sent forth thirteen dukes and thirty-five earls. What house has been so connected with our political and religious annals as that of Howard? The premiers in the roll-call of our nobility, have been also among the most persecuted and ill-fated. Not to dwell on the high-spirited Isabelle, Countess Dowager of Arundel, and widow of Hugh, last Earl of the Albini family, who upbraided Henry III. to his face with "vexing the church, oppressing the barons, and denying all his true-born subjects their rights;" or Richard, Earl of Arundel, who was executed for conspiring to seize Richard II.—we must think with indignation of the sufferings inflicted by Elizabeth on Philip, Earl of Arundel, son of "the great" Duke of Norfolk, beheaded by Elizabeth in[Pg 108] 1572 for his dealings with Mary, Queen of Scots. In the biography of Earl Philip, which, with that of Ann Dacres, his wife, was well edited by the late lamented Duke, we find that he was caressed by Elizabeth in early life, and steeped in the pleasures and vices of her court by her encouragement, to the neglect of his constant wife, whose virtues, as soon as they reclaimed him to his duty to her, rendered him hated and suspected by the Queen, so that she made him the subject of vindictive and incessant persecution, till death released him at the age of thirty-eight. To another Howard, Thomas, son of Earl Philip, the country is indebted for those treasures of the East, the Arundel Marbles; though Lord Clarendon describes him somewhat ill-naturedly, denying him all claims to learning, and even gravity of character.

The sight of the embattled towers of Arundel conjures up before us many historic personages, whom in fancy we can see emerging from their venerable gateways, in all the pride of youth and ancestry, whose mouldered ashes now repose under those grey walls. And there too now lies, alas! added to the number, the late kind-hearted and amiable Duke, snatched away, like so many of his forefathers, in the very prime of manhood.[31]

III. Household Antiquities.

[Pg 109]

THE OLD ENGLISH HOUSE.

itherto we have but glanced at the earlier periods of what may be termed Domestic Life in England. We have attempted to trace our British ancestors in their "woods and caves, and painted skins;" in their rude state, before the Roman colonization; in their advancement under that enlightened sway; and their decadence after their conquerors had left them. To these periods have succeeded the ages of Castle-building, when edifices were built for purposes of defence. In lawless times, might lorded it over right, and stronger places of abode than we regard a *house* were necessary for the security and protection of the inhabitants. Throughout these periods we have few evidences, from their dwellings, of how the *people* lived: from the earth caverns of the Early Britons to the Roman civilization is a dreary picture of rude accommodation; and though the excavation of ancient sites, and the operation of the plough, may bring to light many a splendid pavement and appliances, which denote luxurious life,— these are the remains of the embellished villas of the wealthy Roman, and not of the abodes of the conquered Briton. The Saxons lived so meanly, that it were vain to[Pg 110] expect to find many traces of their dwellings; and of the Danes there are still fewer remains. With these exceptions we have, before the Conquest, no actually existing witnesses.

With the Norman period our series of evidences begins. For some time after the Conquest, strictly domestic remains are very scanty. The great men lived in castles, which are, indeed, domestic so far as men lived in them, but whose architecture is too much affected by military considerations to be called strictly domestic architecture, which is the building of *houses*, whose defence is either not thought of or is something quite secondary. It is clear that houses of this sort, of such pretensions as to possess any architectural character, or to be preserved down to our time, could not well exist, in the open country at least, till the land had become comparatively settled and civilized. Hence, our list of Norman houses in England is very scanty, and they are chiefly formed in walled towers, like Lincoln and Bury St. Edmund's. [The erection of Lincoln Castle by order of William the Conqueror, in 1086, is said to have caused the demolition of 240 houses. Perhaps the only perfect and untouched Norman example is the small unroofed house at Christ Church, in Hampshire. The church is Norman, and the tower is supposed to be of Roman origin.]

Several of the fragments elsewhere have very fine Norman detail; but for Norman architecture exhibiting anything like the real grandeur of the style, we must look to the castles and monasteries. In the thirteenth century our examples are still but few and small, though much more numerous than before. After the age of Edward III. the castle became more like a mansion, as we have seen in the castles of Windsor, Warwick, and Kenilworth.

[Pg 111]

As the character of the times became more peaceful, and law succeeded to the reign of the strong hand, a still further change took place in the construction of these dwellings, and they partook but slightly of the castellated character. Beauty and ornament were consulted by the builders instead of strength; and the convenient accommodation of the in-dwellers, in lieu of the means of disposing of a crowded garrison, and its necessary provision in time of siege. They usually retained the moat and battlemented gateway, and one or two strong turrets, to build which a royal licence was necessary. Thus, the idea of the English manor-house seems to have disengaged itself from that of the castle, and we begin to have a noble series of strictly domestic buildings, defence being quite secondary, and in no way obtruded. They were generally quadrangular in plan, the larger class inclosing two open courts, of which one contained the stables, offices, and lodgings of the household; the second, the principal or statechambers, with the hall and chapel. The windows were large and lofty, reaching almost to the ground, and several of them opening to the gardens on the outside of the building, though these were inclosed by high battlemented walls and a moat. It should, however, be remarked, that the mansion, except in edifices of considerable extent and consequence, seldom contained more than one court.

The hall, in most cases, retained its original design. It was distinguished by its superior elevation, its turreted towers (or lantern), its windows, and projecting bay. The principal doorway entered upon a vestibule or lobby, extending across the edifice, with a door of inferior dimensions at the opposite extremity, having, on one side, the lower wall of the hall, in which were doors leading to the buttery and kitchener's department; and on the other, the screen, or lofty partition[Pg 112] of wood, designed to conceal those doors from the view of persons in the hall. In the Companies' Halls of the City of London, a moveable screen is generally used for this purpose.

The screen was often panelled with wood from top to bottom, and divided into compartments, which were enriched with shields and carved work, having usually two or three arched doorways opening on the lobby. In many instances, the minstrels' gallery was placed above this compartment.

Among the richest specimens extant of the embattled mansions are Wingfield Manor-house, in Derbyshire; Cowdray, in Sussex;[32] Kelmingham Hall, in Suffolk; Penshurst, in Kent; Deene Park, in Northamptonshire; and Thornbury Castle, in Gloucestershire. This period of the transition from the castle to the mansion is considered the best style of English architecture.

Wingfield, near the centre of Derbyshire, was built by Ralph, Lord Cromwell, who, in the time of Henry VI. was Treasurer of England, in allusion to which he had bags or purses of stones carved over the[Pg 113] gateway of Wingfield, as well as on the manor-house of Coly Weston, in Northamptonshire, augmented by this Lord Cromwell. Wingfield Manor-house originally consisted of two square courts—one containing the principal apartments, and the other the offices. It had a noble hall lighted by a beautiful octagon window, and a range of Gothic windows, north and south. The principal entrance is by an embattled gate-house, through a pointed arch, beside the end of the great state apartment lighted by a large and rich pointed window. Here the Earl of Shrewsbury held in his custody Mary Queen of Scots, in a convenient suite of apartments, which communicated with the great tower, whence the ill-starred captive could see her friends with whom she held a secret correspondence. An attempt was made by Leonard Dacre to rescue Mary, after which Elizabeth, becoming suspicious of the Earl of Shrewsbury, directed the Lady Huntingdon to take care of the Queen of Scots in Shrewsbury's house; and had her suite reduced to thirty persons. Her captivity at Wingfield is stated to have extended to nine years, which, however, is questionable.

Thornbury Castle is picturesquely placed twenty-four miles south-west of Gloucester, on the banks of a rivulet two miles westward of "the glittering, red, and rapid Severn, embedded in its emerald vale, and shining up in splendid contrast to the shady hills of the Dean Forest." Thornbury was begun by Edward Stafford, Duke of Buckingham; its completion was prevented by his execution, in the year 1522. It is a castellated group, with battlemented towers and turrets, and enriched chimney-shafts, clothed with luxuriant ivy; its bay-windows are very fine. Buckingham fell one of the earliest victims to the cruel tyranny[Pg 114] of our eighth Henry. The line of his pedigree is marked in blood. His father was beheaded by Richard III.; his grandfather was killed at the battle of St. Albans; his great grandfather at the battle of Northampton; and the father of this latter at the battle of Shrewsbury. More than a century had elapsed since any chief of this great family had fallen by a natural death. Edward was doomed to no nobler fate than his forefathers. Knivett, a discarded officer of Buckingham's household, furnished information to Wolsey, which led to the apprehension of his late master: it was stated that he had consulted a monk about future events; that he had declared all the acts of Henry VII. to be wrongfully done; that he had told Knivett, that if he had been sent to the Tower, when he was in danger of being committed, he would have played the part which his father had intended to perform at Salisbury—where, if he could have obtained an audience, he would have stabbed Richard III. with a knife; and that he had told Lord Abergavenny, if the king had died, he would have the rule of the land. Yet, all this was but the testimony of a spy. Buckingham confessed the real amount of his absurd inquiries from the friar. He was tried in the court of the Lord High Steward, by a jury of one duke, one marquess, seven earls, and twelve barons, who convicted him. The Duke of Norfolk shed tears on pronouncing sentence. The prisoner said: "May the eternal God forgive you my death, as I do." The only favour which he could obtain was, that the ignominious part of a traitor's death should be remitted. He was accordingly beheaded on the 17th of May, 1521; whilst the surrounding people vented their indignation against Wolsey by loud cries of "The butcher's son!" The[Pg 115] half-built and decaying Thornbury has prompted this saddening history of its founder and his ill-fated family.

Longleat, in Wiltshire, the seat of the Marquis of Bath, and built in the reign of Edward VI., is, for its date, esteemed the most regular building in the kingdom. Upon its site was originally a priory, which came into the possession of the Thynne family, in the reign of Henry VIII. The present mansion was commenced by the first proprietor of that family, and completed for his successors by an Italian architect: it consists of three stories, Doric, Ionic, and Corinthian, adorned with rich pilasters, handsome balustrades, and statues; and from the roof rise several cupolas. The apartments are large and sumptuous; and the great hall is two stories in height. The gardens were originally embellished with fountains, cascades, and statues, and laid out in formal parterres; but the whole has been newly remodelled. The entire domain is fifteen miles in circuit; and in magnitude, grandeur, and variety of decoration, Longleat has always been the pride of this part of the country. Its collection of pictures includes many portraits of eminent persons in the reign of Queen Elizabeth and her successors.

In the time of Elizabeth and James I. were erected many mansions upon splendid and extensive scales. John Thorpe built five palaces for Elizabeth's ministers: for Lord Burghley, Theobalds and Burghley; Wimbledon, for Sir Robert Cecil; Hollenby and Kirby, for Lord Chancellor Hatton; and Buckhurst for the Earl of Dorset. Thorpe also built for Sir Walter Cope, Holland House, Kensington, about 1606, which received its name from Henry Rich, Earl of Holland, by whom the mansion was greatly[Pg 116] altered. Its plan is that of half the letter H, of deep red brick, with pilasters and their entablature; the window dressings, and coping, of stone. Few of the apartments retain their original character; some of the interior is supposed to be by Inigo Jones. The gilt room is by Cleyn, an artist largely employed by James I. and Charles I.; the figures over the fireplace are worthy of Parmegiano, and here is a very fine collection of modern busts.

Burghley, Northamptonshire, has the rare fortune of remaining to this time the seat of the descendants of the great Lord Burghley, for whom the mansion was built; the present noble owner being the Marquis of Exeter: in approaching it from Stamford, its singular chimneys, the variety of its turrets, towers, and cupolas, and the steeple of its chapel rising from its centre, give it the appearance more of a small city than a single building.

Hatfield, in Hertfordshire, which has been a palace, episcopal, royal, and noble, for upwards of seven centuries, was mostly built by Thorpe, in 1611. The old palace was of the twelfth century: here is the chamber in which the Princess Elizabeth was kept for some time a state prisoner; and in the present mansion, Charles I. was confined. In plan, Hatfield is in the form of half the letter H: each front differs from the other, but in unity of design the Tudor period is remarkably prevalent, and it is believed that no house in the kingdom erected at so early a date, remains so entire as this.

A stately mansion of this period was erected at Campden, in Gloucestershire, at an expense of 29,000*l.*; it occupied eight acres, was of splendid architecture, and had a large dome rising from the roof,[Pg 117] which was illuminated nightly for the guidance of travellers. Campden was burnt during the Civil War.

Haddon Hall, near Bakewell, in Derbyshire, erected at various periods, affords excellent examples of the several styles of domestic architecture, from the early pointed, to the Tudor and Elizabethan. It was originally a barton, or farm, given by William the Conqueror to his natural son, William Peverell. The mansion is preserved intact: the tapestry and paneling remain; the carved wainscoting and ornamented ceiling of the long gallery are of the time of Elizabeth; the banqueting-hall is equally perfect; the chapel is a good specimen of the early Pointed Gothic. Haddon is one of the curiosities of the Peak country. Many years since Mr. Reinagle painted a picture of this famous old place, which evoked the following poetical tribute to its truthfulness:—

"Gre weeds o'ertop thy ruin'd wall,
Grey, venerable Haddon Hall;
The swallow twitters through thee:
Who would have thought, when, in their pride,
Thy battlements the storm defied,
That Time should thus subdue thee?

"While with a famed and far renown
England's third Edward wore the crown,
Up sprang'st thou in thy glory;

And surely thine (if thou couldst tell,
Like the old Delphian Oracle)
Would be a wondrous story.

"How many a Vernon thou hast seen,
Kings of the Peak thy walls within;
How many a maiden tender;
How many a warrior stem and steel'd,
[Pg 118]In burganet, and lance, and shield,
Array'd with martial splendour.

"Then, as the soft autumnal breeze
Just curl'd the lake, just stirr'd the trees,
In the blue cloudless weather,
How many a gallant hunting train,
With hawk in hood, and horse in rein,
Forsook thy courts together!

"The grandeur of the olden time
Mounted thy towers with pride sublime,
Enlivening all who near'd them;
From Hippocras and Sherris sack
Palmer or pilgrim turn'd not back
Before thy cellars cheer'd them.

"Since thine unbroken early day,
How many a race hath pass'd away,
In charnel vault to moulder—
Yet Nature round thee breathes an air
Serenely bright, and softly fair,
To charm the awed beholder.

"The past is but a gorgeous dream,
And Time glides by us like a stream,
While musing on thy story;
And sorrow prompts a deep alas!
That, like a pageant thus, should pass
To wreck all human glory."

It is now time to speak more in detail of the main apartment—the chief feature of an ancient residence of every class—the Great Hall, which often gave its name to the whole house. A very able writer has thus lucidly yet briefly told its history:—"In the early houses, the hall is almost the whole house; there is nothing besides, except the requisite offices and a room or two for the lord and the lady. The mass of the[Pg 119] household slept how they might in the hall. Gradually, as civilization increased, the accommodation in a house became greater, and the relative importance—sometimes the positive size—of the Hall gradually diminishes. The family gradually deserted it, and the modern luxury of the dining-room was introduced. The *with*drawing-room, that into which they withdrew from the hall, had already appeared. At last, in the sixteenth century, the Hall, though still a grand feature, became, as now, a mere entrance, often with rooms over it."

Sometimes, the Great Hall was raised upon an undercroft of stone vaulting, as we see in the Guildhall, the undercroft of which is the finest specimen of its class in the metropolis. Gerard's Hall, in Basing-lane, built by John Gisors, pepperer, Mayor of London in 1245, and is described by Stow as "a great house of old time, builded upon arched vaults, and with arched gates of stone, brought from Cane, in Normandy."

Aubrey, writing in the seventeenth century, thus describes, in his quaint way, the characteristics of the old manorial or hall houses of the times of the Plantagenets and Tudors: "The architecture of an old English gentleman's house (especially in Wiltshire and thereabouts) was a high strong wall, a gate-house, a Great Hall, and parlours, and within the little green court, where you come in, stood on one side the *barne*. *They then thought not the noise of the threshold ill musique.*"

To come to details. The Great Hall corresponded to the refectory of the abbey. The principal entrance to the main building, from the front or outer court, opened into a *thorough lobby*, having on one side several[Pg 120] doors or arches, leading to the buttery,[33] kitchen, and domestic offices; on the other side, the Hall, parted off by a screen, generally of wood, elaborately carved, and enriched with shields and a variety of ornaments, and pierced with several arches, having folding-doors. Above the screen, and over the lobby, was the minstrels' gallery; on its front were usually hung armour, antlers, and similar memorials of the family exploits.

The Hall itself was a large and lofty room, in the shape of a parallelogram; the roof, the timbers of which were framed with pendants, generally richly carved and emblazoned with arms, formed one of the most striking features. "The top beam of the Hall," in allusion to the position of his coat-of-arms, was a symbolical manner of drinking the health of the master of the house. At the upper end of the apartment, furthest from the entrance, the floor was usually raised a step, and this part was styled the *daïs*, or high place. On one side of the daïs was a deep embayed window, reaching nearly down to the floor; the other windows ranged along one or both sides of the Hall, at some height above the ground, so as to leave room for wainscoting, or arras, below them. We see this arrangement to great advantage in the Great Hall at Hampton Court Palace, where the wall beneath the windows is hung with Flemish tapestry, in eight compartments, the arabesque borders of which are very beautiful; the subject is the History of Abraham. The tapestry at the entrance of the Hall is of much earlier date, being in the school of Albert Durer: the subject, Justice and Mercy pleading before Kings or Judges. The withdrawing-room is also hung with tapestry, the subjects mostly mythological; and the oriel-window is filled with armorial stained glass.

The Hall windows generally were enriched with stained glass,[Pg 121] representing the armorial bearings of the family, their connexions, and royal patrons; and between the windows were hung full-length portraits of the same persons. The windows were not, however, permanently glazed till the fifteenth century. Before that, it was the custom for the glazed casements to be carried about from manor to manor along with the other furniture; every man of rank, whether civil or ecclesiastical, was in the habit of travelling with all his retinue, from one estate to another, so as to consume the produce of each estate upon the spot. It is this custom, or rather necessity, which explains the multitude of manorial houses possessed by every mediæval magnate, and the constant migrations from one to the other. Royal writs and documents are frequently dated from the most insignificant places where the court, on its progress from one royal manor to another, might happen to be staying.[34]

To return to the Hall. The Royal arms usually occupied a conspicuous station at either end of the room. The head-table was laid for the lord and principal guests on the raised place, parallel with the upper end wall; and other tables were ranged along the sides for inferior visitors and retainers. Tables, thus placed, were said to stand *banquet-wise*. In the centre of the Hall was the rere-dosse, or fire-iron, against which fagots were piled, and burnt upon the stone floor, the smoke passing through an aperture in the roof immediately overhead, which was generally formed into an elevated lantern, a conspicuous ornament to the exterior of the building. In later times, a wide-arched fireplace was formed in the wall on one side of the room.

The Halls, in fact, of our colleges, at either University, and the Inns[Pg 122] of Court, still remain as in Aubrey's time, accurate examples of the ancient and baronial and conventual Halls: preserving not merely their original form and appearance, but the identical arrangement and service of the table. Even the central fire has been, in some instances, kept up, being of charcoal, burnt in a large braziere, in lieu of the rere-dosse. The open fire was so kept up, at Westminster School, so late as 1850. The Halls of the temple, Gray's Inn, and Staple Inn, have their lanterns; and even the Hall of Barnard's Inn, the oldest and the smallest, has its lantern; the newly built Hall of Lincoln's Inn has a very ornamental one; and the new roof of the Guildhall is to have a lantern with a lofty spire. The lantern of Westminster Hall is large and picturesque; it is modern, of cast-iron, but is an exact copy of the original one, erected near the end of the fourteenth century. As the existing lanterns are no longer required for the egress of smoke, they are glazed.

In other respects, probably, little, if anything, has been altered since the Tudor era; and he who is anxious to know the mode in which our ancestors dined in the reigns of the Henrys and Edwards, may be gratified by attending that meal in the Great Halls of Christchurch or Trinity, and tasking his imagination to convert the principal and fellows at the upper table, into the stately baron, his family, and guests; and the gowned commoners at the side-tables, into the liveried retainers. The service of the kitchen, buttery, and cellar is conducted, at the present day, precisely according to the ancient custom.[35]

Gradually, the solar or private sitting-room of the matron or mistress[Pg 123] of the house increased in importance. Its most usual position was at one end of the Hall, on an upper level, raised above an apartment which was used as a cellar or a store-room.

The Hall is, of course, the part of a house or castle where the art of architecture proper has the best opportunity of displaying itself. So, in a monastery, the refectory comes next in grandeur to the church and chapter-house. Indeed, some of the early Halls were built not unlike churches, with two rows of pillars. In a wooden construction this is not uncommon both in halls and barns; but the examples we mean have two regular aisles with stone pillars and arches. Such was the original Westminster Hall, till Richard II. threw it into one body under the present magnificent single roof. The finest existing example is perhaps that superb one at Oakham Castle, of the best architecture of the end of the twelfth century. In the next century we have the Hall of the Royal[Pg 124] Palace at Winchester used like that at Oakham, for an assize-court. Of single-bodied halls of the fourteenth century, nothing can surpass those of Caerphilly Castle in Glamorganshire, and Mayfield Palace in Sussex. Mayfield has, and Caerphilly seems to have been designed to have, a very effective arrangement of stone arches thrown across at intervals to support the roof, and to produce something of the effect of actual vaulting. The same is the case at Conway. Most of these examples are ruined.[36] Mayfield has lately been restored.

The gallery was brought into use with the Elizabethan style of architecture, and became a prominent feature among the apartments of houses in that style. The gallery at Hatfield, with a magnificently gilded ceiling—a blaze of gold—is a fine specimen: it was regilt just previous to the visit of Queen Victoria to Hatfield in 1846: a state ball was given in this gallery, and we remember to have been told the day after the Royal visit, that during the dance there fell from Her Majesty's hand a rose, which was immediately taken up by a gentleman of the company; on bended knee he presented it to the Queen, who most graciously returned the flower, which, we doubt not, is preserved.

The extensive passages in some ancient houses have, no doubt, been originally similar to the open galleries round our old inns, of which we have examples, year by year, diminishing in number. These passages were ultimately inclosed for comfort and convenience. The staircases, in ancient times, were usually cylindrical, and were carried up in a separate turret: it was not until the age of Elizabeth that the massive staircase, with its broad hand-rails, balustrades, and enriched[Pg 125] ornaments, was introduced into the mansion; that of a later period is familiarly known as a "Queen Anne staircase."

The royal parlour of Eltham is a perfect specimen of the banqueting-hall, and was the frequent residence of our kings before Henry VIII.; and here they held their great Christmas feasts. Two thousand guests in 1483 were entertained here at Christmas, by Edward IV., the royal builder of the Hall. His badges—the falcon, the fetterlock, and rose-en-soleil—are sculptured over the chief entrance; and Edward is represented by Skelton as saying:

"I made Nottingham a palace royal, Windsor, Eltham, and many mo'."

Princesses have been cradled here, Parliaments have met in the Great Hall, and kings and queens have betaken themselves here to meditate upon the waning earthly greatness. The gloomy Henry VII. at intervals retired to Eltham; Queen Mary or Queen Elizabeth would spend a few days in the almost forsaken palace; and James I. had been known to pass a morning here.

Eltham is now a regal ruin. "The fair pleasaunce, the echoing courts, the king's lodging, presence and guard chamber, and the rooms in which the royal attendants lodged, have all disappeared. The gateway and high walls of ruddy brick only remain to mark the site of the tilt-yard. The moat is half dry, and the sluggish stream is still spanned by the bridge of four arches, which is contemporaneous with the Hall; but 'the gateway and the fair front towards the moat,' built by Henry VII., have been replaced by two modern houses; and another, with three barge-board gables, and corbelled attics, to the east end of the Hall, retains the[Pg 126] designation of the Buttery. There is a view of the Hall by Buck, dated 1735, which represents a great portion of the palace, with its quaint water-towers and moated walls still standing; but, although Parliament in 1827 spent £700 upon the repairs, the state of the Hall is sad enough now: full of litter of every sort, its windows unglazed or bricked up; with damp fastenings in the naked walls, and rough rafters stretching across from side to side, and reaching above the corbels. It is now used as a barn. It was at once an audience-chamber and refectory, 100 feet in length, 55 in height, and 36 feet broad. But the windows now admit broad streams of cheerful sunshine, which light up the thick trails of ivy that flow over the empty panes; its deep bay-window, now stripped of glazing, but enriched with groining and tracery which flanked the daïs, betoken the progress which elegance and security had made at the period of their erection: the lofty walls continue to support a high pitched roof of oak, in tolerable preservation, with hammer-beams, carved pendants, and braces supported on corbels of hewn stone; and although the royal table, the hearth, and louvre have disappeared, there are still remains of the minstrels' gallery, and the doors in the oak screen below it, which lead to the capacious kitchen, the butteries, and cellars, to tell each their several tale of former state."[37]

Hitherto, we have mostly spoken of palaces and mansions. It is, however, very difficult to discover any fragments of houses inhabited by the gentry, before the reign, at soonest, of Edward III., or even to trace them by engravings in the older topographical works; not only from the dilapidations of time, but because very few considerable mansions had[Pg 127] been erected by that class. It is an error to suppose that the English gentry were lodged in stately, or even in well-sized houses. They usually consisted of an entrance-passage, running through the house, with a hall on one side, a parlour beyond, and one or two chambers above; and on the opposite side, a kitchen, pantry, and other offices. Such was the ordinary manor-house of the fifteenth and sixteenth centuries. "In the remains of the fourteenth and fifteenth centuries, Somersetshire is especially rich. Almost every village has a house, a parsonage, or some building or other of this class, to say nothing of extensive monastic remains, as at Glastonbury, Woodspring, Muchelney, and Old Cleve. Among the Somersetshire houses, the original portions of Clevedon Court may claim the first place. Then comes a long list, of which, perhaps, the manor-house and 'fish-house' of Meare, near Glastonbury, are the most curious and beautiful."[38]

Larger houses were erected by men of great estates during the reigns of Henry VI. and Edward IV.; but very few can be traced higher; and Mr. Hallam, in his *History of the Middle Ages*, conceives it to be difficult to name a house in England, still inhabited by a gentleman, and not of the castle description, the principal apartments of which are older than the reign of Henry VII. There may be a few solitary specimens of earlier date. The Rev. Mr. Lysons says:—"The most remarkable fragment of early building which I have anywhere found mentioned, is at a house in Berkshire, called Appleton, where there is a sort of prodigy—an entrance-passage with circular arches in the Saxon (?[Pg 128] Norman) style, which must, probably, be as old as the reign of Henry II. No other private house in England, as I conceive, can boast of such a monument of antiquity."

Wood and stone were the earliest materials used in house-building; but as great part of England affords no stone fit for building, her oak-forests were thinned, and less durable dwellings were erected with inferior timber. Stone houses are, however, mentioned as belonging to the citizens of London, even in the latter half of the twelfth century. Flints bound together with strong cement were employed in building manor-houses. Hewn stone was employed for castles, and the larger mansions: much stone was, in early times, brought from Normandy. Chestnut was much employed. Evelyn, in his *Sylva*, states that "The chestnut is, next the oak, one of the most sought after by the carpenter and joiner. It hath formerly built a good part of our ancient houses in the City of London, as does yet appear. I had once a very large barn near the City, framed entirely of this timber; and certainly the trees grew not far off, probably in some woods near the town; for in that description of London, written by Fitz-Stephen, in the reign of Henry II. he speaks of a very noble and large forest which grew on the boreal [north] part of it."[39]

Ducarel, in his *Anglo-Norman Antiquities*, says: "Rudhall, near Ross,[Pg 129] in Herefordshire, is built with chestnut, which probably grew on the estate, although no tree of the kind is now to be found growing wild in that part of the country. The old houses in the city of Gloucester are constructed of chestnut, derived assuredly from the chestnut-trees in the forest of Dean. In some of the oldest houses of Faversham much genuine chestnut as well as oak is employed. In the nunnery of Davington, near Faversham (now entire), the timber consists of oak, intermingled with chestnut."

In the fourteenth century, ornamental carpentry had reached a high degree of excellence. There are many examples of ancient timber houses yet remaining in this country: they have massive beams and timbers, and are generally of unnecessary strength. The intermixture of wood, brick, and stone, or wood and plaster, in the exterior of houses, was, for a considerable period, the common style of building in the fifteenth and sixteenth centuries. Weatherboard—that is, planks overlapping each other—was formerly much used for house-fronts, and possessed great durability. Overhanging roofs, walls of plaster with lofty gables, bay-windows, and porches of timber, with each story projecting beyond the other, are so many characteristics of a mixed style, when the rude dangers of the timber houses became progressively intermingled with the massive architecture of a subsequent period; and the external use of timber in the walls continued to prevail for a very long time. Beaconsfield Rectory, of the sixteenth century, has the basement story completely built of glazed bricks in chequered patterns; the superincumbent story has elevated roofs and gables, and is constructed with massive timbers placed near together, and plastered between. The[Pg 130] staircase, which is semi-cylindrical and composed of timber, is added to the north side of the house. The entire structure forms three sides of a quadrangle, with a lofty wall and entrance on the fourth; its interior is rude and massive.

In an account of a topographical excursion in 1634, the hall of Kenilworth is described with a roof "all of Irish wood, neatly and handsomely framed;" in it are five chimneys, "answerable to so great a room:" then we read of the Guard, Presence, and Privy chambers, fretted above richly with coats of arms, and all adorned with fair and rich chimney-pieces of alabaster, black marble, and joiners' work in curiously carved wood; all the fair and rich rooms and lodgings in the spacious tower not long since built, and repaired at great cost by Leicester. "The priuate, plaine, retiring-chamber wherein o^r renowned Queene of euer famous memory, alwayes made choice to repose her Selfe. Also the famous, strong old tower, called Julius Cæsar's, on top whereof was view'd the pleasant, large Poole continually sporting and playing on the Castle: the Parke, and the fforest contiguous thereto." Kenilworth has been already described at pp. **101-103**.

Many a middle-aged reader can recollect the disappearance of rows of gabled houses, with timber and plaster fronts, from the metropolis: great part of the High-street of Southwark, built in this manner, was taken down between 1810 and 1831; at the latter period, some houses with ornamental plaster fronts disappeared. In Chancery-lane, a very old thoroughfare, several houses of this class have been taken down within memory; and many an old house-front, with ornamental carving, is missed from the Strand; a few linger in Holywell-street and Wych-street. And,[Pg 131] in 1865, was taken down one side of Great Winchester-street, stated to be one of the oldest specimens of domestic architecture remaining in the metropolis. The casement hung on hinges was the earliest form of window, properly so called. Sash-windows were not introduced till the early part of the reign of Charles I., and were not general till the latter part of the time of Queen Anne.

In the construction of farm-houses and cottages there have been, probably, fewer changes than in large mansions. Cottages in England seem to have generally consisted of a single room, without division of stories. The Spaniards who came to England in Queen Mary's time, wondered when they saw the large diet used by the inmates of the most homely-looking cottages. "The English, they said, make their houses of sticks and dirt, but they fare as well as the king; whereby it appeareth (says Harrison), that they like better of our goode fare in such coarse cabins, than of their own thin diet in their princelike habitations and palaces."

In various counties we can scarcely fail to be struck with the difference in the forms of the cottages, as in the height of the building, the pitch of the roof, as well as the materials. Only let the traveller on the Brighton railway look out after he has passed Redhill, and he may see evidence of the truth of the above remark. Cobbett has left us this charming picture of the Sussex cottages in one of his *Rural Rides*:—

"I never had," he writes, "that I recollect, a more pleasant journey, or ride, than this into Sussex. The weather was pleasant, the elder-trees in full bloom, and they make a fine show; the woods just in their greatest beauty; the grass-fields generally uncut; and the little gardens of the labourers full of flowers;[Pg 132] the roses and honeysuckles perfuming the air at every cottage door. Throughout all England, these cottages and gardens are the most interesting objects that the country presents, and they are particularly so in Kent and Sussex. This part of these counties has the great blessing of numerous woods; these furnish fuel, nice, sweet fuel, for the heating of ovens and all other purposes: they afford materials for the making of pretty pigsties, hurdles, and dead fences, of various sorts; they afford materials for making little cow-sheds; for the sticking of peas and beans in the gardens; and for giving to everything a neat and substantial appearance. These gardens, and the look of the cottages, the little flower-gardens, which you everywhere see, and the beautiful hedges of thorn and of privet,— these are the objects to delight the eyes, to gladden the heart, and to fill it with gratitude to God, and love for the people; and as far as my observation has gone, they are objects to be seen in no other country in the world. Those who see nothing but the nasty, slovenly places in which labourers live round London, know nothing of England. The fruit-trees are all kept in the nicest order; every bit of paling or wall is made use of, for the training of some sort or other. At Lamberhurst, which is one of the most beautiful villages that ever man set his eyes on, I saw what I never saw before, namely, *a gooseberry-tree trained against a house.* The house was one of those ancient buildings, consisting of a frame of oak-wood, the interval filled up with brick, plastered over. The tree had been planted at the foot of one of the perpendicular pieces of wood; from the stem which mounted up this piece of wood were taken side limbs, to run along the horizontal pieces. There were two windows, round the frame of each of which the limbs had been trained. The height of the highest shoot was about ten feet from the ground, and the horizontal shoots from each side were from eight to ten feet in length. The tree had been judiciously pruned, and all the limbs were full of very large gooseberries, considering the age of the fruit. This is only one instance out of thousands that I saw of extraordinary pains taken with the gardens."

Those who love the picturesque will excuse our halting to sketch an episode from the history of the royal forest of Ashdown, in Sussex, once possessed by John of Gaunt, and hence called "Lancaster great Park." Upon the borders of the forest lies the manor of Brambertie of Domesday,[Pg 133] and Brambletye of Horace Smith; the home of the Comptons, and in the tale of fiction, as in fact, dismantled by Parliament troopers, and within two centuries a ruin. Richard Lewknor is the first person described as of Brambletye. He most probably built in one of the forest glens the moated mansion known as "Old Brambletye House," which, with its gables and clustered chimneys, and its moat and drawbridge, long remained an interesting specimen of the fortified manor-house of the reign of Henry VII. We remember the old place, some sixty years since, but it has long been taken down. Towards the middle of the seventeenth century, Brambletye came into the possession of the Comptons, an ancient Roman Catholic family; and here Sir Henry Compton built himself, from an Italian design, another Brambletye House, of the white stone of the country. Over the principal entrance to the mansion were sculptured the coat-armour of Compton, with the arms of Spencer, in a shield, on the dexter side: and on the upper story was cut in stone, C. H. M. 1631. This fixes the period when the house was built; and when Sir Henry Compton, who had before inhabited the old moated house in the neighbourhood, abandoned it to take up his residence in this once elegant and substantial baronial mansion.

From the court-rolls of the manor, it does not appear who succeeded the Comptons in the property; but Sir James Rickards, in his patent of baronetcy, 1683-4, is described as of Brambletye House. The story goes, that "a proprietor of the mansion being suspected of treasonable purposes, officers of justice were dispatched to search the premises, when a considerable quantity of arms and military stores was discovered[Pg

134] and removed; he was out hunting at the time, but receiving intimation of the circumstance, deemed it most prudent to abscond." The historical version is, that in the Civil War, Sir John Compton, a true Royalist, took an active part against the Parliament armies: although never capable of any regular defence, yet Brambletye, being partially fortified, refused the summons of the Parliamentary Colonel Okey, by whom it was invested and speedily taken. The mansion was subsequently deserted. From a sketch taken in 1780, the principal front was nearly entire: it consisted of three square towers, the entrance doorway being in the central tower; the two wings had handsome bay-windows; the three towers were surmounted with cupolas and weather-vanes; but one had half its cupola shattered away, and was internally blackened, as if with gunpowder. In front of the house were an inclosed courtyard and two entrance-gates, one flanked by two massive, square towers, with cupolas. Horace Smith having named his romance *Brambletye House*, the opening scenes being laid there, has sent hundreds of tourists to pic-nic among the ruins; but the spoilers were constantly at work. Some fifteen years ago, "all that remained of Brambletye House was one of the towers clothed with stately ivy, and little more than one story of each of the other towers; the intervening portions, with their bay-windows, had disappeared. Nature had, however, lent a helping hand: by the shrubby trees and the ivy, the ruins had gained that picturesqueness which so often lends a graceful charm to scenes of decaying art."[40]

THE ENGLISHMAN'S FIRESIDE.

ealthful Warmth and Ventilation are to this day problems to be worked out; and few practical subjects have so extensively enlisted ingenious minds in their service. Yet, much remains to be done.

Dr. Arnott, the worthy successor of Count Rumford[41] in *heat philosophy*, when seeking to shame us out of using ill-contrived fireplaces and scientific bunglings, tells us that the savages of North America place fire in the middle of the floor of their huts, and sit around in the smoke, for which there is escape only in the one opening in the hut, which serves as chimney, window, and door. Some of the peasantry in remote parts of Ireland and Scotland still place their fires in the middle of their floors, and, for the escape of the smoke, leave only a small opening in the roof, often not directly over the fire. In Italy and Spain, almost the only fires seen in sitting-rooms are large dishes of live charcoal, or braziers, placed in the middle,[Pg 136] with the inmates sitting around, and having to breathe the noxious carbonic-acid gas which ascends from the fire, and mixes with the air in the room; there being no chimney, the ventilation of the room is imperfectly accomplished by the windows and doors. The difference between the burned air from a charcoal fire, and smoke from a fire of coal or wood, is that in the latter there are added to the chief ingredient, carbonic acid, which is little perceived, others which disagreeably affect the eyes and nose, and so force attention.

With these facts before us, it is not difficult to imagine how our ancestors tolerated the nuisance of wood smoke filling their rooms till it found its way through the roof lantern, as was generally the case until the general introduction of chimneys late in the reign of Elizabeth. It should, however, be mentioned that the temperature of their apartments was kept considerably below that of our sitting-rooms in the present day. Before the fourteenth century, except for culinary and smithery purposes, robust Englishmen appear to have cared little about heating their dwellings, and to have dispensed with it altogether during the warmer months of the year. Even so late as the reign of Henry VIII. it seems that no fire was allowed in the University of Oxford: after supping at eight o'clock, the students went to their books till nine in winter, and then took a run for half an hour to warm themselves previously to going to bed. Therefore, all ideas of the firesides of our forefathers should be confined to four centuries.

The usage of making the fire in the middle of the hall, a lover of olden architecture says, "was not without its advantages: not only was a greater amount of heat obtained, but the warmth became more generally[Pg 137] diffused, which, when we consider the size of the hall, was a matter of some importance. The huge logs were piled upon the andirons or thrown upon the hearth, and the use of wood and charcoal had few of those inconveniences which would have resulted from coal;" an opinion strangely at variance with that of the heat philosopher already quoted.

We are now approaching the age of Chimneys. A practical writer has thus pictured the domestic contrivance, *ad interim*: "The hearth recess was generally wide, high, deep, and had a large flue. The hearth, usually raised a few inches above the floor, had sometimes a halpas or daïs made before it, as in the King's and Queen's chambers in the Tower. Before the hearth recess, or on the halpas, when there was one, a piece of green cloth or tapestry was spread, as a substitute for the rushes that covered the lower part of the floor. On this were placed a very high-backed chair or two, and foot-stools, that sometimes had cushions; and above all high-backed forms, and screens, both most admirable inventions for neutralizing draughts of cold air in these dank and chilling apartments. Andirons, fire-forks, fire-pans, and tongs were the implements to supply and arrange the fuel. Hearth recesses with flues were common in the principal chambers and houses of persons of condition; and were superseding what Aubrey calls flues, like loover holes, in the habitations of all classes. The adage that 'one good fire heats the whole house,' was found true only in the humbler dwellings; for in palace and mansion, though great fires blazed in the presence-chamber, or hall, or parlour, the domestics were literally famishing with cold. This discomfort did not, however, proceed from selfish or stingy housekeeping, but rather from an affectation of[Pg 138] hardihood, particularly among the lower classes, when effeminacy was reckoned a reproach. Besides, few could know what comfort really was; but those who did, valued it highly. Sanders relates that Henry VIII. gave the revenues of a convent, which he had confiscated, to a person who placed a chair for him commodiously before the fire and out of all draughts."

On the introduction of chimneys, in the year 1200, only one chimney was allowed in a manor-house, and one in the great hall of a castle or lord's house: other houses had only the rere-dosse, a sort of raised hearth, where the inmates cooked their food. Harrison, in a passage prefixed to *Holinshed's Chronicle*, writes in the reign of Elizabeth: "There are old men dwelling in the village where I remayne, who have noted three things to be marvellously altered in England, within their sound remembrance. One is the multitude of chimneys lately erected; whereas, in their younger days, there was not about two or three, if so many, in most uplandish towns of the realm (the religious houses and manor places of the lords always excepted, and peradventure some great personage's); but each made his fire against a reré-dosse in the hall, where he dined and dressed his meat."

Numerous instances, however, remain of fireplaces and chimneys of the fourteenth century, even in the hall, though they were more usual in the smaller apartments. In the hall at Meare, in Somersetshire, the fireplace had a hood of stone, perfect, finely corbelled out; and by the side of the fireplace is a bracket for a light, ornamented with foliage.

It is curious to find chimneys constructed of so combustible a material as wood. In the *Liber Albus* of the City of London, 1419, it is ordered by Wardmote "that no chimney be henceforth made, except of stone, tiles,[Pg 139] or plaster, and *not of timber*, under pain of being pulled down."

In the metropolis, we possess a hall of the fifteenth century, which has a fireplace, the existence of which, in a hall of this age, is singular, if not unique. In the north wall of the celebrated hall of Crosby Place, Bishopsgate Street, is a fireplace with a low pointed arch. The builder must have possessed a more refined taste than his contemporaries, and feeling the inconvenience attending a fire of the old description (in the middle of the hall) adopted the plan of confining it to the recessed fireplace and the chimney.[42] Here we may mention the "smoke-loft," which seems to mean the wide space in the old-fashioned chimney.

It is curious to find that a tax was once paid upon a fire in England. Such was "the smoke farthings" levied by the clergy upon every person who kept a fire. The "hearth money" was a similar tax, but was paid to the king: it was first levied in 1653, and its last collection was in 1690.

In the Tapestry room of St. James's Palace is a stone Tudor arched fireplace, sculptured with H. A. (Henry and Anne), united by a true lover's knot, surmounted by the regal crown and the lily of France, the portcullis of Westminster, and the rose of Lancaster.

By a record of 1511, it appears that the hall-fire was discontinued on Easter Day, then called God's Sunday. In the *Festival*, published in the above year, we read: "This day is called, in many places, *Goddes Sundaye*: ye know well that it is the maner at this daye to do the fire out of the hall, and the black wynter brondes, and all thynges that is foule with fume and smoke, shall be done awaye, and where the fyre was[Pg 140] shall be gayly arayed with fayre floures, and strewed with grene rysshes all aboute." The andirons being cleared away, the space whereon the fire was made, on the hearth, was strewed with green rushes; whence the custom, in our time, of decorating, in the country, stove-grates with evergreens, and flowers, and paper ornaments, when they are not used for fires. Rushes were, at this time, much in use. At Canterbury, one of the oldest cities in England, at the end of Mercery-lane, is pointed out the site of the ancient *rush-market*, in which stood a great cross, painted and gilt. We still employ rushes made into matting, for the floors of churches.

Coal is first mentioned in 1245; but the smoke was supposed to corrupt the air so much, that Edward I. forbade the use of that kind of fuel by proclamation; and among the records in the Tower, Mr. Astle found a document, importing that in the time of Edward I. a man had been tried, convicted, and executed, for the crime of burning sea-coal in London.

Coal first came into general use in the north of England.[43] Wood billets, however, long remained the principal fuel of the south; and the contrivance for burning such fuel with economy was the first deviation in metal from the rude simplicity of the rere-dosse towards the close fire-grate. This consisted of useful iron trestles, called hand-irons, or andirons, formerly common in England, and yet occasionally to be met with in old mansions and farm-houses, under the appellation of *dogs*. Originally, these articles were not only found in the houses of persons of good condition, but in the bedchamber of the king himself. Strutt, writing in 1775, says: "These awnd-irons are used at this day, and are[Pg 141] called cob-irons: they stand on the hearth, where they burn wood, to lay it upon; their fronts are usually carved, with a round knob at the top; some of them are kept polished and bright; anciently many of them were embellished with a variety of ornaments." In another place, giving an inventory of the bedchamber of Henry VIII. in the palace of Hampton Court, including awnd-irons, with fire-fork, tongs, and fire-pan, Strutt adds, "of the awnd-irons, or as they are called by the moderns, cob-irons, myself have seen a pair which in former times belonged to some noble family. They were of copper, highly gilt, with beautiful flowers, enamelled with various colours disposed with great art and elegance." At Hever Castle in Kent,—the family seat of the Boleyns, as well as the property of Anne of Cleves, and which Henry VIII. with matchless cupidity claimed in right of a wife from whom, previously to her being beheaded, he had been divorced,—is a pair of elegant andirons, bearing the royal initials H. A. and surmounted with a royal crown. And, in an inventory of Henry's furniture in the Tower of London, we find mentioned "two round pairs of irons, upon which to make fire in, and for conveying fire from one apartment to another."

Shakspeare thus minutely describes a pair of andirons belonging to a lady's chamber:—

"Two winking Cupids
Of silver, each on one foot standing,
Depending on their brands nicely."—*Cymbeline.*

A middle sort of irons, called creepers, was smaller, and usually placed within the dogs, to keep the ends of the wood and brands from the[Pg 142] hearth, that the fire might burn more freely. A pair of these irons is thus described in one of the early volumes of the *Gentleman's Magazine*: "There being in a large house a variety of rooms of various sizes, the sizes and forms of the andirons may reasonably have been supposed to have been various too. In the kitchen, where large fires are made, and large pieces of wood are laid on, the andirons, in consequence, are proportionately large and strong, and usually plain, or with very little ornament. In the great hall, where the tenants and neighbours made entertainment, and at Christmas cheerfully regaled with good plum-porridge, mince-pies, and stout October, the andirons were commonly larger and stronger, able to sustain the weight of the roaring Christmas fire; but these were more ornamented, and, like knights with their esquires, attended by a pair of younger brothers far superior to, and therefore, not to be degraded by, the humble style of creepers; indeed, they were often seen to carry their heads at least half as high as their proud elders. A pair of such I have in my hall: they are of cast-iron, at least two and a half feet high, with round faces, and much ornamented at the bottom."

At Cotehole House, in Cornwall, may be seen a pair of richly ornamented brass dogs, upwards of four feet high; and a few years since we remember to have seen, in Windsor Castle, a pair of andirons faced with richly wrought silver. Yet these articles are eclipsed by some costly items in a list of wedding presents in the reign of James I. wherein is described "an invention," namely, "fire-shovel, tongs, and irons, creepers, and all furniture of a chimney, of silver, and a cradle of silver to burn sea-coal." This expensiveness of material, in all probability, was not matched by the manufacture, a disproportion which reminds us of the[Pg 143] *silver furniture* in some districts of South America, where the earth yields tons of that metal. Thus the proprietor of a productive silver mine in Peru is known to have ejected from his house all articles of glass or crockery ware, and replaced them by others made of silver. Here, likewise, might be seen pier-tables, picture-frames, mirrors, pots and pans, and even a watering-trough for mules—all of solid silver!

To return to the invention of grates. As the consumption of coal increased, the transition from andirons to fire-grates composed of connected bars, was obvious and easy. The andirons formed the end-standards, which supported the grate itself, a sort of raised cradle. Besides these supports, the back-plate, cast from a model of carved-work (often with the arms of the family), was added; and generally under the lowest bar was a filigree ornament of bright metal, which, under the designation of a fret, still retains its place in modern stoves. Movable fireplaces of the above description may be met with about two hundred years old; for at this period, as the quotation of the time of James I. proves, implements for the fireplace were in use. A magnificent fireplace of the above description has been manufactured for St. George's Hall, in Windsor Castle, so as to harmonize with the architectural character of that noble apartment.

Convenience soon suggested the fixing of fireplaces, which led to their being made with side-piers, or hobs, so as to fill the whole space within the chimney-jambs; till the snug cosy chimney-corner is only to be met with in farm-houses, where *dogs* are used to this day.

It would be tedious to follow the improvements in fireplaces from the first introduction of stoves, about the year 1780, to the present time:[Pg 144] from straight unornamental bars and sides, to elegant curves, pedestal hobs, and fronts embellished with designs of great classic beauty. Indeed, in no branch of manufacture are the advantages of our enlarged acquaintance with the fine arts more evident than in the taste of ornaments displayed in the stove-grates of the present day. The tasteful display at the Great Exhibition of 1851 will doubtless be remembered by the reader. "Grates," says the Supplementary Report of the Juries on Design, "rank among the principal works in hardware to which ornamental design is applied, at least on the English side; and there by far the best specimens, both as to design and workmanship, are to be found: this was to be expected from the general necessity for warmth in our cold and variable climate; an Englishman's love for his fireside having passed into a proverb."

By fire-irons are understood a shovel, a poker, and pair of tongs. These implements were not all found on the ancient hearth; nor were they necessary when wood alone was burnt. In the time of Henry VIII. the only accompaniment of the andirons was the fire-fork with two prongs, a specimen of which is preserved in Windsor Castle; still, in the apartments for the upper classes, the irons for trimming the fire were more complete. The use of coal and of close fireplaces led to the adoption of the poker; and about the same period were introduced fenders, the first of which were bent pieces of sheet-iron placed before the fire, to prevent the brands or cinders from rolling off the hearth-stone upon the wooden floors; but fenders have been improved with stoves, till the display of our fireplace is the chief ornamental feature of our rooms.

With these changes, however, the chimney-corner has disappeared, and is[Pg 145] but remembered in poetry, or the pages of romance.

A great deal has been written of late years in disparagement of the open coal fire and the chimney, in comparison with the stove and flue; but Professor Faraday has shown the chimney to possess very important functions in sanitary economy. Thus, a parlour fire will consume in twelve hours forty pounds of coal, the combustion rendering 42,000 gallons of air unfit to support life. Not only is that large amount of deleterious product carried away, and rendered innoxious by the chimney, but five times that quantity of air is also carried up by the draught, and ventilation is thus effectually maintained.

Since the ascent of smoke up a chimney depends on the comparative lightness of the column of air within to that of an equal column without, the longer the chimney the stronger will be the draught, if the fire be sufficiently great to heat the air; but if the chimney be so long that the air is cooled as it approaches the top, the draught is diminished.

It must not be supposed that the modes we have described were the only means of heating houses with which our ancestors were familiar. The Romans in England evidently employed flue-tiles for the artificial heating of houses or baths. In 1849, a course of flue-tiles was found upon a farm near Reigate, in Surrey; they were shown to have been taken from some Roman site in the neighbourhood, and had been used on the farm to form a drain; the apertures for heated air being covered by pieces of Roman wall-tile, or stone, to prevent the soil falling into the flues. One of these flue-tiles is ornamented with patterns, not scored, but impressed by the repetition of stamps, to produce an elaborate design.[Pg 146]Several varieties of flue-tiles have been found: one from a Roman bath in Thames Street; and a remarkable double flue-tile, found in the City of London, and preserved in Mr. Roach Smith's collection in the British Museum. These tiles were arranged one upon the other, and carried up the inner sides of the walls of the rooms, to which artificial heat was to be given from the hypocaust, or subterranean stove, by which means it was easy to regulate the temperature. Pliny describes a bedchamber in his villa warmed by the hypocaust and the tiles, with narrow openings. Sometimes the floor and sides were entirely coated with these tiles.

The Curfew, or *Couvre-feu*, should be mentioned as an appurtenance to the fireplaces in the Anglo-Norman times. The *couvre-feu* formerly in the collection of the Rev. Mr. Gostling, and so often engraved, passed into the possession of Horace Walpole, and was sold at Strawberry Hill, in 1842, to Mr. William Knight. It is of copper, riveted together, and in general form resembles the "Dutch-oven" of the present day. In the same lot was a warming-pan of the time of Charles II. In February 1842, Mr. Syer Cuming purchased of a curiosity-dealer in Chancery-lane a *couvre-feu* closely resembling Mr. Gostling's; and Mr. Cuming considers both specimens to be of the same age—of the close of the fifteenth or early part of the sixteenth century; whereas Mr. Gostling's specimen was stated to be of the Norman period. A third example of the *couvre-feu* exists in the Canterbury Museum; and early in 1866, a *couvre-feu*—reputed date, 1068—was sold by Messrs. Foster, in Pall Mall.

The *Couvre-feu* is stated to have been used for extinguishing a fire, by raking the wood and embers to the back of the hearth, and then[Pg 147] placing the open part of the *couvre-feu* close against the back of the chimney. The notion that all fires should be covered up at a certain hour, was a badge of servitude imposed by William the Conqueror, is a popular error; since there is evidence of the same custom prevailing in France, Spain, Italy, Scotland, and many other countries of Europe, at this period: it was intended as a precaution against fires, which were very frequent and destructive, when so many houses were built of wood. Besides, the curfew was used in England in the time of Alfred, who ordained that all the inhabitants of Oxford should, at the ringing of the curfew-bell at Carfax, cover up their fires and go to bed. It is, therefore, concluded that the Conqueror revived or continued the custom which he had previously established in Normandy: in fact, it was, in both countries, a beneficial law of police.[44]

PRIVATE LIFE OF A QUEEN OF ENGLAND.

[Pg 148]

ne of the most interesting records of the domestic life of our ancestors that we remember to have read, is a series of "Notices of the Last Days of Isabella, Queen of Edward II. drawn from an Account of the Expenses of her Household," and communicated to the Society of Antiquaries, by Mr. E. A. Bond, of the British Museum. Nothing can exceed the minuteness of this memorial of the domestic manners of the middle of the fourteenth century—*the private life of five hundred years since.* No court circular ever chronicled the movements of royalty more circumstantially than does this household account; nor can any roll among our records detail more closely the personal expenses of the sovereign than do the notices before us.

It will be recollected by the attentive reader of our history, that, after the deposition and murder of King Edward II., we hear little of the history of the chief mover of these fearful events.[45] The ambitious Mortimer expiates his crimes on the scaffold. Isabella, the instigator of sedition against her king, the betrayer of her husband, survives her accomplice; but, from the moment that her career of guilt is arrested, she is no more spoken of. Having mentioned the execution of Mortimer, Froissart tells us that the King soon after, by the advice of his council, ordered his mother to be confined in a goodly castle, and gave her plenty of ladies to wait and attend on her, as well as knights[Pg 149] and esquires of honour. He made her a handsome allowance to keep and maintain the state she had been used to; but forbade that she should ever go out, or drive herself abroad, except at certain times, when any shows were exhibited in the court of the castle. The Queen thus passed her time there meekly, and the King, her son, visited her twice or thrice a year. Castle Rising was the place of her confinement. This castle, which in part gives name to the town, is believed to have been originally built by Alfred the Great: at any rate, William de Albini, to whose ancestors the Conqueror gave several lordships in the county, built a castle here before 1176; and this edifice appears to inclose a fragment of a more ancient building. There are, to this day, considerable remains: the keep is still standing, though much dilapidated; the walls are three yards thick; and the division and arrangement of the apartments are very obvious. It stands in a ballium or court, surrounded by a moat and an embankment. The general style of the building is Norman, and bears a resemblance to that of Norwich Castle. Here the Queen took up her abode in 1330; after the first two years the strictness of her seclusion was relaxed. She died at Hertford, August 22, 1358, and was buried in the church of the Grey Friars, within Newgate, now the site of Christ's Hospital.

The Account of the Queen's Expenses is one of the Cottonian MSS. in the British Museum, and embraces, in distinct divisions, the Queen's general daily expenses; sums given in alms; miscellaneous necessary expenses; disbursements for dress; purchases of plate and jewellery; gifts; payments to messengers; and imprests for various services. In the margin[Pg 150]of the general daily expenses are entered the names of the visitors during the day, together with the movements of the household from place to place. From these notices, in addition to the light they throw upon the domestic life of the period, we gain some insight into the degree of personal freedom enjoyed by the Queen and her connexions; the consideration she obtained at the Court of the great King Edward III. her son; and even into her personal disposition and occupations. These particulars relate to her last days.

It appears that at the beginning of October 1357, the Queen was residing at her castle of Hertford, having not very long before been at Rising. The first visitor mentioned, and who sups with her, was Joan, her niece, who visited the Queen constantly, and nursed her in her last illness. Hertford Castle was built by Edward the Elder, about 905 or 909. In the civil war of the reign of John, this fortress was taken, after a brave defence, by the Dauphin Louis, and the revolted barons: it subsequently came to the crown, and was granted in succession to John of Gaunt, and to the Queens of Henry IV., Henry V., and Henry VI. Jean II. King of France, and David, King of Scotland, spent part of their captivity here during the reign of Edward III. Queen Elizabeth occasionally resided and held her court in the castle.

About the middle of October, Queen Isabella set out from Hertford on a pilgrimage to Canterbury. She rested at Tottenham, London, Eltham, Dartford, and Rochester; in going or returning visited Leeds Castle, and was again at Hertford in the beginning of November. She gave alms to the nuns—Minoresses without Aldgate; to the rector of St. Edmund's in London, in whose parish her hostel was situated—it was in Lombard Street; and to the prisoners in Newgate. On the 26th of October, she[Pg 151] entertained the King and Prince of Wales, in her own house in Lombard Street; and we have recorded a gift of thirteen shillings and fourpence to four minstrels who played in their presence.

On the 16th of November, after her return to Hertford Castle, she was visited by the renowned Gascon warrior, the Captal de Buche, cousin of the Comte de Foix. He had recently come over to England with the Prince of Wales, having taken part, on the English side, in the great battle of Poitiers: and subsequent entries record the visits of several noble captives taken in that battle.

On the following day is recorded a visit, at dinner, of the "Comes de la March," considered to be Roger Mortimer, Earl of March, the grandson of her favourite. He was high in Edward the Third's confidence, and appears to have been in England at the present time: under the head of donations is notice of a sum paid to four minstrels of the Earl of March. His visit was, as we find, subsequently twice repeated, and then in company with the King (by whom, as Froissart tells us, "he was much loved") and the Prince of Wales. "And thus," says Mr. Bond, "we have an indication that time has scarcely weakened Isabella's fidelity to a criminal attachment; and that, although the actual object of it had been torn from her, she still cherished his memory, and sought her friends among those most nearly allied to him."

On the 28th of November, and two following days, the Queen entertained the Earl of Tancarville, one of the captives at Poitiers; and with him the Earl of Salisbury, who was connected with the Mortimers, being brother-in-law to the existing Earl of March, although his father had personally acted a principal part in arresting Isabella's paramour in Nottingham Castle. On the 15th of December, the Queen was visited by the[Pg 152] Countess of Pembroke, one of Isabella's closest friends. And, again, what can we infer but a clinging on her part to the memory of Mortimer, when we find that this lady was his daughter? and thus visits were received by Isabella from a daughter, the grandson, and grandson's brother-in-law, of her favourite, within the space of one month.

On the 10th of February, messengers arrive from the King of Navarre, to announce, as it appears elsewhere, his escape from captivity; an indication that Isabella was still busy in the stirring events in her native country. On the 20th of March, the King comes to supper. On each day of the first half of the month of May, during the Queen's stay in London, the entries show her guests at dinner, and her visitors after dinner and at supper, as formally as a court circular of our own time.

Of the several entries we can only select a few of the more interesting. Here we may remark that on three occasions in March, the guests came to *supper* with the Queen: these are Lionel, Earl of Ulster; the King; and the Earl of Richmond. The supper of that period was given, probably, at five o'clock, three hours earlier than the royal dinner of our time.[46]

In April, we find reference to the Queen's journey to Windsor; upon[Pg 153] which Mr. Bond remarks: "There is no room for doubt, therefore (though the chroniclers make no mention of the circumstance), that the object of Isabella's journey was to be present at the festivities held at Windsor by Edward III. in celebration of St. George's Day, the 23d of April—festivities set forth with unwonted magnificence, in honour of the many crowned heads and noble foreigners then in England, and to which strangers from all countries were offered safe letters of conduct." From an entry in May, we find a donation of the considerable sum of six pounds thirteen shillings (equal in value to about ninety pounds of the present currency) to a messenger from Windsor, certifying her of the conclusion of terms of a peace between Edward III. and his captive, John of France; and the same sum is given by Isabella, the same day, to a courier bearing a letter from Queen Philippa, conveying the same intelligence.

On May 14, Isabella left London, and rested at Tottenham, on her way to Hertford; and a payment is recorded of a gift of six shillings and eightpence to the nuns of Cheshunt, who met the Queen at the cross in the high road, in front of their house.

On the 4th of June, Isabella set out on a pilgrimage to Canterbury, and a visit to Leeds Castle. At Canterbury, on the 10th and 11th, she entertained the Abbot of St. Augustine's; and under Alms are recorded the Queen's oblations at the tomb of St. Thomas: the crown of his head (the part having the tonsure, cut off by his assassins), and point of the sword (with which he had been slain); and her payment to minstrels playing "in volta;" as also her oblations in the church of St. Augustine, and her donations to various hospitals and religious houses in Canterbury.

Respecting Isabella's death, she is stated by chroniclers to have sunk,[Pg 154] in the course of a single day, under the effect of a too powerful medicine, administered at her own desire. From several entries, however, in this account, she appears to have been in a state requiring medical treatment for some time previous to her decease. She expired on August 22; but as early as February 15, a payment had been made to a messenger going on three several occasions to London for divers medicines for the Queen, and for the hire of a horse for Master Lawrence, the physician; and again, for another journey by night to London. On the same day a second payment was made to the same messenger for two other journeys by night to London, and two to St. Albans, to procure medicines for the Queen. On the 1st of August, payment was made to Nicholas Thomasyer, apothecary, of London, for divers spices and ointment supplied for the Queen's use. Among the other entries is a payment to Master Lawrence of forty shillings, for attendance on the Queen and the Queen of Scotland, at Hertford, for an entire month.

It is evident that the body of the Queen remained in the chapel of the castle until November 23, as a payment is made to fourteen poor persons for watching the Queen's corpse there, day and night, from Saturday, the 25th of August, to the above date, each of them receiving twopence daily, besides his food. While the body lay at Hertford, a solemn mass was performed in the chapel, when the daily expenditure rose from the average of six pounds to fifteen and twenty-five pounds. The Queen's funeral took place on the 27th: she was interred in the choir of the church of the Grey Friars, the Archbishop of Canterbury officiating, and the King himself being present at the ceremony. Just twenty-eight years[Pg 155]before, on nearly the same day, the body of her paramour Mortimer was consigned to its grave in the same building.

We now reach the Alms, which amount to the considerable sum of 298*l*., equivalent to about 3,000*l*. of present money. They consist of chapel offerings; donations to religious houses; to clergymen preaching in the Queen's presence; to special applicants for charity; and to paupers. The most interesting entry, perhaps, is that of a donation of forty shillings to the abbess and minoresses without Aldgate, in London, to purchase for themselves two pittances on the anniversaries of Edward, late King of England, and Sir John, of Eltham (the Queen's son), given on the 20th of November. And this is the sole instance of any mention in the Account of the unhappy Edward II.

Among these items is a payment to the nuns of Cheshunt for meeting the Queen in the high road in front of their house: and this is repeated on every occasion of the Queen's passing the priory in going to or from Hertford. There is more than one entry of alms given to poor scholars of Oxford, who had come to ask it of the Queen. A distribution is made amongst a hundred or fifty poor persons on the principal festivals of the year, amongst which that of Queen Katharine is included. Doles also are made among paupers daily and weekly throughout the year, amounting in one year and a month to 102*l*. On the 12th of September, after the Queen's death, a payment of twenty shillings is made to William Ladde, of Shene (Richmond), on account of the burning of his house by an accident, while the Queen was staying at Shene.

Under the head of "Necessaries," we find a payment of fifty shillings to[Pg 156] carpenters, plasterers, and tilers, for works in the Queen's chamber, for making a staircase from the chamber to the chapel, &c. Afterwards we find half-yearly payments of twenty-five shillings and twopence to the Prioress of St. Helen's, in London, as rent for the Queen's house in Lombard Street; a purchase of two small "catastæ," or cages, for birds, in the Queen's chamber; and of hemp-seed for the same birds. From an entry under Gifts, it appears that two small birds were given to Isabella by the King, on the 26th of November. Next are payments for binding the black carpet in the Queen's chamber; for repairs of the castle; lining the Queen's chariot with coloured cloth; repairs of the Queen's bath, and gathering of herbs for it. Also, payments to William Taterford, for six skins of vellum, for writing the Queen's books, and for writing a book of divers matters for the Queen, fourteen shillings, including cost of parchment; to Richard Painter, for azure for illuminating the Queen's books; the repayment of sum of 200*l.* borrowed of Richard Earl of Arundel; the purchase of an embroidered saddle, with gold fittings, and a black palfrey, given to the Queen of Scotland; a payment to Louis de Posan, merchant, of the Society of Mallebaill, in London, for two mules bought by him at Avignon for the Queen, 28*l.* 13*s.*: the mules arrived after the Queen's death, and they were given over to the King.

The division of the account relating to her jewels is chiefly interesting as affording an insight into the personal character of Isabella, and showing that the serious events of her life and her increasing years had not overcome her natural passion for personal display. The total amount expended on jewels was no less than 1,399*l.*, equivalent to about 16,000*l.* of our present currency; and, says Mr.[Pg 157] Bond, "after ample allowance for the acknowledged general habit of indulgence in personal ornaments belonging to the period, we cannot but consider Isabella's outlay on her trinkets as exorbitant, and as betraying a more than common weakness for those vain luxuries." The more costly of them were purchased of Italian merchants. Her principal English jewellers appear to have been John de Louthe and William de Berking, goldsmiths, of London. In a general entry of 421*l.* paid for divers articles of jewellery to Pardo Pardi, and Bernardo Donati, Italian merchants, are items of a chaplet of gold, set with "bulays" (rubies), sapphires, emeralds, diamonds, and pearls, price 105*l.*; divers pearls, 87*l.*; a crown of gold, set with sapphires, rubies of Alexandria, and pearls, price 80*l.* The payment was not made till the 8th of August; but there can be little doubt that these royal ornaments were ordered for the occasion of Isabella's visit to Windsor, at the celebration of St. George's Day. Among other entries, is a payment of 32*l.* for several articles: namely, for a girdle of silk, studded with silver, 20*s.*; three hundred doublets (rubies), at twentypence the hundred; 1,800 pearls, at twopence each; and a circlet of gold, of the price of 16*l.* bought for the marriage of Katharine Brouart; and another of a pair of tablets of gold, enamelled with divers histories, of the price of 9*l.*

The division of Dona, besides entries of simple presents and gratuities, contains notes of gifts to messengers, from acquaintances; and others, giving us further insight into the connexions maintained by the Queen. Notices of messengers bringing letters from the Countesses of Warren and Pembroke, are very frequent. Under the head of Prestita, moreover, is an entry of a sum of 230*l.* given to Sir Thomas de la March, in money,[Pg 158] paid to him by the hands of Henry Pikard, citizen of London (doubtless the magnificent Lord Mayor of that name, who so royally entertained King John of France, the King of Cyprus, and the Prince of Wales, at this period), as a loan from Queen Isabella, on the obligatory letter of the same Sir Thomas: he is known as the victor in a duel, fought at Windsor, in presence of Edward III., with Sir John Viscomte, in 1350. To the origin of Isabella's interest in him we find no clue. Several payments to couriers refer to the liberation of Charles, King of Navarre, and are important, as proving that the Queen was not indifferent to the events passing in her native country, but that she was connected with one who was playing a conspicuous part in its internal history—Charles of Navarre, perhaps the most unprincipled sovereign of his age, and known in his country's annals under the designation of "the Wicked."

Among the remaining notices of messengers and letters, we have mention of the King's butler coming to the Queen at Hertford, with letters of the King, and a present of three pipes of wine; a messenger from the King, with three casks of Gascon wine; another messenger from the King, with a present of small birds; John of Paris, coming from the King of France to the Queen at Hertford, and returning with two volumes of Lancelot and the Sang Réal, sent to the same King by Isabella; a messenger bringing a boar's head and breast from the Duke of Lancaster, Henry Plantagenet; William Orloger, Monk of St. Albans, bringing to the Queen several quadrants of copper; a messenger bringing a present of a falcon from the King; a present of a wild boar from the King, and of a cask of Gascon wine; a messenger, bringing a present of twenty-four bream from the Countess of Clare; and payments to messengers bringing[Pg 159] new year's gifts from the King, Queen Philippa, the Countess of Pembroke, and Lady Wake.

Frequent payments to minstrels playing in the Queen's presence occur, sufficient to show that Isabella greatly delighted in this entertainment; and these are generally minstrels of the King, the Prince, or of noblemen, such as the Earl of March, the Earl of Salisbury, and others. And we find a curious entry of a payment of thirteen shillings and fourpence to Walter Hert, one of the Queen's "vigiles" (viol-players), going to London, and staying there, in order to learn minstrelsy at Lent time; and again, of a further sum to the same on his return from London, "de scola menstralcie."

Of special presents by the Queen, we have mention of new year's gifts to the ladies of her chamber, eight in number, of one hundred shillings to each, and twenty shillings each to thirty-three clerks and squires; a girdle to Edward de Ketilbergh, the Queen's ward; a donation of forty shillings to Master Lawrence, the surgeon, for attendance on the Queen; a present of fur to the Countess of Warren; a small gift to Isabella Spicer, her god-daughter; and a present of sixty-six pounds to Isabella de St. Pol, lady of the Queen's bedchamber, on occasion of her marriage with Edward Brouart. Large rewards, amounting together to 540*l.* were given after Isabella's death, by the King's order, to her several servants, for their good service to the Queen in her lifetime.

The division of Messengers contains payments for the carriage of letters to the Queen's officers and acquaintances. Among them we find mention of a letter to the Prior of Westminster, "for a certain falcon of the Count of Tancarville lost, and found by the said Prior."

We have only to add that the period of the account is from the 1st of October to the 5th of December in the following year, the same being[Pg 160] continued beyond the date of the Queen's death. The totals of the several divisions of the account are:—

	£	s.	d.
The Household Expenses amount to	4,014	2	11½
Alms	298	18	7½
Necessaries	1,395	6	11
Great wardrobe	542	10	4½
Jewels	1,399	0	4
Gifts	1,248	5	2½
Messengers	14	12	10
Imprests	313	4	3½

Making a general total of more than 9,000*l.*

NOTE.—*Murder of Edward II.*—In 1837, the Rev. Joseph Hunter communicated to the Society of Antiquaries some new circumstances connected with the apprehension and death of Sir Thomas de Gournay, charged as one of the murderers of King Edward II. Before the measures taken for Gournay's apprehension, he had escaped to the Continent, where, it was alleged, by one old chronicler, that he was taken at Marseilles; by another, at Burgos, in Spain; that his journey to England, in custody, was commenced, and that, by the orders of some influential persons in England, he was beheaded on board ship, on the voyage, lest he might implicate others, if brought to trial in England. Mr. Hunter has, however, found in Rymer's *Fœdera*, minute record that Gournay was taken at Burgos, and that Edward III. dispatched a commissioner to demand him from the Spanish authorities, who, for several months, put off giving up the prisoner; and when the order for his delivery was obtained, Gournay had found means to escape from Burgos. The commissioner endeavoured to discover the fugitive's retreat, but after an absence of more than twelve months, he returned to England without success. Subsequently, Gournay was made prisoner at Naples, on some local charge; on hearing which Edward III. dispatched another messenger, with a letter to the King of Sicily, demanding the custody of the prisoner for trial in England. This demand was complied with; and Gournay set off, in custody, on his journey hither. He is then traced to several places on the route, until his arrival at Bayonne, where he fell ill, died, and was buried. Notwithstanding the long existence of the *Fœdera*, this historical blunder of his having been beheaded was not rectified until the above date by Mr. Hunter.

THE ENGLISH HOUSEWIFE.

early two centuries and a half ago, Gervase Markham wrote a very useful and entertaining tract, entitled "The English Housewife, containing the inward and outward virtues which ought to be in a compleate woman. As her skill in physick, surgery, cookery, extraction of oyles, banquetting stuffe, ordering of great feasts, preserving of all sorts of wines, conceited secrets, distillations, perfumes, ordering of wooll, hempe, flax, making cloth, and dyeing; the knowledge of dayries, office of malting of oates, their excellent uses in a family, of brewing, baking, and all other things belonging to a household."

By aid of a contemporary[47] we are enabled to present a curious portrait of the Housewife from this authentic source. It should first be mentioned that the profusion of provisions in the banquets of the time bordered upon the barbarous magnificence, compared to the elegant modes of preparing dishes in the present day, and called for dining-halls and kitchens of sufficient dimensions to avoid the terrible confusion that must otherwise have occurred. Hence, the superintendence of the household was a labour of great extent and responsibility. It was held that a woman had no right to enter the state of matrimony unless possessed of a good knowledge of Cookery: otherwise she could perform but half her vow: she might love and obey, but she could not cherish. To[Pg 162] be perfect in this art she must know in which quarter of the moon to plant and gather all kinds of salads and herbs throughout the year; she must also be cleanly, have "a quick eye, a curious nose, a perfect taste, and a ready eare;" and be neither butter-fingered, sweet-toothed, nor faint-hearted: for if she were the first of these, she would let everything fall; if the second, she would consume that which she should increase; and if the third, she would lose time with too much niceness. For an ordinary feast with which any good man might entertain his friends, about sixteen dishes were considered a suitable supply for the first course. This included such substantial articles as a shield of brawn with mustard, a boiled capon, a piece of boiled beef, a chine of beef roasted, a neat's tongue roasted, a pig roasted, baked *chewets* (minced chickens made into balls), a roasted goose, a roasted swan, a turkey, a haunch of venison, a venison pasty, a kid with a pudding in it, an olive-pie, a couple of capons, and custards. Besides these principal dishes, the housewife added as many salads, fricassees, *quelquechoses*, and *devised pastes* as made thirty-two dishes, which were considered as many as it was polite to put upon the table for the first course. Then followed second and third courses, in which many of the dishes were for show only, but were so tastefully made as to contribute much to the beauty of the feast.

The banquets given by princes or nobles were much more important affairs. They were served in this manner:—First the grand sallet was to be marshalled in by gentlemen and yeomen-waiters, then green sallets, boiled sallets, and compound sallets; these were followed by all the fricassees, such as collops, rashers, &c.; then by boiled meats and fowls; then by the roasted beef, mutton, goose, swans, veal, pig, and[Pg 163] capon; next were ushered in the hot baked meats, such as fallow-deer in pasty, chicken or calves'-foot pie, and dowset; then the cold baked pheasants, partridges, turkey, goose, and woodcocks; lastly, carbonadoes both simple and compound. These were all arranged upon the table in such a manner that before each trencher stood a salad, a fricassee, a boiled meat, a roasted meat, a baked meat, and a carbonado,—a profusion that must have been almost overwhelming. The second course comprised the lesser wild and land fowl, which were again followed up with the larger kinds, as herons, shovellers, cranes, bustards, peacocks, &c.; and these by cold baked red-deer, hare-pie, gammon of bacon pie, wild boar, roe-pie; and scattered among these were the "conceited secrets" in the way of confectionery and sweet pastry, which were the pride of the good housewife's heart; besides whatever fish was available, which was to be distributed according to the manner in which it was dressed, with the respective courses, the fried with the fricassees, the broiled with the carbonadoes, the dry with the roast meats, and those stewed in broths with the boiled meats. The carbonadoes consisted of any meat scotched on both sides and sprinkled with seasonings in various combinations, and then either broiled over the fire or before it. Roasted geese were stuffed with gooseberries—hence the term; and, if we were to enter into the given details of the various modes of dressing these numerous dishes, we could mention many as long disused. Some of the terms employed are as startling to modern ears as the ingredients: to take one instance, pie-dishes were called coffins.

We are not to conclude that the above profusion was an every-day fact. There are hints here and there that this was by no means the case.[Pg 164] Oatmeal is called the crown of the housewife's garland, as being the largest item of consumption in the household; and whigge (whey) is praised as an excellent cool drink, and as wholesome as any other with which to slake a labouring man's thirst the whole summer long. On the other hand, we know this whigge was looked upon in a somewhat similarly scornful light as that in which we regard small beer, because it was adopted to distinguish the political body opposed to the Tories. And the constant supervision of the mistress of the house over every undertaking would also be a surety against the practice of extravagance. Although there were good men-maltsters in the land, there was no beer to compare with that made by the mistress and her maids. These made both beer and ale; cider from apples; perry from pears; mead and metheglin from honey and herbs. The wines, too, were in her care. It is curious to note the kind of care they experienced at her hands. Every *fatt* (vat) of foreign wine was dosed with several gallons of milk and eggs beaten up, and each was flavoured with some gallons of another, in a mode that must have much bewildered the palates of King Charles's lieges. If claret lost its colour, she stewed some damsons or black bullaces, and poured their syrup into the hogshead, when all came right again. If sack ran muddy, she took some rice, flour, and camphor, and popped that mixture into the butt; if any wine became hard, she knew how to make it mellow with honey and eggs: the same with muskadine and malmsey.

The indefatigable mistress of the house was as omnipresent in the bakehouse as elsewhere, and saw to the making up the various kinds of bread, both for the family and the hinds or servants. There were several kinds in use; wheat bread, rye bread, rye and wheat mixed, and barley[Pg 165] and wheat mixed: into the servants' barley-bread she adroitly mixed two pecks of peas and a peck of malt. She also looked in at the dairy, saw that it was kept as clean as a prince's chamber, and gave an eye to the profits. She could send several cheeses to table,—new milk cheese, nettle-cheese, floaten milk cheese and eddish or after-math cheese.

By way of relaxation to these serious duties, which, with the necessary supervision of the dressing and spinning of wool, hemp, and flax, must have kept the good dame pretty fully employed, she prescribed for any of her household that were indisposed, compounded her own remedies, and made stores of scented bags to lay among her hoarded-up linen, scented waters for different ornamental purposes, perfumes to burn, washing-balls, perfumed gloves, rosemary-water to preserve the complexion (called the bath of life), violet-water, herb-water for weak eyes, and other distillations. Plasters, ointments, lotions of all kinds, were among her cunning secrets. These occupations serve to show why the offices were so spacious and my lady's closet so small. Markharn gives scores of quaint recipes no housewife could ignore who was at all sensitive as to her reputation for skill. In these we are reminded of the absence of really scientific knowledge in the peculiar value set upon valueless distinctions. The milk of a red cow, for instance, was deemed more efficacious than that of any other colour for medicinal purposes; butter made in May without any salt in it was esteemed a sovereign cure for wounds, strains, or aches, although that made in any other month possessed no such virtue; and again, it was of no use to apply certain remedies unless the moon was on the wane. This portion of the volume is dedicated to the Right Honourable and most[Pg 166] Excellent Lady, Frances, Countess Dowager of Exeter.

Before we leave this Dinner-table of other days, we should add to the Housewife's duties the Art of Carving, which, until our time, was performed by the mistress of the house. We gather from Lord Wharncliffe's edition of the *Correspondence of Lady Mary Worthy Montague*, that, in the last century, this task must have required no small share of bodily strength, "for the lady was not only to invite—that is, urge and tease—her company to eat more than human throats could conveniently swallow, but to carve every dish, when chosen, with her own hands. The greater the lady, the more indispensable the duty,—each joint was carried up in its turn, to be operated upon by her, and her alone; since the peers and knights on either hand were so far from being bound to offer their assistance, that the very master of the house, posted opposite to her, might not act as her croupier; his department was to push the bottle after dinner. As for the crowd of guests, the most inconsiderable among them—the curate, or subaltern, or squire's younger brother—if suffered through her neglect to help himself to a slice of the mutton placed before him, would have chewed it in bitterness, and gone home an affronted man, half inclined to give a wrong vote at the next election. There were then professed carving masters, who taught young ladies the art scientifically; from one of whom Lady Mary Wortley Montague said she took lessons three times a week, that she might be perfect on her father's days; when, in order to perform her functions without interruption, she was forced to eat her own dinner alone an hour or two beforehand."

A HEREFORDSHIRE LADY IN THE TIME OF THE CIVIL WAR.

[Pg 167]

bout two centuries ago, there lived in the good old city of Hereford, one Mrs. Joyce Jefferies, of whose singular establishment, during nine years, a minute record has been preserved. In a cathedral town, olden features of English life may be traced more considerably than in other towns of less antiquity and extent. Hereford is thought to be derived from the British Hêre-fford, signifying the "old road." It has its Mayor's Court, view of Frankpledge, and court of Pie Pondre; though it has lost its monastic edifices; and, two centuries ago, its castle, built by Harold, was in ruins, which, as materials, were worth no more than 85*l*. One of the gateways of the town walls has been fitted up as a prison. There are several hospitals or alms-houses. Its Saxon cathedral occupies the site of a former church of wood; it is dedicated to St. Ethelbert, whose name was given to its nine days' fair; two of its fairs are "for diversions." In short, amidst broad streets, and red brick houses, and other modern aspects, are many interesting traces of old times and habits, furnished with its two crosses and a stone pulpit. Its river, the Wye, teems with salmon[48] and grayling; the whole county appears like one orchard; cider and perry are made everywhere; and there[Pg 168] is a good deposit of tobacco pipe clay. In one of its towns, on Shrove Tuesday, a bell rings at noon as a signal for the people to begin frying their pancakes; and among its festal records is that of a Morrice dance, performed by ten persons—a "nest of Nestors"—whose united ages recorded one thousand years.

In this old city, then, lived Mrs. Jefferies, upon an income averaging 500*l*. a year, in a house in Widemarch Street—the street in which Garrick, the actor, was born—which she built at a cost of 800*l*. but which was ordered to be pulled down in the time of the Rebellion, under Charles I., and the materials sold for 50*l*. This was a calamitous loss. Besides, the old lady lived beyond her means, not by self-indulgence in costly luxuries, but in indiscriminate gifts; and three-fourths of the entries in her accounts consist of sums bestowed in presents, of loans never repaid, or laid out in articles to give away. She continued in the city till the year 1642, when, driven by stress of war, she abandoned it, and sought refuge in the dwellings of others. Ultimately, in 1644, she gave up housekeeping to the day of her death.

The household establishment of Mrs. Jefferies is by no means, for a single person, on a contracted scale. Many female servants are mentioned; two having wages from 3*l*. to 3*l*. 4*s*. per annum, with gowns of dark stuff at Midsummer. Her coachman, receiving 40*s*. per annum, had at Whitsuntide, 1639, a new cloth suit and cloak; and, when he was dressed in his best, exhibited fine blue silk ribbon at the knees of his hose. The liveries of this and another man-servant were, in 1641, of fine Spanish cloth, made up in her own house, and cost upwards of nine pounds. Her man of business, or steward, had a salary of 5*l*.16*s*. A horse was kept for him, and he rode about to collect her rents and dues, and to see to her agricultural concerns. She appeared abroad in a coach drawn by two mares; a nag or two were in her stable; one that a widow lady in Hereford purchased of her, she particularly designated as "a rare ambler."

Mrs. Jefferies had a host of country cousins; for, in those days, family connexions were formed in more contracted circles than at present, and the younger people intermarried nearer home; and she was evidently an object of great interest and competition among such as sought for sponsors to their children. She seems to have delighted in the office of gossip, or *God-sib*, that is, *sib*, as related, by means of religion. The number of her god-children became a serious tax upon her purse. A considerable list of her christening gifts includes, in 1638, a silver tankard to give her god-daughter, little Joyce Walsh, 5*l*. 5*s*. 6*d*.; "at Heriford faier, for blue silk ribbon and taffetary lace for skarfs," for a god-son and god-daughter, 8*s*.; and 1642, "paid Mr. Side, gouldsmith in Heriford, for a silver bowle to give Mrs. Lawrence daughter, which I found, too, called Joyse Lawrence, at 5*s*. 8*d*. an oz., 48*s*. 10*d*." But to Miss Eliza Acton she was more than maternally generous and was continually giving proofs of her fondness in all sorts of indulgence, supplying her lavishly with costly clothes and sums of money—money for gloves, for fairings, for cards against Christmas, and money repeatedly to put in her purse.

We have mentioned Mrs. Jefferies' loans. She had various sums placed out at interest, on bond and mortgage, varying from three hundred pounds and upwards, and one of eight hundred pounds. The securities were frequently shifting; and the number of persons who paid to her irregularly enough, in this way, in two years, was little short of one hundred. The borrowers of these moneys were knights, yeomen, gentry, farmers, and tradesmen; burgesses, and aldermen, and Mayors of Hereford, with many others. The collection of interest upon principal so detached and widely dispersed, must have been attended with difficulty. The principal itself must have incurred risk of diminution; but the convenience of the Three per Cents. was then unknown, and eight per cent. was the interest upon these loans. This practice of lending money in small sums must formerly have been more general than at the present day: there were then few modes of employing money so as to realize fair interest; it was often hoarded by "making a stocking," and various modes of concealment.

Some of Mrs. Jefferies's entries respecting those who do not repay loans are curious. Thus, M. Garnons, an occasional suitor for relief, she styles "an unthrifty gentleman;" amuses herself in setting down a small bad debt; and, after recording the name of the borrower, and the trifling sum lent, adds, in a note by way of anticipation, "which he will never pay." In another case, that of a legal transaction, in which a person had agreed to surrender certain premises to her use, and she had herself paid for drawing the instrument upon which he was to have acted, she observes, "but he never did, and

I lost my money." In all matters she exhibits a gentle and generous mind. It was natural enough that she should describe the Parliamentary folks who pulled down her house as "fearful soldiers."

Here is a slight sketch of the personal appearance of Mrs. Jefferies in a specimen or two of her dress, among many that occur in her book of accounts. Her style of dress was such as became a gentlewoman of her[Pg 171] condition. In 1638, in her palmy days, she wore a tawny camlet coat and kirtle, which, with all the requisite appendages, trimmings, and making, scrupulously set down, cost 10l. 17s. 5d. She had, at the same time, a black silk calimanco loose gown, petticoat, and bodice, and these, with the making, came to 18l. 1s. 8d. Next month, a Polonia coat and kirtle cost in all 5l. 1s. 4d. Tailors were then the dressmakers: she employed those in Hereford, Worcester, and London; and, strange to say, sometimes the dresses were so badly made in London that they had to be altered by a country tailor. She had, about the same period, a head-dress of black tiffany, wore ruff-stocks, and a beaver hat with a black silk band, and adopted worsted hose of different colours—blue, and sometimes grass-green. Among the articles of her toilet were false curls, and curling-irons; she had Cordovan (Spanish leather) gloves, sweet gloves, and gold embroidered gloves. She wore diamond and cornelian rings, used spectacles, and carried a whistle for a little dog, suspended at her girdle by a yard of black loop lace. A cipress (Cyprus?) cat, given to her by a Herefordshire friend, was, no doubt, a favourite; and she kept a throstle in a twiggen cage.

A young lady who resided with her was dressed at her expense in a manner more suited to her earlier time of life: for instance, she had a green silk gown, with a blue satin petticoat. At Easter, she went to a christening arrayed in a double cobweb lawn, and had a muff. Next, she was dressed in a woollen gown, "spun by the coock's wife, Whooper," liver-coloured, and made up splendidly with a stomacher laced with twisted silver cord. Another article of this young lady's wardrobe was a gown of musk-coloured cloth; and when she rode out she was decked in a scarlet safeguard coat and hood, laced with red, blue, and yellow lace;[Pg 172] but none of her dresses were made by female hands.

Of the system of housekeeping we get a glimpse. In summer, she frequently had her own sheep killed; and at autumn a fat heifer, and at Christmas a beef or brawn were sometimes slaughtered, and chiefly spent in her house. She is very observant of the festivals and ordinances of the Church, while they continue unchanged; duly pays her tithes and offerings, and, after the old seignorial and even princely custom, contributes for her dependants as well as herself, in the offertory at the communion at Easter; has her pew in the church of All Saints at Hereford dressed, of course, with flowers at that season by the wife of the clerk; gives to the poor-box at the minster, and occasionally sends doles to the prisoners at Byster's Gate. Attached to ancient rules in town and country, she patronizes the fiddlers at sheep-shearing, gives to the wassail and the hinds at Twelfth Eve, when they light their twelve fires, and make the fields resound with toasting their master's health, as is done in many places to this day. Frequently in February, she is careful to take pecuniary notice of the first of the other sex, among those she knew, whom she met on Valentine's Day, and enters it with all the grave simplicity imaginable: "Gave Tom Aston, for being my valentine, 2*s*. Gave Mr. Dick Gravell, cam to be my valentine, 1*s*. I gave Timothy Pickering of Clifton, that was my valentine at Horncastle, 4*d*." Sends Mr. Mayor a present of 10*s*. on his "law day;" and on a certain occasion dines with him, when the waits, to whom she gives money, are in attendance at the feast; she contributes to these at New Year and Christmas tide, and to other musical performers at entertainments or fairs; seems fond of music, and strange sights, and[Pg 173] "rarer monsters." "Gave to Sir John Giles, the fiddler, and to 2 others on 12th day;" "to a boy that did sing like a blackbird." She was liberal to Cherilickcome "and his Jack-an-apes," some vagrant that gained his living by exhibiting a monkey; and at Hereford Midsummer Fair, in 1640, "to a man that had the dawncing horse." To every one who gratified her by a visit, or brought her a present, she was liberal; as well as to her own servants and attendants at friends' houses. She provided medicine and advice for those who were sick and could not afford to call in medical aid; and she took compassion on those who were in the chamber of death and house of mourning, as may be seen in this entry: "1648, Oct. 29. For a pound of shugger to send Mrs. Eaton when her son Fitz Wm. lay on his death-bed, 20*d*."

Our Herefordshire Lady's Diary takes us through nine years of the time of the dispute between Charles I. and the Parliament: it, accordingly, possesses much historic interest. In 1638, she paid the unpopular impost of Ship-money, unsuccessfully opposed by Hampden, as well as another tax, called "the King's provision;" and she finds a soldier for her farm, and for her property in Hereford, when the Trained Bands are called out and exercised. Now, too, old ancestral armour, or Train-band equipments, that hung rusting in manor-houses, were taken down and repaired. And when Prynne, Burton, and Bastwick had been agitating, Laud impeached and imprisoned, and Lord Strafford tried and beheaded, she took a decided interest in passing events, and sent for some of the pamphlets and newspapers that swarmed from the press. Thus, we find paid for a book of Strafford's Trial, and his portrait, and Laud's, and some other portraits, 4*s*. 1*d*. And when the Parliament soldiers discharged[Pg 174] their muskets, at or near her dwelling, we find this item: "Gave the sowldiers that shott off at my window, 1*s*. and beer." Then we find her, amidst great confusion, packing up her beds, furniture, and boxes, and taking flight in her carriage: but she was mercilessly plundered of "much goods, two bay coach mares, and some money, and much linen and clothes."

How her possessions were made away with at Hereford is a sad tale. Sir Henry Slingsby, a noted Royalist officer, mentions the havoc in terms of much regret. The orchards, gardens, trees, and houses were all destroyed. Before her house was pulled down, she sent her steward to save some part of the property, and make presents of the produce of her gardens, "gardin salitts," &c.

As years advance, symptoms of infirmity appear. The spectacles, and favourite "guilt spoone," and diamond ring, are missing, and found and brought by her attendants, who always have a reward. It has been related of Prince Eugene of Savoy, that his servants took dexterous advantage of his foible of immoderate anger, and threw themselves in the way of his fits of passion, that they might get a sound beating from him, and its never-failing accompaniment, a reward to make it up. Thus, probably, the attendants of Mrs. Jefferies, though in a different method, might make profit of her failing memory, by hiding and reproducing the above valuables, in order to a remuneration. Then, a fair is held at Worcester, and the maids from Horncastle of course attend it: our lady gives each a shilling, when Barbara, the dairy-maid, pretends that she had lost her shilling, and her mistress gave her another. But the maids were always in favour, and not content with making them presents at stated times, she invented vicarious means of slipping vails into their[Pg 175] hands.

Age seems to have abated nothing of her generous feeling, or of the ardour of her domestic affections. In all those events which usually bring joy to families, and occasion entries in our parish registers, she heartily sympathised. A marriage, even of a servant, was an occurrence that always appeared highly to interest her. When Miss Acton was married, she gave her a handsome portion, arranged the settlement, and defrayed incidental expenses; and to the entries she adds, "God bless them both." The clerks in the solicitors' offices are not forgotten; and, "Paid the butcher for a fatt weather to present this bride wooman at her wedding-day, 6*s*. 6*d*." The portion was made up in instalments, and on the last payment, she notes: "So I praise God all the 800*l*. is paid, and we are even." Then, what joy was there at a christening, when "ould Mrs. Barckley and myself Joyse Jeffreys were Gossips. God bless hitt: Amen." Also, "Gave the midwyfe, good wyfe Hewes, of Vpper Jedston, the christening day, 10*s*.;" and, "Gave nurse Nott ye same day, 10*s*."

Thus did she continue to go on, with blessings upon her lips and her right hand full of gifts, without intermission, till the grave closed over all that was mortal, and amiable, and singular in the character and conduct of one whose parallel is not easy to be found.

As respects herself, little did she think that, in compiling these accounts, she was about to present, after a lapse of upwards of two centuries, a more expressive memorial of her virtues than any that her surviving relatives could have placed upon her tomb.

"And so it has fallen out, that nothing appears to have been hitherto[Pg 176] done to mark the spot where she lies; neither has the exact period of her decease been ascertained, though the codicil of her will carries her forward to 1650, and it has been shown that she was buried in the chancel of the parish church of Clifton-upon-Teme, on the borders of Worcestershire. But her memory is still revered by those to whom her existence and character are known: and a brass tablet has been placed near the spot where she is believed to have been interred, with an inscription transmitting the name and virtues of Mrs. Joyce Jefferies to future times."[49]

HOUSE-FURNISHING IN THE MIDDLE AGES.

n accomplished illustrator of our Domestic History in describing the mode of furnishing houses in the Middle Ages, tells us that there were tables of Cyprus and other rare woods, carved cabinets, desks, chess-boards, and, above all, the Bed—the most important piece of furniture in the house, and of which Ralph Lord Basset said, "Whoever shall bear my surname and arms, according to my will, shall have my great bed for life." There was the "standing bed," and the "truckle bed;" on the former lay the lord, and on the latter his attendant. In the daytime the truckle bed, on castors, was rolled under the standing bed. The posts, head-boards, and canopies or spervers of bedsteads were sometimes carved, or painted in colours, but they are generally represented covered by rich hangings. King Edward III. bequeathed to his heir an entire bed marked with the arms of France and England, and Richard, Earl of Arundel, to his wife Philippa, a blue bed, marked with his arms, and the arms of his late wife; to his son Richard a standing bed called clove, also a bed of silk embroidered with the arms of Arundel and Warren; to his son Thomas, his blue bed of silk embroidered with griffins, &c.

The great chamber was often used as a sleeping-room by night and a reception-room by day. Shaw, in his *Decorations of the Middle Ages*, gives the interior of a chamber in which Isabella of Bavaria receives from Christine of Pisa her volume of poems. The Queen is seated on a couch covered with a stuff in red and gold, and there is a bed in the room furnished with the same material, to which are attached three shields of arms. The walls of the chamber were either hung with tapestry or painted with historical subjects. Chaucer, in his Dream, fancies himself in a chamber—

"Full well depainted,
And al the walles with colors fine
Were painted to the texte and glose,
And all the Romaunte of the Rose."

The beds of the better classes were sumptuous and comfortable. Mattresses were used, but sometimes, to receive the bed, loose straw was spread on the sacking. The order for making the royal savage's own lair says, "A yoman with a daggar is to search the strawe of the kynges bedde that there be none untreuth therein—the bedde of downe to be cast upon that." The lower classes were contented with straw alone; but, as appears from Holinshed's account, more from an ignorant contempt for a pleasant bed, and a soft pillow, than from lack of means to obtain the indulgence. The windows had curtains, and were glazed in the manner described by Erasmus; but in inferior dwellings, such as those of copyholders and the like, the light-holes were filled with linen, or with a shutter.

Early in the fourteenth century one Thomas Blaket, or Blanket, of Bristol, introduced the woollen fabric which still goes by his name. The word *worsted* comes from the village so named, near Norwich, where that kind of stuff began to be extensively manufactured for wall-hangings in[Pg 179] the fourteenth century. A still richer fabric similarly used, called *baudekin*, a kind of brocade, is said to have derived its name from Baldacus, in Babylon, whence, says Blount, it was originally brought.

Few objects of antiquarian curiosity acquired more notoriety than a bedstead or bed, of unusually large dimensions, preserved at Ware, twenty miles from London, on the road to Cambridge. Shakspeare employs it as an object of comparison in his play of *Twelfth Night*, bearing date 1614, where Sir Toby Belch says: "As many lies as will lie in this sheet of paper, though the sheet were big enough for the bed of Ware in England." (Act iii. sc. 2.) Nares, in his *Glossary*, says: "This curious piece of furniture is said to be still in being, and visible at the Crown or at the Bull in Ware. It is reported to be twelve feet square, and to be capable of holding twenty or twenty-four persons." And he refers to Chauncey's*Hertfordshire* for an account of the bed receiving at once twelve men and their wives, who lay at the top and bottom in this mode of arrangement,—first two men, then two women, and so on alternately,—so that no man was near to any woman but his wife. Clutterbuck, in his History, places the great bed at the Saracen's Head Inn, where a large bedstead is preserved. It is twelve feet square, of carved oak, and has the date 1463 painted on the back; but the style of the carving is Elizabethan—a century later, at least. It was*traditionally* sold among other movables which belonged to Warwick, the King-maker, at Ware Park, to suit which story the date is thought to have been painted. Again, it is placed at three inns—the Crown, the Bull, and Saracen's Head, at Ware, each of which may have had its "great bed."

Formerly, wealthy persons travelled with their bed in their carriage.[Pg 180] Mr. Beckford, of Fonthill, was, probably, the last person who so travelled, in England, some forty years since, when the writer's informant saw the unpacking of the bed, at the inn-door, at Salt Hill.

The Warming-pan did not make its appearance till the Tudor times. In the inventory of the goods of Sir William More, of Loseley, in Surrey, A.D. 1556, occurs "a warmynge," considered to be a warming-pan, and the earliest recorded mention of that article. The old warming-pans were often engraved with armorial bearings, mottoes, and inscriptions. In the *Welsh Levite tossed in a Blanket*, 1691, we read: "Our garters, bellows, and warming-pans wore godly mottoes, &c." We find a warming-pan engraved with the arms of the Commonwealth, and the motto: "ENGLANDS . STATS . ARMES." Another warming-pan has the royal arms, C. R. and "FEARE GOD HONNOR Y^E KINGE. 1662." Some years ago, there was purchased at the village of Whatcote, in Warwickshire, a warming-pan engraved with a dragon, and the date 1601; probably brought from Compton Wyniatt, the ancient seat of the Earl (now Marquis) of Northampton; the supporters of the Compton family being dragons.

The seats were mostly forms, but Chairs were sometimes used. A MS. of the fourteenth century has this item:—"To put wainscote above the dais in the king's hall, and to make a fine large and well sculptured chair." The early chair was a single seat without arms. The fauldsteuel (fauteuil in modern French) was originally a folding stool of the curule form, but afterwards the form alone was preserved; examples remain from the time of Dagobert up to a late period. Dagobert's seat is considered by some to be of much greater antiquity than his time, and the back and[Pg 181] arms are certainly of a later period than the rest. The so-called Glastonbury chair is much to be commended for simplicity of form, perfect strength, and adaptation for comfort.

In the earlier times, chairs and benches were not stuffed but had cushions to sit upon and cloths spread over them: afterwards, as the workmanship improved, they were stuffed and covered with tapestry, leather, or velvet. The forms and workmanship of these seats were generally very rude, but the stuffs that covered them were of great richness and value, and tastefully trimmed with fringes and gimps, fastened with large brass studs or nails.

The description of the furniture in the great chamber at Hengrave, the seat of Sir Robert Kytson, *temp.* Henry VII., enumerates very minutely the various articles; among which are, the carpet, the tables, the cupboards, the chairs, the stools, two great chairs, silk and velvet coverings, curtains to the windows and doors, a great screen, the fire-irons, branches for lights, &c.

The floors, which at an early period were laid with rushes, were at a later one covered with a carpet, called the bord carpet. Still, carpets were used very early in the castles and mansions of the wealthy. The manufacture of carpets is of great antiquity: we read of them in the sacred writings, they were found in the ruins of Pompeii, they were introduced from the East to Spain, from Spain they passed to France and England, and when Eleanor of Castile arrived in London, in 1255, the rooms of her abode were covered with carpets; they were used generally in the palace in the reign of Edward III. Turkey carpets were first advertised for sale in London in 1660. The manufacture of carpets was introduced into France by the celebrated Colbert, in 1664. A manufactory[Pg 182] was opened in England during the reign of Henry VIII., but this branch of industry was not permanently established until 1685, when the revocation of the Edict of Nantes drove half a million of Protestants from France, many of whom, settling in this country, established the manufacture of carpets. Brussels carpets were introduced from Tournay into Kidderminster, in 1745.

We have already described the Hall. At the further end of this apartment was generally placed a cupboard called the "Court cupboard," in which the service of plate, such as salvers and gold drinking cups, were arranged on shelves or stages, answering in some respects to our sideboards of the present day. These cupboards, though originally of rude construction, afterwards became elaborate and beautiful pieces of furniture, richly carved in oak: they are often alluded to in old documents. On grand occasions temporary stages, as cupboards, were also erected. At the marriage of Prince Arthur, son of Henry VII., in the hall was a triangular cupboard, five stages high, set with plate valued at 1,200*l.* entirely ornamental; and in the "utter chamber," where the princess dined, was another cupboard set with gold plate, garnished with stones and pearls, valued at 20,000*l.*

In the inventory of Skipton Castle, in Yorkshire, the furniture of the great hall is thus given:—"Imprimis, 7 great pieces of hangings, with the Earl's arms at large in every one of them, and powdered with the several coates of the house. 3 long tables on standard frames, 6 long forms, 1 short ditto, 1 Court cupboard, 1 fayre brass lantern, 1 iron cradle with wheels for charcoal, 1 almes tubb, 20 long pikes."

There is no mention of Mirrors, but they were used at this time, though[Pg 183] very small, and of metal polished. The coffre or chest which contained the ladies' trousseaux, was subsequently much ornamented. The wardrobes, so called, were generally small rooms fitted with cupboards called armoiries. In 1253, "the sheriff of Southampton was ordered to make in the king's upper wardrobe, in Winchester Castle, where the king's cloths were deposited, two cupboards or armoiries, one on each side of the fireplace, with arches and a certain partition of board across the same wardrobe."[50]

DRESS.—PERSONAL ORNAMENTS.

rom the old accounts of the Laundry we gather some idea of mediæval clothing and personal cleanliness. Four shirts was a large allowance for a nobleman in the fifteenth century; and youths of noble rank were sent to college without a change of linen. It is upon record that Bishop Swinfield, for himself and his whole household, in the thirteenth century, only spent forty-three shillings and twopence for washing; and the Duke of Northumberland's establishment, in the time of Henry VIII. consisting of one hundred and seventy persons, only cost forty shillings for the laundry expenses of a whole year. On the other hand, the institution of "tubbing" was not unknown. Baths are frequently mentioned in the romances, and are occasionally depicted in illuminations. They were large tubs with a curtain over them, after the manner of a modern French bed.

With respect to what we now call "comfort," it is certain that all the appliances of tapestried hangings were far inferior to the modern devices of double walls, sashes, and French casements, &c. as means of excluding draughts of air. But then the costume was suited to the houses. The modern drawing-room life was scarcely possible in a mediæval mansion. It was a necessity to dress more warmly; and, as may be seen in very many mediæval illuminations, almost every one, of either sex, went with covered heads. Just in the same way, in a modern farm-house or cottage, it is common enough for hats and bonnets to be worn habitually indoors.

The flannel in general use, the wadded petticoats, and worsted stuffs and brocaded silks (so thick as almost to stand alone) for gowns, were much better calculated to resist cold and damp than the cobweb fabrics worn by modern females; and the men's clothes were of a more substantial texture, and made much fuller than the scanty modern corresponding garments of thin superfine broadcloth. The thick woollen dresses of the monks also were well contrived for preserving a comfortable portable climate. No part but the face was exposed to the external air, and this was protected by the cowl, so that they were always defended from currents of cold air in the cloisters and vaulted aisles of the now desolate monastic edifices.

Woollen cloths were long the chief material of male and female attire. When new the nap was generally very long; and after being worn for some time it was customary to have it shorn; indeed, this process was repeated as often as the stuff would bear it. Thus we find the Countess of Leicester sending Hicque, the tailor, to London, to get her robes reshorn. Among the materials for dress mentioned, are linen, sindon, which has been variously interpreted to mean satin or very fine linen; scarlet and rayed or striped cloths, of Flemish, French, or Italian make; *pers*, or blue cloth, for the manufacture of which Provence was famous; russet, say or serge, and blanchet or blanket, a name which, it is believed, was given to flannel. The furs named are squirrel and miniver.

Among the minor objects of personal use which appear to have belonged to Margaret de Bohun, in the fifteenth century, the "poume de ambre," or scent-ball, in the composition of which ambergris formed a principal[Pg 186] ingredient, deserves notice; this being, perhaps, the earliest evidence of its use. We here learn also that a nutmeg was occasionally used for the like purpose; it was set with silver, decorated with stones and pearls, and was evidently an object rare and highly prized. Amongst the valuable effects of Henry V. according to an inventory dated A.D. 1423, are enumerated a musk-ball of gold, weighing eleven pounds, and another of silver-gilt. At a later period the Pomander was very commonly worn as the pendant of a lady's girdle. The *peres de eagle* were the stones supposed to be found in the nest of the eagle, to which various medicinal and talismanic properties were attributed. Nor are we cognizant of an earlier mention of coral than that which occurs in this inventory: namely, the paternoster of coral, with large gilded beads, which belonged to Margaret de Bohun, and the three branches of coral which Alianmore de Bohun possessed. Among her effects also is the wooden table "painted for an altar;" it formed part of the movable chapel furniture which persons of rank took with them on journeys, or used when, through infirmity, the badness of roads, or some other cause, valid in those days, they were prevented from attending public worship. Licences to use such portable altars are of frequent occurrence on the older episcopal registers.

John Evelyn, regretting "the simple manners that prevailed in his younger days, and which were now fast fading away," thus describes old-fashioned country life about the middle of the seventeenth century:—

"Men courted and chose their wives for their modesty, frugality, keeping at home, good housewifery, and other economical virtues then in reputation; and the young damsels were taught all these in the country[Pg 187] and in their parents' houses. They had cupboards of ancient, useful plate, whole chests of damask for tables, and stores of fine Holland sheets, white as the driven snow, and fragrant of rose and lavender for the bed; and the sturdy oaken bedstead and furniture of the house lasted one whole century; the shovel-board and other long tables, both in hall and parlour, were as fixed as the freehold; nothing was movable save joint-stools, the black jacks, silver tankards, and bowls.... The virgins and young ladies of that golden age, *quæsiverunt lanam et linum*, put their hands to the spindle, nor disdained they the needle; were obsequious and helpful to their parents, instructed in the managery of the family, and gave presages of making excellent wives. Their retirements were devout and religious books, and their recreations in the distillatory, the knowledge of plants and their virtues, for the comfort of their poor neighbours and use of their family, which wholesome, plain diet and kitchen physic preserved in perfect health." As the quaint old ballad hath it—

"They wore shoes of a good broad heel,
And stockings of homely blue;
And they spun them upon their own wheel,
When this old hat was new."

PINS AND PIN-MONEY.

etal pins are said to have been introduced into this country from France in the fifteenth century: as an article of commerce they are not mentioned in our statutes until the year 1483. Before this date, we are told that ladies were accustomed to fasten their dresses by means of skewers of boxwood, ivory, or bone; this statement has been doubted, but we are assured that, to this day, the Welsh use as a pin the thorn from the hedge.

Stow assigns the first manufacture of metal pins in England to the year 1543; and they seem to have been then so badly made that in the thirty-fourth year of King Henry VIII. (1542-3), Parliament enacted that none should be sold unless they be "double-headed, and have the headdes soudered faste to the shanke of the pynne." In short, the head of the pin was to be well smoothed, the shank well shapen, and the point well rounded, filed, canted, and sharpened. The Act of Parliament, however, appears to have produced no good effect, for in the thirty-seventh year of the same reign it was repealed.

The manufacture of pins was introduced into several towns of Great Britain by individuals who, in some cases, are called the inventors of the article. The pin-makers of former days seem to have been a body somewhat difficult to please, of whom

Guillim, in his *Display of Heraldry*, writes:—"The Society of Pinmen and Needlers, now ancient, or whether incorporated, I find not, but only that, in the year 1597, they[Pg 189] petitioned the Lord Treasurer against the bringing in of foreign pins and needles, which did much prejudice to the calling." The Pinners' Company was incorporated by Charles I. in 1636; the Hall is on part of the ancient Priory of the Augustine, or Austin Friars; it has been, since the reign of Charles II., let as a Dissenting meeting-house: it is in Pinners'-hall-court, Old Broad-street.

The manufacture of pins formed early a lucrative branch of trade. Sixty thousand pounds, annually, is said to have been paid for them to foreign makers, in the early years of Queen Elizabeth; but, as we have seen, long before the decease of that princess, they were manufactured in this country in great quantities; and in the time of James I., the English artisan is regarded to have "exceeded every foreign competitor in the production of this diminutive, though useful article of dress."

Pennant, in his description of old London Bridge, states that "most of the houses were tenanted by pin or needle makers, and economical ladies were wont to drive from the St. James's end of the town to make cheap purchases." But Thomson, in his minute *Chronicles of London Bridge*, does not mention pin-makers among the trades common on the bridge; haberdashers, who came here *late* from the Chepe, however, sold pins.

Yet vast quantities of early pins have been recovered from the Thames near the site of the old Bridge. In 1864, Mr. Burnell exhibited to the British Archæological Association fifteen brass pins, varying in length from one inch and three-eighths to five inches and a half, stated to have been found on the paper on which they now are, in a cellar on the northern bank of the Thames, in excavating for the foundations of the[Pg 190] South-Eastern Railway bridge. Most, if not all, of these pins have solid globose heads. At the same meeting, Mr. Syer Cuming exhibited two brass pins recovered from the mud of the Thames some years since. One is little less than two inches and a half in length, the other full seven inches and three-quarters long. The heads of both are formed with spiral wire; the shortest being globose, the other somewhat flattened. Mr. Cuming stated that quantities of such early pins as those then produced have been found in and along the banks of the river, some of them measuring upwards of a foot in length. These great pins may have been employed in securing the wide-spreading head-dresses of the Middle Ages, and fastening the ends of the pillow-case, a use not quite obsolete in the time of Swift, who speaks of "corking pins," for this purpose, in his *Directions to Servants*.

For some time after their introduction pins must have been costly, for we find that they were acceptable New Year's gifts to ladies, and that presents of money were made for buying pins; whence money set apart for the use of ladies received the name of *pin-money*.

In France, three centuries ago, there was a tax for providing the queen with pins; from whence the term of *pin-money* has been, undoubtedly, applied by us to that provision for married women, with which the husband is not to interfere. In Bellon's *Voyages*, 1553, we read:—"Quand nous donnons l'argent a quelque chambrière, nous *disons pour ses épingles*."

Pins must soon have been made and sold at a very cheap rate, to justify the common remark, "Not worth a pin," and equivalent expressions in some[Pg 191] of our early writers, such as Tusser:

"His fetch is to flatter, to get what he can;
His purpose once gotten, a *pin* for thee than."

Pins are of various sizes, from the blanket-pin, three inches in length, to the smallest ribbon-pins, of which 300,000 only weigh one pound. Insect-pins, used by entomologists, are of finer wire than ordinary pins, and vary in length from three inches to a size smaller than ribbon-pins. It has been calculated that ten tons of pins are made every week in England alone, requiring from fourteen to fifteen tons of brass-wire.

"What becomes of all the pins?" a question every day asked, received an answer, a few years since, upon the opening of an old sewer for repair, in Rea-street, Birmingham. At the bottom of it was a deposit as hard as the "slag" from a blast furnace, and in this deposit a vast number of pins were embedded: a piece about the size of a man's fist bristled with them, and this was but a specimen of a great mass of such matter. In another way, too, the deposit was a curiosity; for, independently of the pins, it inclosed a heterogeneous collection of old pocket-knives, marbles, buttons, &c.

Anciently, there were local springs, known as *Pin Wells*, in passing which the country maids dropped into the water a crooked pin to propitiate the fairy of the well. In some places, rich and poor believed this superstition.

PROVISIONS:

BREAD-MAKING, GROCERY, AND CONFECTIONERY.

nder the designation of *Panis*, Mr. Hudson Turner thinks that grain and flour, as well as bread, were included. It would appear that bread of different degrees of fineness was used. Thus, in the Household Expenses of Eleanor, Countess of Leicester, third daughter of King John, and wife of the celebrated Simon de Montfort, 1265, "the earliest known memorial of the domestic expenditure of an English subject," we find that there was "bread purchased for the Countess," and "bread for the kitchen." Loaves or cakes were made of bolted flour, are twice mentioned, as well as cakes, or wastells, perhaps biscuits; on one occasion half a quarter of flour is set down for pastry. It is inferred that the bread generally used in the family was made of a mixture of wheat and rye. As the dogs were fed with corn, it may be concluded that the servants fared no worse: at any rate there is no distinct notice of bread made of barley, oats, or the more inferior grain which were commonly used in France and other countries.

It is not clear that their bread was leavened with yeast, as that article occurs but once, and then in connexion with malt. The price of the quarter of wheat or rye varied from 5*s*. to 5*s*. 8*d*.; of oats,[Pg 193] from 2*s*. to 2*s*. 4*d*.; twenty-five quarters, however, were bought at Sandwich, at 1*s*. 10*d*. When grain was brought from the Countess' manors, some of the prices were rather below the average. The bailiff of Chalton was allowed 5*s*. the quarter for wheat, 4*s*. for barley, and 2*s*. 4*d*. for oats; the bailiff of Braborne had 4*s*. 4*d*. for wheat, and 1*s*. 3*d*. for oats.

The Manchet is a fine white roll, named, according to Skinner, from *michette*, French; or from *main*, because small enough to be held in the hand:

"No manchet can so well the courtly palate please
As that made of the meal fetch'd from my fertil leaze."
Drayton's *Polyolbion*.

Here are two olden recipes for manchets:

"*Lady of Arundel's Manchet.*—Take a bushel of fine wheat-flour, twenty eggs, three pound of fresh butter; then take as much salt and barm as to the ordinary manchet; temper it together with new milk pretty hot, then let it lie the space of half an hour to rise, so you may work it up into bread, and bake it: let not your oven be too hot."—*True Gentlewoman's Delight*, 1676.

"Take a quart of cream, put thereto a pound of beef-suet minced small, put it into cream, and season it with nutmeg, cinnamon, and rose-water; put to it eight eggs and but four whites, and two grated manchets; mingle them well together and put them in a buttered dish; bake it, and being baked, scrape on sugar, and serve it."—*The Queene's Royal Cookery*, 1713.

Manchets are used in the colleges of Oxford and Cambridge to this day. The manchets and cheese, and fine ale, of Magdalen College are well known.

[Pg 194]

The Manciple, a purveyor of victuals, a clerk of the kitchen, or caterer, still subsists in the universities, where the name is therefore preserved; but Archdeacon Nares believed nowhere else. One of Chaucer's pilgrims is a manciple of the Temple, of whom he gives a good character for his skill in purveying.

It is curious to find that one of the domestic arts which is somewhat neglected in the households of the present generation, should, in the last century, have been considered an accomplishment of such importance as to be taught in schools: this was Pastry-making. There was then resident in London one of the ancient family of the Kidders, of Maresfield, in Sussex, and a descendant of Richard Kidder, Bishop of Bath and Wells. This was Edward Kidder, a pastrycook, or, as he calls himself, "pastry-master," who carried on his business in Queen Street, Cheapside, and was induced to open two schools in the metropolis to teach the art of making pastry, one at his own place of business, and the other in Holborn. He also gave instructions to ladies at their private houses. So popular did his system of teaching become, that he is said to have instructed nearly 6,000 ladies in this art. He also published a book of *Receipts of Pastry and Cookery*, for the use of his scholars, printed entirely in copper-plate, with a portrait of himself, in the full wig and costume of the day, as a frontispiece. He died in 1739, at the age of seventy-three. By will, he gave to his wife, Mary Kidder, a gold watch, a diamond ring, and all the other rings and trinkets used by her, and also all the furniture of the best room in which she lay in the house in Queen Street; and to his daughters, Elizabeth and Susan, he bequeathed all his money, bank-stock, plate, jewellery, &c. Susan, among other bequests, gave to her cousin, George[Pg 195] Kidder, of Canterbury, pastrycook, 150*l*. and the copper-plates for the receipt-book.

Some dishes of the olden dinner-table are not very inviting. Our ancestors had no objection to stale fish; and blubber, if they could get it from a stray whale, or grampus or porpoise, was considered a delicacy. Yet some of the old dishes have stood the test of ages, as we see in the case of a Christmas Pie, the receipt to make which is preserved in the books of the Salters' Company, in the City of London.

"For to make a moost choyce Paaste of Gamys to be eten at ye Feste of Chrystemasse" (17th Richard II. A.D. 1394). A pie so made by the Company's cook in 1836 was found excellent. It consisted of a pheasant, hare, and capon; two partridges, two pigeons, and two rabbits; all boned and put into paste in the shape of a bird, with the livers and hearts, two mutton kidneys, forced-meats, and egg-balls, seasoning, spice, catsup, and pickled mushrooms, filled up with gravy made from the various bones.

We must, however, remember that Cookery flourished in the reign of Richard II., who rebuilt Westminster Hall, and gave therein a *house-warming*, at which old Stow says, "he feasted ten thousand persons." Richard is also said to have kept 2,000 cooks, who left to the world their famous cookery-book, the "Form of Cury, or, a Roll of English Cookery," compiled about the year 1390, by the master-cooks of the Royal Kitchen.

Sugar was at first regarded as a spice, and was introduced as a substitute for honey after the Crusades. It was sold by the pound in the thirteenth century, and was procurable even in such remote towns as Ross and Hereford. Before the discovery of America, however, Sugar was a costly luxury, and only used on rare occasions. About 1459, Margaret Barton, writing to her husband, who was a gentleman and landowner of[Pg 196] Norfolk, begs that he will vouchsafe "to buy her a pound of sugar." Again: "I pray that ye will vouchsafe to send me another sugar-loaf, for my old one is done." The art of refining sugar, and what is called loaf-sugar, was discovered by a Venetian about the end of the fifteenth, or the beginning of the sixteenth century. Sugar-candy is of much earlier date; for in Marin's *Storia di Commercio de Veneziani*, there is an account of a shipment made at Venice for England, in 1319, of 100,000 pounds of sugar, and 10,000 pounds of sugar-candy. Refined or loaf-sugar is thus mentioned in a roll of provisions in the reign of Henry VIII.: "two loaves of sugar, weighing sixteen pound two ounces, at —— per pound." A letter from Sir Edward Wotton to Lord Cobham, dated Calais, March 6, 1546, informs him that he had taken up for his lordship twenty-five sugar-loaves, at six shillings a loaf, "which is eightepence a pounde." Up to the close of the fifteenth century its price varied from one-and-sixpence to three shillings a pound, "or, on an average, to a sum equivalent to about thirty shillings at present." Sugar has become to us almost a necessary of life. "We consume it in millions of tons; we employ thousands of ships in transporting it. Millions of men spend their lives in cultivating the plants from which it is extracted, and the fiscal duties imposed upon it add largely to the revenue of nearly every established government. It may be said, therefore, to exercise a more direct and extended influence, not only over the social comfort, but over the social condition, of mankind, than any other production of the vegetable kingdom, with the exception, perhaps, of cotton alone."—*J. F. W. Johnston, M.A.*[51]

Coffee is mentioned in Burton's *Anatomy of Melancholy*, date 1621,[Pg 197] several years before coffee-houses were introduced into England. The first coffee-house was opened in 1650, at Oxford, by Jacobs, a Jew, "at the Angel; and there it (coffee) was, by some who delighted in novelty, drunk." About this time, Mr. Edwards, a Turkey merchant, brought from Smyrna to London, one Pasqua Rosee, a Ragusan youth, who prepared this drink for him every morning. But the novelty thereof, drawing too much company to him, he allowed his said servant, with another of his son-in-law, to sell coffee publicly, and they set up the first coffee-house in London, in St. Michael's Alley, in Cornhill. The sign was Pasqua Rosee's own head.

Tea was first sold in London by Thomas Garway, in Change Alley, in 1651, at from 16s. to 50s. per pound; it had been previously sold at from six pounds to ten pounds per pound. Pepys, in his *Diary*, tells, Sept. 25, 1669, of his sending "for a cup of Tea, a China drink he had not before tasted." Henry Bennet, Earl of Arlington, about 1666, had introduced Tea at Court. And, in Sir Charles Sedley's *Mulberry Garden*, we are told that "he who wished to be considered a man of fashion always drank wine-and-water at dinner, and a dish of tea afterwards."[52]

Spices and other condiments are mentioned in the Countess of Leicester's[Pg 198] accounts, viz., anise, cinnamon, ginger, pepper, cloves, cummin, dried fennel, saffron, sugar, liquorice, mustard, verjuice, and vinegar, the prices of which were very low. It must not be supposed, from the low prices of some of these articles, that they were generally used in the country; the arrival of a ship laden with spices was an event of such importance, and perhaps rarity, that the King usually hastened to satisfy his wants before the cargo was landed. Thus in the 10th of Henry the Third, the bailiffs of Sandwich were commanded to detain, upon their coming to port, two great ships laden with spices and precious merchandises, which were expected from Bayonne; and not to allow anything to be sold until the King had had his choice of their contents.

Among the glories of olden confectionery was March-pane, a biscuit composed of sugar and almonds, like those now called Macaroons. It is also called *massepain* in some old books. The word March-pane exists, with little variation, in almost all the European languages; yet the derivation of it is uncertain. In the Latin of the Middle Ages, March-panes were called *Martii panes*, which gave occasion to Hermolaus Barbaras to inquire into their origin, in a letter to Cardinal Piccolomini, who had some sent to him as a present. Balthazar Bonifacius says they were named from Marcus Apicius, the famous epicure. Minshew, following Hermolaus, will have them originally sacred to Mars, and stamped with a castle.

Whatever was the origin of their name, the English receipt-books show that they were composed of almonds and sugar, pounded and baked together. Here is a receipt:

"*To make a March-pane.*—Take two pounds of almonds, being[Pg 199] blanched, and dryed in a sieve over the fire, beate them in a stone mortar, and when they bee small, mix them with two pounds of sugar beeing finely beaten, adding two or three spoonefuls of rose-water, and that will keep your almonds from oiling: when your paste is beaten fine, drive it thin with a rowling pin, and so lay it on a bottom of wafers; then raise up a little edge on the side, and so bake it; then yce it with rose-water and sugar, then put it into the oven againe, and when you see your yce is risen up and drie, then take it out of the oven and garnish it with pretie conceipts, as birdes and beasts being cast out of standing-moldes. Sticke long comfits upright into it, cast bisket and carrowaies in it, and so serve it: you may also print of this march-pane paste in your moldes for banqueting dishes. And of this paste our comfit makers at this day make their letters, knots, armes, escutcheons, beasts, birds, and other fancies."—*Delightes for Ladies* 1608.

March-pane was a constant article in the desserts of our ancestors, and appeared sometimes on more solemn occasions. When Elizabeth visited Cambridge, the University presented their chancellor, Sir William Cecil, with two pairs of gloves, a march-pane, and two sugar-loves. In the old play of *Wits* we find a reference to

"——dull country madams that spend
Their time in studying recipes to make
March-pane and preserve plumbs."

Castles and other figures were often made of march-pane for splendid desserts, and were demolished by shooting or throwing sugar-plums at them.

Almonds are an olden delicacy of our table, and have for ages been very extensively used in a variety of preparations. Almond-milk, composed of almonds ground and mixed with milk or other liquid, was a favourite beverage, as was also almond-butter and almond-custard. The antiquity of the practice of serving almonds and raisins together at dessert seems to be shown from the name Almonds-and-raisins being given as that of an old English[Pg 200] game in *Useful Transactions in Philosophy*, 1700.

Biscuits (originally Biskets) of various kinds were in use in the sixteenth and seventeenth centuries; among which that most in repute was called Naples Biscuit, from the place where it was first made: it occurs in the Carpenters' Company's books in 1644.

Orange-Flower Water has been a favourite perfume in England since the reign of James I. It occurs in Copley's *Wits, Fits, and Fancies*, 1614; and in the *Accomplished Female Instructor*, 1719, is the following recipe:—Take two pounds of orange-flowers, as fresh as you can get them, infuse them in two quarts of white wine, and so distil them, and it will yield a curious perfuming spirit.—*Orange Butter* was made, according to the *Closet of Rarities*, 1706, by beating up new cream, and then adding orange-flower and red wine, to give it the colour and scent of an orange.[53]

DESSERT FRUITS.

The only kinds of fruits named in the Countess of Leicester's Expenses, are apples and pears: three hundred of the latter were purchased at Canterbury; probably from the gardens of the monks. It is believed, however, that few other sorts were generally grown in England before the latter end of the fifteenth century; although Matthew Paris, describing the bad season of 1257, observes that "apples were scarce, and pears scarcer, while quinces, vegetables, cherries, plums, and all shell-fruits, were entirely destroyed." These shell-fruits were probably the common hazel-nut, walnuts, and perhaps chestnuts: in 1256, the Sheriffs of London were ordered to buy two thousand chestnuts for the King's use. In the Wardrobe Book of the 14th of Edward the First, before quoted, we find the bill of Nicholas, the royal fruiterer, in which the only fruits mentioned are pears, apples, quinces, medlars, and nuts. The supply of these, from Whitsuntide to November, cost 21*l.* 14*s.*[Pg 201] 1½*d.* This apparent scarcity of indigenous fruits naturally leads to the inquiry, what foreign kinds besides those included in the term spicery, such as almonds, dates, figs, and raisins, were imported into England in this and the following century? In the time of John and of Henry the Third, Rochelle was celebrated for its pears and conger eels: the Sheriffs of London purchased a hundred of the former for Henry, in 1223.

In the 18th of Edward the First, a large Spanish ship came to Portsmouth; out of the cargo of which the Queen bought one frail of Seville figs, one frail of raisins or grapes, one bale of dates, and two hundred and thirty pomegranates, fifteen citrons, and seven ORANGES. The last item is important, as Le Grand d'Aussy could not trace the orange in France to an earlier date than 1333; here we find it known in England in 1290; and it is probable that this was not its first appearance. The marriage of Edward with Eleanor of Castile naturally led to a greater intercourse with Spain, and, consequently, to the introduction of other articles of Spanish produce than the leather of Cordova, olive-oil, and rice, which had previously been the principal imports from that fertile country, through the medium of the merchants of Bayonne and Bordeaux. It is to be regretted that the series of Wardrobe Books is incomplete, as much additional information on this point might have been derived from them. At all events it appears certain that Europe is indebted to the Arab conquerors of Spain for the introduction of the orange, and not to the Portuguese, who are said to have brought it from China. An English dessert in the thirteenth century must, it is clear, have been composed chiefly of dried and preserved fruits—dates, figs, apples, pears, nuts,[Pg 202] and the still common dish of almonds and raisins.

The garden of the Earl of Lincoln, now in the midst of one of the most densely-peopled quarters of London, was highly kept long before the Earl's mansion became an Inn of Court. His Lordship's bailiff's accounts, in the reign of Edward I. (1295-6), show the garden to have produced apples, pears, hedge nuts, and cherries, sufficient for the Earl's table, and to yield by sale in one year, 135*l.*, modern currency. The vegetables grown were beans, onions, garlick, leeks; hemp was grown; the cuttings of the vines were much prized; of pear-trees there were several varieties: the only flowers named are roses. In the previous reign (Henry III.) a considerable quantity was cultivated as gardens within the walls of the metropolis; and we read, from time to time, in the coroners' rolls, of mortal accidents which befel youths attempting to steal apples in the orchards of Paternoster Row and Ivy Lane, almost in the shadow of St. Paul's Cathedral.

ORNAMENTAL FRUIT TRENCHERS.

The usages of social life amongst our ancestors present us with several interesting instances of their ingenuity in keeping before them the rule of life by monitory inscriptions, or texts, placed over doorways, upon walls, and upon articles in daily domestic use, thus making it "plain upon the tables, that he may run that readeth it." We find this good advice upon the curiously-ornamented Fruit-trenchers in fashion during the sixteenth century. The only set of tablets, or trenchers, of this description, rectangular in form, hitherto noticed, are in the possession of Mrs. Bird, of Upton-cum-Severn. They are twelve in number,[Pg 203] formed of thin leaves of light-coloured wood, possibly lime-tree, measuring about 5¾ inches by 4½ inches, and inclosed in a wooden case, formed like a book, with clasps, the sides decorated like bookbinding.

On removing a sliding-piece, the upper tablets may be taken out. They are curiously painted and gilt; every one presenting a different design, and inscribed with verses from Holy Writ, conveying some moral admonition. Each tablet relates to a distinct subject. These legends are inclosed in compartments, surrounded by various kinds of foliage, and the old-fashioned flowers of an English garden—the campion, honeysuckle, and gillyflower—each tablet being ornamented with a different flower. One trencher bears the oak-leaf and acorns, and the texts inscribed upon it relate to the uncertainty of human life. Upon the others are found admonitions against covetousness, hatred, malice, gluttony, profane swearing, and evil speaking; with texts in which the virtues of benevolence, patience, chastity, forgiveness of injuries, and so forth, are inculcated.

The following are the texts in the centre, relating to inebriety, the spelling modernized:—"Woe be unto you that rise up early to give yourselves to drunkenness, and all your minds go on drinking, that ye sit swearing thereat until it be night. The harp, the lute, the tabour, the thalme, and plenty of wine are at your feasts, but the Word of the Lord do ye not behold, neither consider ye the work of His hands." In the four compartments of the margin: "Take heed that your heart be not overwhelmed with feasting and drunkenness." "Through gluttony many perish." "Through feasting many have died, but he that eateth measurably[Pg 204] prolongeth life." "Be no wine-bibber." The sides thus ornamented, were coated with a hard transparent varnish; the reverse, which probably was the side upon which the fruit or comfits were laid, is smooth and clear, without varnish or colour. These curious fruit-trenchers were found amongst a variety of old articles at Elmley Castle, Worcestershire, about forty years since. They were exhibited during the Meeting of the Archæological Institute at Winchester, in 1845, and brought to light other sets of fruit-trenchers. One of these, belonging to Jervoise Clarke Jervoise, Esq., of Idsworth Park, Hants, consisted of ten trenchers, in the form of roundels, ornamented like those just described, and inclosed in a box, which bears upon its cover the royal arms, France and England quarterly, surmounted by the Imperial crown. The supporters are the lion and the dragon, indicating that these roundels are of the time of Queen Elizabeth. On each are inscribed a rhyming stanza and Scripture texts. Thus, under the symbol of a skull, is (modernized)—

"Content thyself with thine estate,
And send no poor wight from thy gate;
For why this counsel I ye give,
To learn to die, and die to live."

These roundels have been described as trenchers for cheese or sweetmeats. Some antiquaries, however, consider them as intended to be used in some social game, like modern conversation-cards: their proper use appears to be sufficiently proved by the chapter on "Posies" in the *Art of English Poesie*, published in 1589, which contains the following:—"There be also another like epigrams that were sent usually for New Yeare's gifts, or to be printed or put upon banketting dishes of[Pg 205] sugar-plate, or of March-paines, &c.; they were called Nenia or Apophoreta, and never contained above one verse, or two at the most, but the shorter the better. We call them poesies, and do paint them now-a-days upon the back sides of our fruit-trenchers of wood, or use them as devices in ringes and armes."

It was customary in olden times to close the banquet with "confettes, sugar-plate, fertes with other subtilties, with Ipocrass," served to the guests as they stood at the board after grace was said. The period has not been stated at which the fashion of desserts and long sittings after the principal meal of the day became an established custom. It was, doubtless, at the time when that repast, which, during the reign of Queen Elizabeth, had been at eleven before noon, amongst the higher classes in England, took the place of the supper, usually served at five, or between five and six, at that period.[54] The prolonged revelry, once known as the "reare supper," may have led to the custom of following up the dinner with a sumptuous dessert. Be this as it may, there can be little question that the concluding service of the social meal—composed, as Harrison, who wrote about the year 1579, informs us, of "fruit and conceits of all sorts,"—was dispensed upon the ornamental trenchers above described.

In the Doucean Museum, at Goodrich Court, there is a set of roundels, similar to the above, which appear, by the badge of the rose and the pomegranate conjoined, to be of the early part of the reign of Henry VIII. Possibly, they may have been introduced with many foreign "conceits" and luxuries from France and Germany, during that reign. In[Pg 206] the times of Elizabeth, mention first occurs of fruit dishes of any ornamental ware, the service of the table having previously been performed with dishes, platters, and saucers of pewter, and "treens," or wooden trenchers; or, in more stately establishments, with silver plate. Shakspeare makes mention of "china dishes;" but it is more probable that they were of the ornamental ware fabricated in Italy, and properly termed *Majolica*, than of Oriental porcelain. The first mention of "porselyn" in England occurs in 1587-8, when its rarity was so great, that a porringer and cup of that costly ware were selected as New Year's gifts presented to the Queen by Burghley and Cecil. Shortly after, mention is made by several writers of "earthen vessels painted; costly fruit dishes of fine earth painted; fine dishes of earth painted; such as are brought from Venice."

Those elegant Italian wares, which in France appear to have superseded the more homely appliances of the festive table, about the middle of the sixteenth century, were doubtless adopted at the tables of the higher classes in our own country, towards its close.

The wooden fruit-trencher was not, however, wholly disused during the seventeenth century; and amongst sets of roundels which may be assigned to the reign of James I. or Charles I. may be mentioned a set exhibited in the Museum formed during the meeting of the Archæological Institute at York, in 1846. They were purchased at a broker's shop at Bradford, Yorkshire: in dimensions they resemble the trenchers of the reign of Elizabeth, already described; but their decoration is of a more ordinary character. On each tablet is pasted a line engraving, of coarse[Pg 207] execution, and gaudily coloured, representing one of the Sibyls.[55]

The common trencher which most of us have seen in use, was a wooden platter employed instead of metal, china, or earthen plates. It was even considered a stride of luxury when trenchers were often changed in one meal. "And with an humble chaplain it was expressly stipulated," says Bishop Hall, "that he never change his trencher twice." The term "a good trencher-man" was then equivalent to a hearty feeder (Nares's *Glossary*). Maple-wood, being soft and white, was formerly in great request for trenchers.

Fosbroke remembered when no other but wooden dishes of this kind were used in farm-houses in Shropshire. The general form of the trencher was round; yet the *trencher-cap* of our Universities has a square top.

VEGETABLES.

Very few esculent plants are mentioned in the Accounts of the Middle Ages. Dried peas and beans, parsley, fennel, onions, green peas, and new beans, are the only species named. Pot-herbs, of which the names are not specified, but which served eleven days, cost 6*d*. There is much uncertainty upon the subject of the cultivation of vegetables, in this country, during the thirteenth and fourteenth centuries. Cresses, endive, lettuces, beets, parsnips, carrots, cabbages, leeks, radishes, and cardoons, were grown in France during the reign of Charlemagne; but it is doubtful whether many of these varieties had penetrated into England at that early period. The most skilful horticulturists of the[Pg 208] Middle Ages were ecclesiastics, and it is possible that in the gardens of monasteries many vegetables were reared which were not in common use among the laity. Even in the fifteenth century, the general produce of the English kitchen garden was contemptible when compared with that of the Low Countries, France, and Italy. Gilbert Kymer can enumerate only, besides a few wild and forgotten sorts, cabbage, lettuce, spinach, beetroot, trefoil, bugloss, borage, celery, purslane, fennel, smallage, thyme, hyssop, parsley, mint, a species of turnip, and small white onions. According to him, all these plants were boiled with meat. He observes also that some were eaten raw, in spring and summer, with olive-oil and spices, but questions the propriety of the custom. This is, perhaps, the earliest notice extant of the use of salads in England.

The subject of the supplies of the table with food is a very large one; and leaves us but space to remark that the condition of food, an important point of its worth, must have suffered from the slow mode of conveyance in former times. The advantages which we enjoy in this age of rapid transit have been thus cleverly illustrated by a contemporary:—"A little more than half a century ago it took about six weeks to drive the herds of cattle from the north of Scotland to the metropolis: now they can be whirled here in a few hours. Fish in great variety may be caught in the morning on the coast of Berwick and Coquet, and be boiling in the kitchens of Belgravia on the same evening for dinner. In exchange for the sheep and beeves from the highlands and Cheviot, the choice fruits and early vegetables of the south are rapidly passed. By means of steamships and other quick sailing vessels, the oranges of Spain and[Pg 209] Portugal, the grapes of France and Italy, and the oxen, sheep, fruits, &c. of other foreign parts are brought in fine condition; and delicacies which were not easily obtained even by the rich are now common amongst the multitude. But for this increased facility of conveyance how would it be possible to feed the immense multitude of London, which, in half a century of time, will in all probability number 5,000,000?"

ANTIQUITY OF CHEESE.

Cheese and curdling of milk are mentioned in the Book of Job. David was sent by his father, Jesse, to carry ten cheeses to the camp, and to see how his brethren fared. "Cheese of kine" formed part of the supplies of David's army at Mahanaim during the rebellion of Absalom. Homer makes cheese form part of the ample stores found by Ulysses in the cave of the Cyclop Polyphemus. Euripides, Theocritus, and other early poets, mention cheese. Ludolphus says that excellent cheese and butter were made by the ancient Ethiopians. Strabo states that some of the ancient Britons were so ignorant that, though they had abundance of milk, they did not understand the art of making cheese. There is no evidence that any of these ancient nations had discovered the use of rennet in making cheese; they appear to have merely allowed the milk to sour, and subsequently to have formed the cheese from the caseous part of the milk, after expelling the serum or whey. As David, when too young to carry arms, was able to run to the camp with ten cheeses, ten loaves, and an ephah of parched corn, the cheeses must have been very small.

Thomas Coghan, in *The Haven of Health*, 1584, says: "What cheese is[Pg 210] well made or otherwise may partly be perceived by an old Latin verse translated thus— 'Cheese should be white as snowe is, nor ful of eyes as Argos was, nor old as Mathusalem was, nor rough as Esau was, nor full of spots as Lazarus.' Master Tusser, in his book of Husbandrie, addeth 'other properties also of cheese well made, which whoso listeth may reade. Of this sort, for the most part, is that which is made about Bamburie in Oxfordshire; for of all the cheese (in my judgment) it is the best, though some prefer Cheshire cheese made about Nantwich, and others also commend more the cheese of other countries; but Bamburie cheese shall goe for my money, for therein (if it be of the best sort) you shall neither tast the renet nor salt, which be two speciall properties of good cheese. Now who is so desirous to eat cheese must eate it after other meate, and in a little quantity. A pennyweight, according to the old saying, is enough; for being thus used it bringeth two commodities. First, It strengthened a weake stomache. Secondly, It maketh other meates to descend into the chief place of digestion; that is, the bosome of the stomache, which is approved in "Schola Salerni." But old and hard cheese is altogether disallowed, and reckoned among those ten manner of meates which ingender melancholy, and bee unwholesome for sick folkes, as appeareth before in the chapter of Beefe.'"

The county of Chester was, ages since, famous for the excellence of its cheese. It is stated that the Countess Constance of Chester (reign of Henry II., 1100), though the wife of Hugh Lupus, the King's first cousin, kept a herd of kine, *and made good cheese*, three of which she presented to the Archbishop of Canterbury. Giraldus Cambrensis, in the[Pg 211]twelfth century, bears honourable testimony to the excellence of the Cheshire cheese of his day.

Cheshire retains its celebrity for cheese-making: the pride of its people in the superiority of its cheese may be gathered from the following provincial song, with the music, published in 1746, during the Spanish war, in the reign of George II.

"A Cheshire-man sailed into Spain,
To trade for merchandise:
When he arrivèd from the main
A Spaniard him espies.

"Who said, 'You English rogue, look here—
What fruits and spices fine
Our land produces twice a year!
Thou hast not such in thine.'

"The Cheshire-man ran to his hold,
And fetched a Cheshire cheese,
And said, 'Look here, you dog! behold,
We have such fruits as these!

"'Your fruits are ripe but twice a year,
As you yourself do say;
But such as I present you here,
Our land brings twice a day.'

"The Spaniard in a passion flew,
And his rapier took in hand;
The Cheshire-man kicked up his heels,
Saying, 'Thou art at my command!'

"So never let a Spaniard boast,
While Cheshire-men abound,
Lest they should teach him, to his cost,
To dance a Cheshire round!"[56]

Next to Cheshire rank Gloucestershire, Wiltshire, and Somerset, for their cheese. In the latter county they have the proverb:

"If you wid have a good cheese, and hav'n old,
You must turn 'n seven times before he is old."

To curdle the milk in cheese-making was formerly used the *Galium verum* of botanists, a wild flower with square stems, shining whorled leaves, and loose panicles of small yellow flowers, popularly known as *Cheese Rennet*.

The practice of mixing sage and other herbs, and the flowers or seeds of plants, with cheese, was common among the Romans; and this led to the herbs, &c. being worked into heraldic devices in the Middle Ages. Charlemagne once ate cheese mixed with parsley-seeds at a bishop's palace, and liked it so much, that ever after he had two cases of such cheese sent yearly to Aix-la-Chapelle. Our pastoral poet of the last century has noted this device:

"Marbled with sage, the hardened cheese she pressed."—GAY.

ALE AND BEER.

The virtues of Saxon ale have already been commemorated, at pp. **66-68**. We return to the subject, at a later period.

"It may be remarked," says Mr. Hudson Turner, "that in the thirteenth century the English had no certain principle as to the grain best suited for brewing. A roll of household expenses of the Countess of Leicester shows that Beer was made indiscriminately of barley, wheat, and oats, and sometimes of a mixture of all. As the Hop was not used we may conjecture that the produce of their brewing was rather insipid, and not[Pg 213] calculated for long keeping: it was drunk as soon as made. To remove the mawkish flatness of such beer it was customary to flavour it with spices and other strong ingredients: long pepper continued to be used for this purpose some time after the introduction of hops. The period at which the last-named plant became an ingredient of English beer is not precisely known. It was cultivated from a very early date in Flanders and Belgium, where it was both employed in brewing, and eaten in salads; and from those countries it was imported into England while the produce of our own hop-grounds was inconsiderable. It would appear, however, that Hops were used in this country for brewing, in the beginning of the fifteenth century, as Gilbert Kymer, in his *Dietary*, pronounces beer brewed from barley, and well hopped, also of middling strength, thin and clear, well fined, well boiled, and neither too new or too old, to be a sound and wholesome beverage. It is pretty certain, nevertheless, that in his time the hop was not *grown* in England. In ancient days brewing was almost solely managed by women, and till the close of the fifteenth century the greater part of the beer-houses in London were kept by females who brewed what they sold."

Ale, the favourite drink of our Saxon forefathers, has been described as a thick, sweet, *unhopped* liquor, and as such distinguished from our modern *hopped* "beer." Gerard says: "The manifold virtues in hops do manifestly argue the wholesomeness of *beer* above *ale*;" and conjectures that the origin of this distinction may be due to the use of the word beer in the Low Countries, from which hops were introduced. It would appear, however, that beer was known in this country, and[Pg 214] specified as such, before the use of hops; which were not imported till 1524, other bitters having supplied their place.

There is an ancient rhyme which says,—

"Turkeys, Carps, *Hops*, Piccarel, and *Beer*,
Came into England all in one year."

The year when all these good things are supposed to have been introduced, was somewhere in the early part of the reign of King Henry VIII. But it is evident that as early as 1440, when the *Parvulorum Promptorium* was compiled, the use of hops was not altogether unknown. Mr. Albert Way supposes that at that time hopped beer was either imported from abroad or brewed by foreigners. And this supposition is certainly supported by the *Promptorium*.

The great hop county of Kent produced better ale than any other; and the large quantity of ale found in the cellars of the Kentish gentry, had much to do with fomenting Jack Cade's rebellion, which arose in Kent.

Unhopped ale, having no bitter principle, would easily run into acetous fermentation. And this is the reason why, in old family receipt-books, we find that our great-grandmothers were in the habit of using alegar where, by the cooks of the present day, vinegar is employed.

In modern usage the distinction between *Ale* and *Beer* is different in various parts of the country. But originally, the distinction was very clearly marked: *Ale* being a liquor brewed from *malt*, to be drunk fresh; *Beer*, a liquor brewed from *malt and hops*, intended to keep.

The above distinction is clearly observed in Johnson's *Dictionary*, where *ale* is defined, "A liquor made by infusing *malt* in hot water,[Pg 215] and then fermenting the liquor:" *Beer*, "Liquor made *from malt and hops*;" "distinguished from ale either by being older or smaller." Ale thus defined answers to the description given by Tacitus of the drink of the ancient Germans. The ancient Spaniards had a somewhat similar drink, called by them *Celia*.

M. Alphonse Esquiros writes of our national drink thus amusingly:—"It was the favourite fluid of the Anglo-Saxons and Danes, whom we have seen descend in turn on Great Britain. Before their conversion to Christianity, they believed that one of the chief felicities the heroes admitted after death into Odin's paradise enjoyed, was to drink long draughts of ale from tall cups. Archæologians have made learned and laborious researches to recover the history of beer in Great Britain: it will be sufficient for us to say, that in Wales, ale, even small, was formerly regarded as a luxury, and was only seen on the tables of the great. In England, about the middle of the sixteenth century, Harrison assures us that, when tradesmen and artisans had the good fortune to stumble on a haunch of venison and a glass of strong ale, they believed themselves as magnificently treated as the lord mayor. At the present day, what a change! Ale and porter flow into the pewter pots of the humblest taverns; rich and poor—the poor more frequently than the rich—refresh themselves with the national beverage, as the Israelites in the Desert slaked their thirst at the water leaping from the rock, to quote a minister of the English Church. This abundance compared with the old penury, rejoices the social economist from a certain point of view, for he sees in it the natural movement of science, trade and agriculture, which in time places within reach of the most numerous[Pg 216] class articles which, at the outset, were regarded as luxuries. Not only has beer become more available to the working classes, but the quality has improved, and at the present day English beer knows no rival on the Continent."

The old compound of roasted apples, ale, and sugar, which our ancestors knew as "Lamb's Wool," is thought to have derived its name as follows:—The words La Mas

Ubal are good Irish, signifying the Feast, or day, of the Apple, and, pronounced *Lamasool*, soon passed into Lamb's Wool. The mixture was drunk on the evening of the above day, which was supposed to be presided over by the guardian angel of fruits and seeds.

A less fanciful etymology points to the above drink being named from its smoothness and softness, resembling the wool of lambs. Herrick sings:

"Now crowne the bowle
With gentle lambs-wooll,
Add sugar, and nutmegs, and ginger;"

and in an old play we read of this addition: "Lay a crab in the fire to roast for lamb's-wool."

IV. Peasant Life.[57]

ew inquiries of social interest better show the progress of the English people than glances at their condition at various periods of their history. Here we may trace the rise of the people from rude forms of civilization, through its various grades, to the blessings of industry and independence, which have so materially contributed to the character of our National Life. Commencing with the substratum of these social changes, we are reminded of the truth of Goldsmith's oft-quoted lines:

"Princes and lords may flourish or may fade,
A breath can make them, as a breath has made;
But a bold peasantry, their country's pride,
When once destroy'd, can never be supplied."

In early times freemen formed a mere section of the people, and the bulk of the English population were in a servile condition. Some of the bondmen were captives, or the children of captives; others had been reduced to servitude by distress, by debts, or crimes; but they were not all of them absolute slaves, for even amongst the convicts there were[Pg 218] some who were not slaves, but serfs. Now, in acquiring the use of land, a slave made the first step towards freedom. In this manner a *thrall-bred* man became *boor-bred*, and although still a bondman—he might hope, by good conduct or by the lord's bounty, to rise to the higher condition of a geneatman, or free farmer, and even to become a freeman, and a freeholder,—to become the absolute owner of his little croft.

In Anglo-Saxon times, the political station of a freeman was determined by his *were*—it was his worth or value; and the *wergyld* was the fine paid in compensation of his life. The abolition or disuse of this fine was an encouragement of liberty, since it removed the strongest mark of distinction between freemen and non-freemen.

The free or unfree condition of a man descended to his posterity. At the close of the thirteenth century, many peasants in England were still affected by the crimes or the misfortunes of their remote ancestors. By that time there was an end of absolute slavery, and the bondsmen were all serfs, or the children of serfs.

OPERATIVE TENANTS.

Villenage and operative tenancy were almost extinct at the time of the Reformation. The few villeins, or operative tenants, then remaining, were in the occupation of small plots of land, or were, in fact, agricultural labourers, working for wages, rather than tenants *paying their rent in labour*. They were scarcely to be found except upon Church-lands, or upon lands which had lately belonged to the Church.

An operative tenant of five acres usually worked once a week for the[Pg 219] lord. We learn from Domesday that bordars were tenants of five acres, and that the bordars under the Castle of Ewias worked once a week: the Saxon cottar held at least five acres, and was accustomed to work for the lord every Monday. This custom prevailed in later times. If a tenant worked for the lord once a week, the working-day was commonly Monday. The Monday-men at East Brent, in Somerset, had the following customs in the year 1517:—Each of them, by ancient usage, should annually, in forty days selected by the lord's steward, do forty works of summer and winter husbandry, called Monday-works, working and labouring well each day for six whole hours; each of them receiving, while at work, a halfpenny, the sum of which is twenty pence per annum: and each of them who should do eight autumnal works, working well six hours a day as before said, should receive one penny a day. At the same time there were Monday-men at Limpesham in the same county; and they are noticed in earlier rentals at Castle Combe in Wiltshire, at Leighton in Huntingdonshire, in East Kent, and at Bocking and Hadleigh in the eastern counties.

At Bury St. Edmund's anciently, there were humble servitors called Lancetts, who were bound by their tenure to clean the chambers of the monastery. A tenant of the abbey at Cokefield, whose tenure is not called lancettage, was obliged to thatch, to wattle and daub, to do carpenter's work, to collect compost, to clean houses, &c.—but was not required to clean out the lord's *latrines*.

Although villeins were said to hold their land at the will of the lord, their position was not really precarious; they did not hold at the lord's arbitrary will, but at the will of the lord subject to the custom of the manor. While they paid their dues and performed their[Pg 220] services, the lord could not molest them; if the lord ejected a sick villein, the villein was emancipated. For trivial offences the villein was amerced, or was at the lord's mercy; that is, was obliged to pay a fine assessed by a jury who were sworn to spare no one for love or fear, and to punish no one too severely; for disobedience and disloyalty the lord could set his villein in the stocks; if others then came and broke the stocks to let the villein out, the lord could have an action of trespass: the stocks were chiefly designed for vagrants and unruly servants.

At one time the ties which bound a peasant to his landlord were like those which bound a soldier to his martial chief. Dependence on a lord was thought no degradation, and the state of society made independence impossible. The feudal system was exhausted as soon as the law became strong enough to protect an independent man.

SERVICES OF TILLAGE.

We now proceed to the several services. *Grass-erth*, or the service of Tillage, was in return for the privilege of feeding cattle in the lord's open pastures. The Saxon boor ploughed two acres, and might be allowed to plough more if he required more pasture.

At Sturminster Newton in Dorsetshire, certain tenants came upon the lord's grass-land on the morrow of St. Martin's Day with as many teams of oxen as they could bring, and they ploughed four acres of the land with each team; they brought seed from the hall to sow the land, and afterwards harrowed it. This service entitled them to feed their oxen with the lord's oxen, from the time that the meadows were mown until the[Pg 221] cattle were housed. The lord might, in the meantime, raise no hedge, and might make no several pasture in the fallow-field, to exclude the cattle of the tenantry.

The Saxon boor, in addition to grass-erth, ploughed three acres of gafolyrthe: that is, ploughing alone in satisfaction of his gayfol, or rent; as well as three acres of benyrthe, or optional tillage, done as a *boon* to the lord,—done out of grace and kindness, not in the way of duty.

A large part of the lord's arable land was entirely cultivated by the tenantry. The customary tenants at Cokefield, near Bury, ploughed 200 acres; or rather, they ploughed each acre more than once, and their labour was equal to the single tillage of 200 acres.

In large manors, it was the duty of the reeve to ascertain whether a tenant intended to do the service, or chose rather to pay for a substitute. The reeve had to deal with persons of both sexes, and of all conditions. Some of the contributors of labour were knights, and gentlemen, and ladies of quality; others were independent yeomen, surly farmers, and poor widows. This arrangement was called an *arable precation*. The *gathering of the ploughs* must have been a remarkable sight. Soon after dawn, on the appointed day the tenants met the lord's officers in the field. Tenants who came without oxen, were employed in delving and in making fences; tenants who came with single oxen or with less than an entire team, were associated with others; and thus all the oxen and cart-horses present were sorted in teams of about eight animals. The teams were marshalled by a beadle, who carried his wand of office, not quite a bare symbol of authority, for, we dare say, it was used upon inert husbandmen as well as upon inert oxen. The reeve took care that each team did its full work: that the ploughmen worked as well[Pg 222] for the lord as they would work for themselves; and that the teams were not unyoked until the work had been fairly done. The day's work was supposed to be completed at the ninth hour,—three in the afternoon, according to our reckoning. This hour was called high noon, and the meal then taken was called a noonshun or nuncheon. Some of the ploughmen had a meal from the lord, but there was no regular feast; a tenant employed in the lord's service was not usually entitled to a meal, unless the service kept him occupied an entire day. A boon-harrowing, with horses, succeeded; each horse that harrowed was allowed two or three handfuls of oats. In due time there followed a bedweding, or weeding boon.

There were small services, such as threshing, thatching, delving, building, and enclosing. A tenant made two perches, or eleven yards, of dyke. A tenant at Darent, near Rochester, in the thirteenth century, did two perches of enclosure around the court, and seven perches of Racheie around the lord's corn. Then there was the service of enclosing the hall-garth or courtyard. The tenants are still obliged to keep up a stone wall round the site of the manor-house at Brotherton, in Norfolk; the mansion itself disappeared long ago. The fencing of a park was in some places distributed among a number of townships, each undertaking to maintain so many rods of paling; this was the custom at Pilton, in Somerset, where there was a deer-park belonging to the Abbot of Glastonbury. The churchyard at Bradley, in Staffordshire, is said to be still enclosed by the parishioners associated in this manner,—that is, each person is bound to finish a certain portion of paling. The tenants also made or maintained the lord's sheepfold. Each hyde at Thorpe in[Pg 223] Essex had to make a certain number of rods for the fold out of the lord's wood.

At times, the tenants had to spread composts in the lord's field. They also collected stubble out of the corn-fields, and reeds out of the marsh; reeds and straw were strewn in apartments, and used for thatching or fuel. In many places they were required to gather nuts in the woods for the lord; the nuts were for making oil, and a quarter of nuts answered to a gallon of oil. Nutting was rather a pastime, or holiday task, than a service. The nutting expeditions at Wickham, in Essex, were to be made on three feast days, which are not named, but Holyrood Day, the 14th of September, may have been one of them:

"This day, they say, is called Holy-Rood Day,
And all the youth are now a nutting gone."
Grim, the Collier of Croydon.

To make malt for the lord was usually the chief service of the poorer tenants in the immediate neighbourhood of a monastery, as at Darent and other places near Rochester, and at Battle; tenants at a distance, instead of making malt, in some places paid a tax called *malt-silver*. The cottagers carried their lord's malt to the flour mill to be crushed, for they were not allowed to keep hand-mills or mortars, which might be used in grinding corn. The malt might be dried at home, for kilns were common in old houses; but in some manors the lord had a public kiln, which the tenants were bound to make use of.

OLDEN HARVEST.

A *bedrip*, *reaping boon*, or *autumnal precation*, was a more pompous festival than an *arable precation*. In old times, as in our own, the Harvest was made a season of merriment, if not of thanksgiving:

"In tyme of harvest mery it is ynough;
The hayward bloweth mery his horn,
In eueryche felde ripe is corn."
Romance of King Alexander.

In the illustrations of an old Saxon Calendar, in the Cotton Library, the hayward is shown standing on a hillock, cheering the reapers with his horn. Slumbering reapers were roused by the sound of a horn in Tusser's time; and the custom of blowing horns at harvest-time endured until the end of the last century, for it is noticed by John Scott, of Amwell. In the thirteenth century, when the rentals were mostly compiled, the lord was aided in harvest, as in seed-time, by tenants of all ranks. A superior tenant rarely sent more than two men to the bedrip, or two men and an *overman*, that is a foreman.

The kindly services rendered to the lord in seed-time and harvest were otherwise called precations, gifel-works, and love-boons. The days on which they were rendered used to be called boon-days, and occasionally love-days: a love-day more commonly meant a law-day, a day set apart for a leet or manorial court, a day of final concord and reconciliation; as we read in the *Coventry Mysteries*:

"Now is the love-day mad of us foure fynially
Now may we leve in pes as we were wonte."

Love-boons are described by the Law authorities as "the voluntary labour[Pg 225] of the inhabitants of the neighbouring townships."

The memorable truce between the Yorkists and Lancastrians, in 1458, was called a love-day.

A customary tenant, in some places, was bound to appear on the grandest day with his whole family, except the housewife, who stayed at home and spun; sometimes excepting the nurse as well the mistress. In the neighbourhood of Oxford, in the year 1279, all the men who held yard-lands, and all who held half-yard-lands, came to two autumnal precations, each of them with one man; and to the third precation each of them with his whole family, excepting his wife and shepherd, and was regaled by the lord on this third day,—not on the two former days; and all the customary tenants were obliged to ride beyond the lord's crops, to see that they were reaped safe and well. They rode in saddles, with bridles and spurs; if they failed in any part of this equipment, they were fined. These mounted overseers were called reap-reeves. In the time of Edward the Third, the tenant of an estate called Fawkner Field was bound to ride among the reapers in the lord's demesnes, at Isleworth, on the bederepe day, in autumn, with a sparrow-hawk upon his wrist. The officers of the court were entitled to a share of the crop. In some places, the sicklemen received a worksheaf each; each man was expected to reap half an acre, called a deywine (day-win), or day's labour. In the accounts of the tenures at Booking, in Essex, there is a curious estimate of the cost of these autumnal precations. The expense of the food provided for the reapers is weighed against the value of their work, and the balance is found to be fivepence and three-farthings.

[Pg 226]

A yard-lander at Chalgrave, in Oxfordshire, reaped at the two precations in autumn with all his household but his wife and shepherd; if he brought three labourers, he walked with his rod, or rode, in front of the reapers; if he brought no labourers, he worked in person; for two repasts, at nones, a wheaten loaf, pottage, meat, and salt; at supper, bread and cheese and beer, and enough of it, with a candle while the guests were inclined to sit. The last day was always the grand day, when, at Piddington, the tenants and their wives came with napkins, dishes, platters, cups, and other necessary things.

In the reign of Henry III., the ploughmen and other officers, at East Monkton, near Warminster and Shaftesbury, were allowed a ram for a feast on the Eve of St. John the Baptist, when they used to *carry fire round the lord's corn*. This form of the Beltane superstition was observed in the north of England, and in Scotland, about fifty years ago. The Beltane flourishes at the uttermost ends of Europe, in the Scilly Islands, and in Russia; and even the main of Madagascar, who holds his head to other stars, is accustomed to kindle bonfires on the day which we have dedicated to St. John. We learn from the *Popular Antiquities* that in our time, in Gloucestershire and Herefordshire, on the eve of Twelfth Day, fires used to be lit at the ends of the lands, in fields just sown with wheat.

Tenants in old times were required to cut and clear the lord's hay-field. A tenant at Bradbury, for one day's mowing, received a meal of bread and cheese twice in the course of the day; and for carrying the same meadow, a bundle of hay, for his pains. The mowers also received among them twelvepence or a sheep, which they were to choose out of the[Pg 227] lord's fold by sight, not by touch. In other places the mower was allowed as much grass as he could raise up on his scythe, without breaking its handle; and a haymaker received as much hay as he could grasp with both arms. At Sturminster, a tenant, after mowing and carrying, received a knitch of hay,—that is, as much hay as the hayward could raise with one finger to the height of his knees.

In the year 1308, it was the rule at Borley that the mowers and haymakers should have two bushels of wheat for bread, a wether worth eighteenpence, a gallon of butter, the second-best cheese out of the lord's dairy, salt and oatmeal for their pottage, and the morning's milk of all the cows; and a mower as much grass as he could lift upon the point of his scythe. In 1222 they had in common a cheese and a good ram. A sheep was commonly the reward of work in the hay-field. Old English husbandmen were very fond of mutton, and the hay-harvest fell about St. John's Day, when mutton was considered in season.

HOCK-DAY.

The second Tuesday after Easter, was another very important day in bygone times. At Chingford, the ward-staff was presented in court on Hock-day. John Ross, of Warwick, records that, on the death of Hardicanute, England was delivered from Danish servitude; and to commemorate this deliverance, on the day commonly called Hock Tuesday, the people of the villages are accustomed to pull in parties at each end of a rope, and to indulge in other jokes. The Hock-tide sports were kept up at Hexton, in Hertfordshire, in the time of Elizabeth, and are[Pg 228] described in Clutterbuck's Hertfordshire. Hock-day was usually set apart for a love-day, law-day, or court-leet. This court could be held but twice in the year, and was generally held at Hock-tide and Michaelmas, or Martinmas, since a court on these days would not interfere much with agricultural operations. Leets, like most other gatherings, ended with good cheer. In the thirteenth century, when the officers of East Monkton attended the Hundred courts at Deverell—which were held at Hock-tide and Martinmas—they were allowed a loaf and a piece of meat each. A feast following a court-leet or law-day, was called a leet-ale, or scot-ale, as ale is said to mean no more than a feast. There were leet-ales and scot-ales, church-ales, clerk-ales, bid-ales, and bride-ales. Scot-ales were often abused, and made means of extortion. The bishops, the judges, and all the king's men in vain tried to suppress them. All persons present at a scot-ale paid *scot*,—that is, a fine, or fee; the money raised nominally furnished a feast, but was really for the benefit of the chief officer of the court—the portreeve, head borough, or third borough. In some places, leet-ale was not entirely supported by subscription. In Tollard, on the edge of Cranborne Chase, the steward was allowed on the law-day to have a course at a deer out of Tollard Park. At Bovey Tracy, the profits of the Portreeve's Park defrayed the expenses of the annual revel. The Glastonbury Rental describes the mode of keeping the scot-ales in Wiltshire, in the thirteenth century. The customs are very like those of ancient Guilds. By the rules of the Guild of the Holy Ghost at Abingdon, members who sat down at dinner paid one rate, and members who stood for want of room paid another.

[Pg 229]

SHEEP-SHEARING.

This was another service imposed upon the tenantry. Though hard and heavy work to wash and shear sheep, in the thirteenth century it was done by women, who are called "shepsters" in the *Vision* of Piers Plowman. The sheep were washed in the mill-pond. Shearers were usually entitled to the wambelocks, or loose locks of wool under the belly of the sheep; or at Weston, in Oxfordshire, a penny instead of the locks. The finest part of the fleece is the wool about the sheep's throat, called in Scotland the haslock, or hawselocks:

"A tartan plaid, spun of good hawslock woo',
Scarlet and green he sets, the borders blew."
The Gentle Shepherd.

Up in the North they call a sheep-shearing the clipping-time; and to come in clipping-time is to come as opportunely as at sheep-shearing, when there are always mirth and good cheer. In the middle of the seventeenth century, clippers always expected a joint of roasted mutton. In the *Winter's Tale*, the clown ponders:

"Let me see, what am I to buy for our sheep-shearing feast? Three pounds of sugar, five pounds of currants, rice—what will this sister of mine do with rice? But my father hath made her mistress of the feast, and she lays it on.... I must have saffron to colour the warden pies; mace; dates, none! That's out of my note. Nutmegs, seven; a race or two of ginger—but that I may beg; four pounds of prunes, and as many of raisins o' the sun."

The old customs of clipping-time were observed by Sir Moyle Finch, at Walton, near Wetherby, in the time of Charles I., and are thus described by Henry Best:

"Hee hath usually fower severall keepinges shorne altogether in the Hall-garth.... He hath had 49 clippers all at once, and their wage is, to each man 12*d.* a day, and when they have done, beere[Pg 230] and bread and cheese; the traylers have 6*d.* a day. His tenants the graingers are tyed to come themselves, and winde the well; they have a fatte wether and a fatte lambe killed, and a dinner provided for their paines; there will be usually three score or fower score poore folkes gatheringe up the lockes; to oversee whom standeth the steward and two or three of his friends or servants, with each of them a rodde in his hande; there are two to carry away the well, and weigh the roll so soone as it is wounde up, and another that setteth it downe ever as it is weighed; there is 6*d.* allowed to a piper for playing to the clippers all the day; the shepheards have each of them his bell-weather's fleece,"—the "bellys" allowed to the shepherd by the old Saxon laws.

Sheep-shearing was thus celebrated in ancient times with feasting and rustic pastimes; at present, excepting a supper at the conclusion of the sheep-shearing, we have few remains of the older custom. Nevertheless, it is interesting to revert to these pictures of pastoral life and rusticity, more especially as we find them embellished by the charms of poetry, and enlivened by a simplicity of manners which, to whatever period it may belong, is always entertaining, if not productive of better fruit. The season of the shearing is thus laid down by Dyer:

"If verdant Elder spreads
Her silver flowers, if humble Daisies yield
To yellow rowfoot and luxuriant grass,
Gay Shearing Time approaches."

CONVEYANCE SERVICE.

The most irksome tasks were the transport services, called in Scotland the duties of *arriage* and *carriage*. The load of a sumpter-horse was usually eight bushels—the weight of a sack of wool, or a quarter of corn. A wain-load was apparently nine seams. The goods carried were chiefly provisions—grain, pulse, malt, honey, bacon, suet, salt, and wood. A castle or monastery was *farmed*—that is, supplied with[Pg 231] food—by the nearest manors belonging to the lord. The farming was done according to a regular cycle, each manor sending supplies in its turn for so many days or weeks. We have a list of thirty-five villages which took turns to farm Ely Minster—some for three or four days, some for a week, some for a fortnight.

Everything contributed in this manner did not travel in waggons, or packs and panniers; oxen and swine were driven to the head of the barony to be slaughtered, especially at Martinmas; if the drovers came from any distance, they received drove-meat. Arriage and carriage were not very burdensome when fulfilled by the removal of so much wool, or cheese, or corn, or bacon, to a neighbouring town; but they became serious when a tenant had to ride or drive from the heart of England to the coast and home again. Some tenants were called *pouchers*, because they were required to carry goods in a poke, pouch, or bag. In the Channel Islands, on the first spring-tide after the 24th of June, the poor who possess neither cart nor horse have the exclusive right to cut *vraic* (wrack, sea-weed), on consideration that it is conveyed on their backs to the beach. Thus cut and conveyed it is called *vraic à la poche*, and distinguished from *vraic à cheval*.

When fish was wanted at Rochester, the tenants of the four hydes of Hedenham and Cuddington, near Aylesbury, were called out; two of the hydes brought the fish from Gloucester into Buckinghamshire, and the other two hydes carried it on to Rochester: it is likely that they were sent to fetch the dainty lamprey, still sought for at Gloucester. The *langerodes*, or long journeys, were very troublesome to the tenants, but could not be dispensed with while there were no regular mails, and[Pg 232] no public conveyances. A person undertaking a *langerode* either received some remuneration or worked out his rent by serving as a carrier; in general he was not inclined to leave his home and farm, and found it more convenient to pay the price of the service, which enabled the lord to find another carrier. No services were more frequently commuted than the duties of arriage and carriage, and a body of professional carriers was gradually formed by the habit of constant commutation.

WATCH AND WARD.—THE BEADLE.

The wardmen of ancient times were a kind of rural police, whose duty of ward-keeping was connected with their tenure. They were, probably, maintained on the north side of London until the institution of a general system of police in the time of Edward the First. By the statute of Winton, it was ordered that a watch should be kept by six men at each gate of a city, by twelve men in every borough, and by six men or four men in each rural township, every night, from the Feast of the Ascension of our Lord to the Feast of St. Nicholas. The watchmen could detain any one unknown to them; any one who would not stand and declare himself, was pursued with hue and cry—with horn and voice—

> "Swarming at his back the country cried."

We suppose that St. Nicholas became the patron of highwaymen, because the watch was intermitted on the day dedicated to St. Nicholas. The wardmen were occasionally noticed in the Domesday of St. Paul's. The survey of 1279 states, that at Sutton, in Middlesex, each tenant who had cattle on the lord's lands to the value of thirty pence, paid a penny at[Pg 233]Martinmas, called *ward-penny*; but this tax was not due from the watchmen of the ward, who waited at night in the King's highway, and received the ward-staff:—

"They wared and they waked,
And the Ward so kept,
That the king was harmless,
And the country scatheless."

In Essex, the ward-keeper had a rope with a bell, or more than one bell, attached to it: the rope may have been used to stop the way. The ward-staff was a type of authority, cut and carried with peculiar ceremony, and treated with great reverence.

The duties of the beadle (Saxon, *bydel* or *bædel*), in ancient times, lay more on the farm than in the law-court, the state procession, or in the parochial duties of punishing petty offenders, as in the present day.[58] In many places, the bedelry and the haywardship were held together by one person. The beadle was the verger of the manorial court; he likewise overlooked the reapers and carried his rod into the[Pg 234] harvest-field. At Darent, near Rochester, the beadle held five acres as beadle, shepherd, and hayward; he had eighteen sheep and two cows in the lord's pasture; against Christmas he had a *crone*—an old sheep—a lamb with a fleece, and some other allowances. At Ickham, in the same county, the beadle's office was hereditary: the beadle had five acres with a cottage for his service, and made all the citations of the court, and, if he went on horseback into the Weald of Kent, he was allowed provender for his horse; he had pasture for five hogs, five head of cattle, and a horse; he attended in the fields to regulate the labours of the harvest. And such had been the tenure of his father, grandfather, and great-grandfather.

Old English gentlemen were anciently very much afraid of theft and peculation; they believed that "Treste lokes maketh trewe hewen,"—or, to change their maxim into current English, they believed that "firm locks made faithful servants." The barns were to be well closed after August, and no servant was to open them until threshing-time, without the special direction of the landlord or the steward. The strictest accounts were kept. Every person, in any situation of the slightest trust or responsibility, was required to render an account of every penny and every article passing through his hands, to the receiver, or bailiff, whose accounts were revised once a year by auditors, who went round from manor to manor.

OLDEN HOUSE-MARKS.

[Pg 235]

he means by which property has been identified, and denoted by some distinctive mark, at various periods, present us with some curious customs.

In England, individual marks were in use from the fourteenth to the middle of the seventeenth centuries, probably much earlier; and when a yeoman affixed his mark to a deed, he drew a *signum*, well known to his neighbours, by which his land, his cattle, and sheep, his agricultural implements, and even his ducks, were identified. In the 25th year of Queen Elizabeth, a jury at Seaford, in Sussex, convicted John Comber "for markyng of three ducks of Edwd Warwickes and two ducks of Symon Brighte with his own marke, and cutting owt theire markes." Cows and oxen were marked on the near horn. When cattle in bodies of many hundreds ranged over extensive commons, as was formerly the case, the use of marks for identification was more indispensable than at present. Our swans retain their marks to the present day. In Ditmarsh and Denmark the owner's mark was cut in stone over the principal door of the house; it designated not only his land and cattle, but his stall in the church, and his grave when he was no more. At Witney, Oxon, a woolstapler's mark may be seen so incised on a house, with the date 1564; and numerous merchants' marks are at Norwich and Yarmouth. At Holstein, within the memory of man, the beams of the cottages of the bond-servants were[Pg 236] incised with the marks of their masters. A pastor, writing from Angeln, says, "The hides had their marks, which served instead of the names of their owners." In the island of Föhr, a little to the north of Ditmarsh, the mark, cut on a wooden ticket, is always sold with the house; and it is cut in stone over the door; and the same custom is still in use in Schleswig and Holstein. In the Tyrolese Alps, at the present day, the cattle that are driven out to pasturage are marked on the horn with the mark of their owner's land. Marks for cattle are also used in Switzerland, in the Bavarian Alps, and in some parts of Austria.

These house-marks are connected with merchants' and tradesmen's marks, and also with stonemasons' marks, all of which formed a lower kind of heraldry for those not entitled to the bearings of the noble; for, on old houses at Erfurt, double shields, with the marks of the families of husband and wife, are found.

Many of the marks found on old pictures are true house-marks, and not alphabetical monograms. A painting by Wouvermans or Lingelback, in the writer's possession, bears the mark known as the crane's foot. Michelsen considers armorial bearings to have been originally little more than decorated marks, and to have been engrafted, as it were, upon the system: indeed, he asserts that the arms of Pope Hadrian VI., a Netherlander, were framed from house-marks. Some knightly families in Schleswig still retain their house-marks on their coat-of-arms: for instance, the Von Gogerns bear the kettle-hanger, or pot-hook; the Von Sesserns, in 1548, bore the same, which occurred on their family tomb, *anno* 1309. The earliest marks were supposed to represent the most indispensable agricultural implements, as a spade, a plough, a scythe, a[Pg 237] sickle, a dung-hook, the tyres of a barrow; also, anchors, stars, &c.

There was, also, often a supposed connexion between the figurative name of a house and its owner's mark, which was a representation of the object, more or less exact. Michelsen considers that the names and signs of inns are but remnants of the once universal and necessary custom of giving figurative names to houses, which the modern numbers have superseded.

Prof. Michelsen shows that the *cultellum*, which was given by the Franks, Goths, and Germans, in the ninth and tenth centuries, on the transfer of land, with the *signum* cut on a piece of wood, was originally intended for notching the mark on the wood, in the same manner as the inkstand and pen were lifted up with the chart, as symbols of a transfer of land. Among the archives of Nôtre Dame, at Paris, is preserved a pointed pocket-knife of the eleventh century, on the ivory handle of which is engraved the record of a gift of land; and at the same place is preserved a piece of wood, of the ninth century, six inches long and one inch square, attached to a diploma, as was then the custom. A similar knife, with an ivory handle, is still preserved, attached to a charter of Trinity College, Cambridge.

The surrender of copyholds by the rod or glove, and occasionally by a straw, or rush (whence the word "stipulation," from *stipula*, straw), is well known in England; and in the manor of Paris Garden, Surrey, an ebony rod is preserved with a silver head, on which are engraved the royal arms, with E. R. and a crown, and an inscription purporting that it is kept for the surrender of copyholds of the manor. The inscribed sticks, mentioned in Ezekiel xxxv. 16, appear to relate to this ancient mode of conveyancing.

V. Olden Customs and Ceremonies.

[Pg 238]

MAY-DAY CAROL ON MAGDALEN COLLEGE TOWER.

ay customs are nothing more than a gratulation of the spring, to testify universal joy at the revival of vegetation. Hence the universality of the practice; and its festivities being inspired by the gay face of Nature, they are as old as any we have on record. There is at Oxford a May-day ceremony which has a special claim upon our respect and veneration, for nearly four centuries.

Upon the majestic Perpendicular tower of Magdalen College we have many time and oft looked with reverential feeling: seen from every point, it delights the eye with its stately form, fine proportions, and admirable simplicity; and with its history is associated a May-day custom of surpassing interest. For more than three centuries and a half the choristers of the College have assembled upon the top of its tower on a May-day morning, and there performed a most harmonious service, the origin of which has been thus traced by the learned Dr. Rimbault.

In the year 1501, the "most Christian" King Henry VII. gave to Magdalen College the advowsons of the churches of Slymbridge, in Gloucestershire, and Fyndon, in Sussex, together with one acre of land in each parish. In gratitude for this benefaction, the College was accustomed, during the[Pg 239] lifetime of the royal benefactor, to celebrate a service in honour of the Holy Trinity, with the collect still used on Trinity Sunday; and the prayer, "Almighty and everlasting God, we are taught by Thy word that the heart of kings," &c.; and, after the death of the King, to commemorate him in the usual manner.

The Commemoration Service ordered in the time of Queen Elizabeth, is still performed on the 1st of May; when is sung on the College-tower a Latin hymn, which has evidently reference to the original service. The produce of the two acres beforementioned used to be distributed on the same day, between the President and Fellows: it has, however, for many years been given up, to supply the choristers with a festal entertainment in the College-hall.

The arrangement of the ceremony is as follows. At about half-past four o'clock in the morning, the singing boys and men, accompanied by members of Magdalen and different colleges, ascend to the platform of the tower; and the choristers, having put on their surplices, range themselves on the slightly-gabled roof, standing with their faces towards the east. Magdalen bell having tolled five, the choristers sing from their books the Latin hymn, of which the following is a translation:—

"Father and God, we worship Thee,
And praise and bless on bended knee:
With food Thou'rt to our bodies kind,
With heavenly grace dost cheer the mind.

"O, Jesus, only Son of God!
Thee we adore, and praise, and laud:

Thy love did not disdain the gloom
Of a pure Virgin's holy womb.

"Nail'd to the cross, a victim made,
On Thee the wrath of God was laid:
Our only Saviour, now by Thee
Immortal life we hope to see.

"To Thee, Eternal Spirit, rise
Unceasing praise, from earth and skies:
Thy breath awoke the heavenly Child,
And gave Him to His mother mild.

"To Thee, the Triune God, be paid—
To Thee, who our redemption made—
All honour, thanks, and praise divine,
For this great mystery of Thine!"

At the close of the hymn, all heads are covered, and the singers hasten to the belfry, whence the bells ring out a joyful peal. The spectators in the road beneath disperse, the boys blowing tin horns, according to ancient custom, to welcome in sweet May; while others ramble into the fields to gather cowslips and field flowers, which they bring into the town. Occasionally the singing on the tower has been heard, with a favourable wind, at two miles' distance. This being a "gaudy day" for the choristers, they have a dinner of roast lamb and plum-pudding in the College-hall at two o'clock. There is a good representation of the ceremony on the tower, carefully engraved by Joseph Lionel Williams, in the *Illustrated London News*, whence the accompanying representation has been reduced.

Dr. Rimbault, whilst making some researches in the library of Christchurch, Oxford, discovered what appeared to him to be the first draft of the above hymn. It has the following note:—"This hymn is sung every day in Magdalen College Hall, Oxon, dinner and supper throughout the year, for the after grace, by the chaplains, clerks, and choristers there. Composed by Benjamin Rogers, Doctor of Musicke of the University of Oxon, 1685." The author of the hymn is unknown.

At Oxford, formerly, boys used to blow cows'-horns and hollow canes all night, to welcome in May-day; and girls carried about garlands of flowers, which afterwards they hung upon the churches.

Before we leave the sacred ground whereon this holy May-day ceremony is, year by year, performed, we present the reader with a very ably-drawn picture of the locality itself, and its many attractions.

"Probably," says a writer in the *Saturday Review*, "there is no city in the United Kingdom, with the exception of the metropolis, which possesses such a concentration of interest as Oxford. Its historical associations are spread over a long succession of ages. Not to speak of more apocryphal reminiscences, it was a favourite residence of one of our monarchs, and the birthplace of another. It was the scene of important transactions in the troubled reign of Stephen, and witnessed an episode in the equally troubled reign of the third Henry. It beheld the seeds of the Reformation sown by Wycliff, and saw the martyrdom of Cranmer and his fellow-sufferers. It became a confessor for the Church of England as against Puritanism under the second Stuart, and as against Popery under the fourth. It has been, at least since the Reformation, a sort of head-quarters of that Church; and has witnessed, in our own day, the most remarkable theological convulsions which it has experienced since the Reformation. Its outward appearance is in keeping with its history. It bears traces of the architecture of eight centuries—from the rude belfry-tower of St. Michael's, which has been assigned on good authority to the age of the Confessor, to Mr. Scott's exquisite[Pg 242] imitation of the Sainte Chapelle, in its immediate neighbourhood. It is true that it contains no building of the first rank; but it exhibits an almost infinite variety, under the influence of accidental yet harmonious grouping, which has a charm more akin to that of nature than that of art. In its æsthetical as well as in its moral aspect, it betrays a strong spirit of Conservatism, and, occasionally, one of studied Revivalism. We see in Oxford the shadow of the Middle Ages projected far into the region of modern life. A College is a strange compound, half club, half convent, and its daily usages are curiously intermingled with the past. For two centuries after the Reformation, Protestant founders cast their institutions in the mould of Wykeham and Waynflete: the scholastic system appears to have been a living thing at the beginning of the last century, and its ghost still haunts the academic shades. These facts have their parallel in the architecture of Oxford. The revival of mediæval art, which we have ourselves witnessed, had its precursors here in the early part of the seventeenth century. Nowhere in England—we may almost say, nowhere in Europe—shall we find such good and pure Gothic, built at a time when the style was defunct elsewhere, as is presented by the Chapels of Wadham, Lincoln, and Jesus Colleges, and in the staircase of Christchurch Hall; and as was to be seen in the chapel of Exeter College, before its destruction.

"With such attractions, added to that of personal interest, arising out of the past or in direct connexion with the place, it is no wonder that Oxford, at the most pleasant season of the year, draws to itself crowds of visitors from all parts of the country. The only wonder is, that it is not even more popular than it is, when we consider the throngs of[Pg 243] English men and women who are to be met with in the dingy and unsavoury Colleges of continental cities from June till October."

At Saffron Wolden, and in the village of Debden, an old May-day song is still sung by the little girls, who go about in parties carrying garlands from door to door. The first stanza is to be repeated after each of the others by way of chorus:—

"I, I been a rambling all this night,
And some part of this day,
And, now returning back again,
I brought you a garland gay.

"A garland gay I brought you here,
And at your door I stand;
'Tis nothing but a sprout, but 'tis well budded out,
The works of our Lord's hand.

"Why don't you do as I have done
The very first day of May?
And from my parents I have come,
And could no longer stay.

"So dear, so dear as Christ loved us,
And for our sins was slain,
Christ bids us turn from wickedness,
And turn to the Lord again."

The garlands which the girls carry are sometimes large and handsome, and a doll is usually placed in the middle, dressed in white, according to certain traditional regulations: this doll represents the Virgin Mary, and is a relic of the ages of Romanism.

The May-pole still lingers in the village of St. Briavel's, in the picturesque forest of Dean. In the village of Burley in the New Forest,[Pg 244] a May-pole is erected, a fête given to the school children, and a May-queen is chosen by lots; a floral crown surmounts the pole, and garlands of flowers hang about the shaft. Among other late instances are recorded a May-pole, eighty feet high, on the village-green of West Dean, Wilts, in 1836; and in 1844, there was "dancing round the May-pole" in St. James's district, Enfield. William Howitt describes May-poles in the village of Lisby, near Newstead; and in Farnsfield, near Southwell, Derbyshire, May-poles are to be seen. Dr. Parr was a great patron of May-day festivities: opposite his parsonage-house at Hatton, near Warwick, stood the parish May-pole, which was annually dressed with garlands, and the doctor danced with his parishioners around the shaft. He kept its large crown in a closet of his house, from whence it was produced every May-day, and decorated with fresh flowers and streamers, preparatory to its elevation to the top of the pole.

On May-day and December 26th, is distributed the fund bequeathed in 1717 and 1736, by Mr. Raine, a wealthy brewer at St. George's-in-the-East, who founded schools and a hospital for girls, and added marriage portions of 100*l.*, to be drawn by lots: the winner is married to a young man, of St. John's, Wapping, or St. Paul's, Shadwell; the couple dine with their friends, and in the evening an ode is sung, and the marriage portion of one hundred new sovereigns is presented to the bride.

Miss Baker, in her *Northamptonshire Glossary*, tells us that there are very few villages in that county where the May-day Festival is not noticed in some way or other.

BANBURY CAKES.—CONGLETON CAKES, ETC.

[Pg 245]

hat the ancient town of Banbury, lying on the northern verge of the county of Oxford, should have been famed, from time immemorial, for its rich cakes, should not excite our special wonder, seeing that the district has some of the richest pasture land in the kingdom; a single cow being here known to produce 200 pounds of butter in a year! Butter, we need scarcely add, is the prime ingredient of the Banbury cake, giving it the richness and lightness of the finest puff-paste; and, to the paper in which the cakes are wrapped, the appearance of their having been packed up by bakers with well-buttered fingers.

The cause of this cake-fame must, however, be sought in a higher walk of history than in the annals of pastry-making. It appears that the Banbury folks went on rejoicing in the fatness of their cakes until the reign of Elizabeth; from which time to that of Charles II., the people of the town were so noted for their peculiar religious fervour, as to draw upon themselves most unsparingly the satire of contemporary playwrights, wits, and humorists. By some unlucky turn of time, cakes, which were much valued by the classical ancients, and were given away as presents, in the Middle Ages, instead of bread, became looked upon as a superstitious relic by the Puritans, who thereupon abolished the practice. They formed so predominant a party at Banbury, in the reign of Elizabeth, that they pulled down Banbury Cross, so celebrated in our[Pg nursery rhymes. In the face of this historical fact, however, the reputed "zeal" of the Banburians has been attributed to an accidental circumstance, in modern phrase, "an error of the press." In Gough's edition of Camden's *Britannia*, in the MS. supplement, is this note: "Put out the word *zeale* in Banbury, where some think it a disgrace, when a *zeale* with knowledge is the greater grace among good Christians; for it was first foysted in by some compositor or press-man, neither is it in my Latin copie, which I desire the reader to hold as authentic." It was, indeed, printed, as a proverb, "Banbury zeal, cheese, and cakes," instead of "Banbury veal, cheese, and cakes." Gibson, in his edition of Camden, however, gives another version, relating: "There is a credible story—that while Philemon Holland was carrying on his English edition of the *Britannia*, Mr. Camden came accidentally to the press, when this sheet was working off; and looking on, he found, that to his own observation of Banbury being famous for cheese, the translator had added cakes and ale. But Mr. Camden thinking it too light an expression, changed the word *ale* into *zeal*; and so it passed, to the great indignation of the Puritans, who abounded in this town." Barnaby Googe, in his *Strappado for the Divell*, refers to Banbury as

"Famous for twanging ale, zeal, cakes, and cheese."

Better remembered are the lines in his *Journey through England*:

"To Banbury came I, O profane one!
Where I saw a puritane one
Hanging of his cat on Monday
For killing of a mouse on Sunday."

Early in the seventeenth century, the Puritans were very strong in Banbury. In Ben Jonson's *Bartholomew Fair*, Zeal-of-the-Land Busy, the Puritanical Rabbi, is called a *Banbury man*, and described as one who was a baker—"but he does dream now, and sees visions; he has given over his trade out of a scruple that he took, that it spiced conscience, *those cakes he made* were served to bridales, May-poles, morrises, and such profane feasts and meetings:" in other words, he had been a baker, but left off that trade to set up for a prophet; and one of the characters in *Bartholomew Fair* says: "I have known divers of these Banburians when I was at Oxford." And Sir William D'Avenant, in his play of *The Wits*, illustrates this Puritanical character, in

"A weaver of Banbury, that hopes
To entice heaven by singing, to make him lord of twenty looms."

Old Thomas Fuller personifies the zeal in the Rev. William Whately, who was Vicar of Banbury in the reign of James I., and was called "The Roaring Boy." Fuller adds: "Only let them (the Banbury folks) adde knowledge to their zeal, and then the more zeal the better their condition." The Vicar was a zealous and popular preacher, according to his monument:

"It's William Whately that here lies,
Who swam to's tomb in's people's eyes."

In the *Tatler*, No. 220, in describing his "Ecclesiastical Thermometer," to indicate the changes and revolutions in the Church, the Essayist writes, "That facetious divine, Dr. Fuller, speaking of the town of Banbury, near a hundred years ago, tells us, 'it was a place famous for cakes and zeal,' which I find by my glass is true to this day, as to the latter part of this description, though I must confess it[Pg 248] is not in the same reputation for cakes that it was in the time of that learned author."

The Banburians, however, maintained their character for zeal in a grand demonstration made by them in favour of Dr. Sacheverell, whose trial had just terminated in his acquittal; and in the same year, this High Church champion made a triumphal passage through Banbury, on his journey to take possession of the living of Salatin, in Shropshire, which was ridiculed in a pamphlet, with a woodcut illustrative of the procession; and there appeared another pamphlet on the same lively subject.

Thus far the association of cakes with zeal in the case of Banbury. It is worthy of remark that cakes had formerly not unfrequently a religious significance, from their being more used at religious seasons than at other times. The triangular cakes made at Congleton, in Cheshire, have a raisin in each corner, thought to be emblematic of the Trinity; the cakes at Shrewsbury may have had something to do with its old religious shows. Coventry, on New Year's day, has its God-cakes. Then we have the Twelfth-cake with its bean; the Good Friday bun with its cross; the Pancake, with its shroving or confessing; and the Passover cake of the Jews. The minced pie was treated by the Puritans as a superstitious observance; and, after the Restoration, it almost served as a test for religious opinions. According to the old rule, the case or crust of a minced pie should be oblong, in imitation of the cradle or manger wherein the Saviour was laid; the ingredients of the mince being said to refer to the offerings of the Wise Men.

Returning to the Banbury cake: in a *Treatise of Melancholy*, by T.[Pg 249] Bright, 1586, we find the following:—"Sodden wheat is a grosse and melancholicke nourishment, and bread especially of the fine flour unleavened. Of this sort are bag puddings made with flour; fritters, pancakes, *such as we call Banberrie Cakes*; and those great ones confected with butter, eggs, &c., used at weddings; and however it be prepared, rye, and bread made thereof, carrieth with it plentie of melancholie."

At Banbury, the cakes are served to the authorities upon state occasions. Thus, in the Corporation accounts of this town, we find a charge of "Cakes for the Judges at the Oxford Assizes, 2*l*. 3*s*. 6*d*." The present form of the cake resembles that of the early bun before it was made circular. The zeal has died away, but not so the cakes; for in Beesley's *History of Banbury*, 1841, we find that Mr. Samuel Beesley sold, in 1840, no fewer than 139,500 twopenny cakes; and in 1841, the sale increased by at least a fourth. In August, 1841, 5,000 cakes were sold weekly; large quantities being shipped to America, India, and even Australia.

The cakes are now more widely sold than formerly, when the roadside inns were the chief depôts. We remember the old galleried Three Cranes inn at Edgware, noted for its fresh supplies of Banbury cakes; as were also the Green Man and Still, and other taverns of Oxford Road, now Oxford Street.

Banbury Cheese, which Shakspeare mentions, is no longer made, but it was formerly so well known as to be referred to as a comparison. Bishop Williams, in 1664, describes the clipped and pared lands and glebes of the Church "as thin as Banbury cheese." Bardolf, in the *Merry Wives of Windsor*, compares Slender to Banbury cheese, which seems to have been[Pg 250] remarkably thin, and all rind, as noticed by Heywood, in his Collection of Epigrams:—

"I never saw Banbury cheese thick enough,
But I have often seen Essex cheese quick enough."

The same thought occurs in *Jack Drum's Entertainment*, 1601:—

"Put off your cloathes, and you are like a Banbury cheese—nothing but paring."

In the Birch and Sloane MSS., No. 1201, is a curious receipt for making Banbury cheese, from a MS. cookery book of the sixteenth century. A rich kind of cheese, about one inch in thickness, is still made in the neighbourhood of Banbury.

We have already traced the destruction of the Cross at Banbury to the leaven of fanaticism. The nursery rhyme,

"Ride a cock-horse
To Banbury-cross,"

is by some referred to this act; and to signify being over-proud and imperious. Taylor, the Water-poet, has,—

"A knave that for his wealth doth worship get,
Is like the divell that's a-cock-horse set."

The Banburians have rebuilt the Cross to commemorate the marriage of the Princess Royal with the Crown Prince of Prussia. They also exhibit, periodically, a pageant, in which a fine lady on a white horse, preceded by Robin Hood and Little John, Friar Tuck, a company of archers, bands of music, flags and banners, passes through the principal street to the Cross, where the lady (Maid Marian) scatters Banbury cakes among the[Pg 251] people. How far this pageant may be associated with local tradition, time and the curious have hitherto failed to explain.[59]

Other towns, in addition to Banbury, have been celebrated for their cakes, from remote times. The ancient borough of Congleton, upon the Staffordshire border of Cheshire, have already been incidentally mentioned. The streets have an air of antiquity, many of the houses being constructed entirely of timber framework and plaster. The place has long been famed for its silk-mills, and tagged leather laces, called Congleton points. These, however, have been outlived by the sack and cakes, which have, for ages, figured in the festivities of Congleton; eclipsed for a while during the gloomy mayoralty of President Bradshaw, but happily retained to our time.

The Congleton cakes are of triangular form, with a raisin inserted at each corner. These have been used at the Grammar School breaking-up for three-quarters of a century. They have been the orthodox cakes at the quarterly account meetings of the Corporation for more than a century, and are hence called "count cakes." It is conjectured that the three raisins represent the mayor and two justices, who were the governing body under the charter of James I. The trio of raisins have also been deemed symbolical of the Trinity. Be this as it may, Congleton has been noted from time immemorial for these cakes, as well as for its gingerbread; and in the Corporation records we find such convivial items as the following:—"1618. Bestowed upon the Earl of Essex, being money paid for figs and sugar, 1*l*." "1614. Bestowed upon Sir John Byron, one[Pg 252] gallon of sack and one gallon of claret, 5*s*. 8*d*." "1619. A banquet bestowed upon Sir John Savage, being a gallon of sack and a sugar-loaf, 5*s*." "1627. Bestowed upon my Lord Brereton, in wine and beer, 5*s*." "1633. Bestowed on the Earl of Bridgewater, in wine, sack, and sugar, 8*s*." "1632. Paid Randle Rode, of the Swan, for wine, cake, and beer, for a banquet which was bestowed upon the Lord Chief Baron of the Exchequer, 1*l*. 4*s*. 2*d*." "Paid Mr. Drakeford for a pottle of wine, bestowed on Sir B. Wilbraham, 2*s*." "1662. Paid for *sweetmeats* bestowed upon Lord and Lady Brandon, 9*s*. 3*d*., because," as the book says, "he was our great friend." This must have been in reference to the influence exerted by that nobleman, in obtaining a re-grant of the borough charter, which Charles II., on his accession, had thought fit to call in, along with several others, that of London among the rest.

Among the recent celebrations, was the hospitable reception given by the Corporation of Congleton to the Lord Mayor of London, Sir Francis Graham Moon, Bart., in the year 1855, when the entertainment well represented the ancient festivity. On the chairman's table lay the gold and silver maces of the borough, and capacious china Corporation bowls full of sack, and flanked by large old two-handled silver flagons, by which the sack was gradually drawn off, and circulated amongst the company. On every plate was placed a *count cake*, and the centres of the tables were covered with delicate cakes and confectionery, among which was pre-eminent the famous Congleton gingerbread, and a profusion of choice fruit. The brewage of the sack was entrusted to Joseph Speratti, who boasts that he alone possesses the true receipt.

The famous old city of Shrewsbury has also long been celebrated for its[Pg 253] brawn and cakes; the latter are made of much larger size than we are accustomed to see them in the metropolis, and are packed in round boxes made for the purpose.

Around London some of the villages boast of this celebrity. Islington was once as famous for its cheesecakes as Chelsea for its buns; and among its other notabilities were custards and stewed "pruans:" old Wither, in 1628, told us that Islington

"For cakes and cream had then no small resort;"

and to this day the place is noted for its cakes and confectionery. Lower Holloway was once noted for its cheesecakes, which, almost within memory, were regularly cried through the streets of London by a man on horseback.

HORSELYDOWN FAIR, IN THE REIGN OF QUEEN ELIZABETH.

[Pg 254]

orselydown is situate near the bank of the river Thames, about half a mile eastward of London Bridge. "It is difficult," says Mr. Corner, the Southwark antiquary, "to imagine that a neighbourhood now so crowded with wharves and warehouses, granaries and factories, mills, breweries, and places of business of all kinds, and where the busy hum of men at work, like bees in a hive, is incessant, can have been, not many centuries since, a region of pleasant fields and meadows, pastures for sheep and cattle; with gardens, houses, shady lanes, clear streams with stately swans, and cool walks by the river-side. Yet such was the case, and the way from London Bridge to Horselydown was occupied by the mansions of men of mark and consequence, dignitaries of the Church, men of military renown, and wealthy citizens."

Horselydown was part of the possessions of the Abbey of Bermondsey, and was, probably, the common of the manor. After the surrender to Henry VIII. it became the property of private individuals, and, in 1581, was conveyed to the Governors of St. Olave's Grammar School, to whom it still belongs; and it is one of the remarkable instances of the enormous increase in the value of property in the metropolis, that this piece of[Pg 255] land, which was then let as pasturage for 6*l*. per annum, now produces to the governors for the use of the school an annual income exceeding 3,000*l*. Hereon were erected the parish butts for the exercise of archery, pursuant to the statute of 33 Henry VIII.

The Marquis of Salisbury possesses, at Hatfield, a very remarkable picture, which has been supposed to have been painted by the celebrated Holbein, but is really the work of George Hofnagle, a Flemish artist in Queen Elizabeth's time, as is shown by the costume of the figures: it bears the date of 1590, whereas Holbein died in 1554. The picture represents a Fair or Festival, which, from the position of the Tower of London in the background, appears to have been held at Horselydown. In the catalogue of the pictures at Hatfield, in the *Beauties of England and Wales*, the painting is said to represent King Henry VIII. and his Queen, Anne Boleyn, at a country wake or fair, at some place in Surrey, within sight of the Tower of London; but several circumstances, in addition to its situation with respect to the river Thames and the Tower of London, concur to show that the locality is Horselydown, or, as it was then called, Horseydown or Horsedown. This is proved by a curious picture-map, dated 1544. Its centre shows a large open space, now occupied by the diverging Queen Elizabeth Free School, and *Fair* Street. It is not known whether Southwark Fair was ever held on Horselydown; but it is worthy of observation, that when the down came to be built on, about the middle of the seventeenth century, the principal street across it from east to west, and in the line of foreground represented in the picture, was, and is to the present day, called *Fair* Street; and a street or lane of houses running from north to south is called Three Oak Lane, traditionally from three oaks formerly[Pg 256]standing there. The tree-o'ershadowed hostelry, where the feast is being prepared, may indicate the spot. In Evelyn's time, however (*Diary*, 13th Sept. 1666), the fair appears to have been held at St. Margaret's Hill, in the Borough, for he calls it St. Margaret's Fair; and it continued to be held between St. Margaret's Hill and St. George's Church, until the fair was suppressed in 1762.

The portly figure in the centre foreground, with a red beard and a Spanish hat, must have occasioned the idea of its being a representation of King Henry VIII.; but the general costume of the figure is later than his reign, and the date on the picture shows the period of the scene to have been towards the end of Queen Elizabeth's reign.

The principal figures seem rather to represent some of the grave burgesses and young gallants of Southwark, with their wives and families, assembled on Horseydown on some festive occasion, on a bright day in summer. The principal figure is evidently a man of worship, for whom and his company a feast is preparing in the kitchen of the hostelry; while the table is laid in the adjoining apartment, which is decorated with boughs and gaily-coloured ribbons. The principal figure may be one of the Flemish brewers, who settled in the parish in great numbers; one of whom Vassal Webling, dwelt hard by Horseydown, having become possessed of the house of Sir John Fastolfe, called Fastolfe Place. Or, it may be Richard Hutton, armourer, and an alderman of London, an inhabitant of St. Olave's. Whoever it is, he is accompanied by a comely dame, probably his wife, and by two elderly women, and followed by a boy and girl with a greyhound, a servant carrying an infant, and a serving-man with sword and buckler. Near them is a yeoman[Pg 257] of her Majesty's guard, with the Queen's arms on his breast. The citizen, in his long furred gown, accompanied by a smartly-dressed female, crossing behind the principal party, is worthy of notice. The gay trio behind them are also remarkable objects in the picture.

The minister accompanying a lady, is probably Thomas Marten, M.A., parson of the parish. The hawking party behind shows that the neighbourhood of Southwark was at that period sufficiently open for the enjoyment of the sport. The flag-staff, or May-pole, in the left background, is also noticeable, as well as the unfinished vessel at the river side, and the unfortunate transgressor in the stocks.

Two young women and two serving-men are bearing large brass dishes for the coming feast; while in the right foreground a party of five are dancing to the minstrelsy of three musicians seated under a tree. A party are approaching from the right, headed by another minister, who may be the celebrated Robert Browne, a Puritan minister, and founder of the sect of Brownists, who was schoolmaster of St. Olave's Grammar School, from 1586 till 1591. He was connected by family ties with Lord Burghley, which circumstance may account for this picture being preserved at Hatfield, which was built by Robert Cecil, Earl of Salisbury, second son of Lord Burghley.

Behind the musicians are two figures which deserve some attention. It has been suggested that the appearance of the foremost is much that of the portraits of Shakspeare, and the head behind him is not unlike that of Ben Jonson. Nor would there be any improbability in the idea of Shakspeare and Jonson being present at such a fête, as Shakspeare lived in St. Saviour's, and is very likely to have been invited to a festival[Pg 258] in the adjoining parish; but the date of the picture is somewhat too early to be consistent with that notion.

The church-like building with a tower, at the right of the picture, may be "The Hermitage," marked on the plan: it was no uncommon thing for hermitages to have chapels attached to them, as at Highgate, where the hermit was authorized by a royal grant of Edward III. to take toll for repairing the road. The hermitage at Highgate, which had a tower, became a chapel for the devotions of the inhabitants.

Hermitages were generally founded by an individual upon the ground of some religious house, who, after the death of the first hermit, collated a successor; and as those persons devoted themselves to some act of charity, it does not appear so extraordinary that we find hermits living upon bridges, and by the sides of roads, and being toll-gatherers, as numerous records indubitably prove. (Tomlin's *Yseldon*.)

The Hermit of Horselydown, or Dock-head, perhaps, received a toll for keeping in repair the road across the Bermondsey Marshes from Southwark towards Rotherhithe and Deptford.[60]

WAKE FESTIVALS IN THE BLACK COUNTRY.

akes were originally established to commemorate the erection of the church in the parish where they were held. They were then celebrated on the Sunday, and the parson did not deem it "unworthy his high vocation" to enjoy a gambol on the village-green after the morning service. In the larger towns, most of the churches had weekly fairs or markets attached to them, these also being held on the Sabbath. As late as the commencement of the fourteenth century, Wolverhampton had a market every Sunday morning, the shingles being arranged round the old Collegiate Church; and when the voice of worship ceased, the Babel of the Fair began. During the fourteenth century, however, the custom of holding Sunday markets was abolished, but the village Wake continued to be celebrated on the sacred day, until the commencement of the present century. The leading diversions of Wake-time in this district were, as is pretty generally known, bull and badger baiting, cock-fighting, pigeon-flying, boxing, running, and wrestling. There is, we think, a very fair standard of comparison between past and present, presented to us in the subject of Wake festivals; and for this reason we have thought it worth while briefly to compare Wake-time in the Black Country half a century ago with the corresponding season now. We think it will be allowed that, after taking into consideration all educational and other advantages, there has been a progress towards social and moral excellence among our working men and women which is deserving of all praise.

The traditions of Bull-baiting, Cock-fighting, and other exhibitions of brutality which characterised Wakes in this district forty or fifty years ago, have in many cases been so distorted and magnified by frequent repetition that they can no longer be accepted as truthful pictures of the festivals which it was the humour of our ancestors to establish and be pleased with.

During the past half-century, there have been some brutal exhibitions of this class. In the *Staffordshire Advertiser*, November 23, 1833, we read of bulls being shockingly tortured in the neighbourhood of Dudley. At Rowley Regis, a two-year-old bull was worried most brutally, his horns being torn off, and his head and face mangled in the most appalling manner.

In the following year the *Wolverhampton Chronicle* publishes this intelligence:—"At Wilhenhall Wakes, two bulls were baited in the streets of that town, and more than usual cruelty was displayed on the occasion, as one of the bulls died on the night after being baited." At Darlaston Wakes, about the same period, three bulls, three bears, and two badgers underwent baiting simultaneously; to say nothing of dog and cock fights.

These instances might, of course, be multiplied by records of each town in the district, but they will suffice to show the extent of the barbarity which distinguished the Wakes of our forefathers. The ludicrous was sometimes associated with the cruelties in these scenes. At Tipton on one occasion, the bull broke loose, and, dashing madly[Pg 261] through the crowd, entered the open door of a house, at whose fire a huge piece of Wake beef was roasting. From the force of habit, the bull tossed the smoking joint to the ceiling, and disappeared, to the great joy of the affrighted inmate. On another occasion, at Bloxwich, some wag stole the bull at midnight, and when the excited crowd assembled on the morrow, from all parts of the district, they were doomed to disappointment. The circumstance gave rise to a local proverb still in use. When great expectations are baffled, the circumstance is instinctively likened to "the Bloxwich bull." The remembrance of this barbarous pastime is perpetuated in the topographical nomenclature of the district, where, following the example of Birmingham, almost every town and village has its Bull King.

The stronghold of Cock-fighting was at Wednesbury, where the "cookings" were resorted to by persons from all parts of the kingdom. In a *Directory of Walsall*, 1813, we read:—"The cockpit is situate on the left-hand side of the entrance into Park Street, from Digbeth, at the bottom of a yard belonging to Mr. Fox, known by the sign of the New Inn. It is spacious and much frequented at the Wakes, at which period only it is used."

The minor sports and pastimes were the interludes between the tragedies, and served to complete the day's programme of the Black Country Wake-time. Forty years ago it was dangerous to pass through a town during the Wakes. The inhabitants who took active part in these sports were so infuriated with drink and excitement, and their feelings were so hardened by scenes of torture, that they regarded neither the limb nor life of any who happened to offend them. There was no amusement provided[Pg 262] either for young or old but the most vicious and degrading, and the Wakes seldom passed by without some other blood than that of bulls being spilt—the blood of comrades, and too frequently of wives and children, who dared to remonstrate with a furious husband and father in his orgies.

Happily, modern Wakes have been divested of nearly all the characteristics of the olden festivals. The only vestiges which distinguish them are the booths, clowns, and drinking bouts; and these amusements are only indulged in by children and the lowest class of the population. Among the features recently introduced in connexion with district Wakes may be enumerated out-door fêtes, flower-shows, bazaars, and excursions. Temperance Societies and Working Men's Institutes select Wake-time for their celebrations. Two of the most successful exhibitions ever held in the district were inaugurated at the Wakes of Willenhall, in 1857, and at those of Bilston a year or two later, both in connexion with the progress of popular education. The Right Hon. C. P. Villiers, M.P. who was present on both occasions, and who knew this district in its dark days, took occasion to compare the former Wake times with the present, as an evidence of the social advancement of the Black Country. The cultivation of cottage window-flowers, now happily so general throughout the same district, is another refining agency, which has helped in no small degree to root out the love for grosser sports among the people. But, perhaps, the most powerful agent in improving the character of modern Wakes is the influence of popular excursions. The district is fortunate in its situation in this respect. Within easy distance are the lawns and flowers of Enville, Hagley, Shugborough, and [Pg 263] Teddesley, which it is the delight of their noble owners to place at the service of our working men and women; and the more recent facilities for locomotion have also placed the Malvern slopes and Southport sands within their reach. Wake-times are therefore now become seasons of excursions, when hard-working men quit the factory bench and the dark mine, to delight and refine their inner manhood with views of Nature's fairest works. This, we think, is one great step towards the development of a love for art among the artisans of our utilitarian district; and Wake-times so spent will assuredly exert an influence for good through the remainder of the year.[61]

Nevertheless, the Wakes are still disgraced by sad scenes of intoxication and other excesses: the agencies of education and religion are not working in vain in the district; let us hope that the progress, though slow, may be sure.

KEEPING BIRDS IN THE MIDDLE AGES.

lexander Neckam, from whose Treatise the following curious things are derived, was a learned man of the twelfth century: his work, which is written in Latin, has been translated by Mr. Thomas Wright, and published under the direction of the Master of the Rolls. Of Neckam's birth we learn the date from a chronicle formerly existing among the MSS. of the Earl of Arundel, which inform us that "in the month of September, 1157, there was born to the King at Windsor a son named Richard; and the same night was born Alexander Neckam at St. Alban's, whose mother gave suck to Richard with her right breast, and to Alexander with her left breast." Thus was Alexander the foster-brother of the future Cœur de Lion, who was celebrated for his own love of literature and learning; and the position which the circumstance here related by the chronicler gave to Neckam in regard to such a Prince goes far to explain the honourable position he gained in after-life.

Neckam was born and passed his boyhood at St. Alban's: he received his earlier education in the Abbey School there; and such a rapid advance did he make in learning, that whilst still very young, the direction of the school at Dunstable, a dependency of the Abbey of St. Alban's, was entrusted to him. But he soon, of his own accord, sought a larger field[Pg 265] for his mental activities, and proceeded to the then celebrated University of Paris, where he was a distinguished professor as early as the year 1180, when he can have been no more than twenty-three years of age.

He did not long adhere to the scholastic learning of the University, but in 1186 returned to England, and resumed his old post at Dunstable. He subsequently became one of the Augustinian monks of Cirencester, and in 1213 was elected Abbot of Cirencester. He died at Kempsey, near Worcester, in 1217, and was buried in Worcester Cathedral.

Neckam, in these early times, displayed a taste for experimental science. The Treatise from which we quote is a sort of manual of natural science, as it was then taught; and it derives a still greater value for us from the love of its author for illustrating his theme by the introduction of contemporary anecdotes and stories relating to the objects treated of; as well as the mention of popular facts and articles of belief which had come under his observation or knowledge, many of which offer singular illustrations of the condition and manners of the age.

From Neckam we learn how great was the love for animals in the Middle Ages; how ready people, apparently of all classes, were to observe and note the peculiarities of animated nature, and especially how fond they were of tamed and domestic animals. We see that the mediæval castles and great mansions were like so many menageries of rare beasts of all kinds. It is in the stories told by Neckam, also, that we become more than ever acquainted with the attachment of our mediæval forefathers to the chase, and to all the animals connected with it. Beginning with the King of Birds, the Eagle, however, he offers no new facts; though he makes it the subject of numerous moralisings. With the lesser birds of prey he[Pg 266] becomes communicative of his anecdotes. He recounts how a Hawk one day, by craft and accident and not by mere strength, killed an Eagle. "This occurred in Great Britain, the King of which country, with his courtiers, were witnesses of the occurrence. The courtiers applauded the ferocity of the smaller and weaker bird, which, too, had only killed its adversary in self-defence; but the King interfered, reproved his followers for expressing sentiments which justified the employment of force by vassals against their Sovereigns, and ordered the Hawk to be hanged immediately as guilty of treason."

Another anecdote places the reputation of the Hawk in a less obnoxious light. It was one of the characteristics of that bird, as Neckam tells us, in the cold of winter, to seize in its claws a Partridge, wild Chick, or some other bird, and hold it under its belly all night, in order to profit by its warmth; and when the warmth of day returned, the Hawk, however hungry it might be, spared the bird, in consideration of the service thus derived from it, and displayed the noble nature of the bird of prey, the fit representative of the Feudal Baron, by setting it at liberty. Neckam tells another story of a Falcon which revenged itself on an Eagle; and another of a Weasel which caught a Sparrowhawk and dragged it under the water. We may pass over his account of the Phœnix, which is taken from the ancients; but that which he tells us of the Parrot shows how great a favourite it was as a cage-bird even in our islands during the Middle Ages. He speaks especially of its mischievous cunning and of its skill in imitating the human voice, adding that, for exciting people's mirth, it was preferable even to the jongleurs. It must, however, be acknowledged that Neckam's wonderful[Pg 267] anecdotes become at times rather legendary.

Passing by the Peacock, the Vulture, the Pheasant, and Partridge, the often-described Barnacle, supposed to be generated from the gluey substances produced on fir-timber when immersed in the waves of the sea, finds its place here. The qualities of the Swan, which celebrated its own death in sweet song; the Ostrich, said to be devoid of affection for its own offspring; the Nightingale, which was so capricious in its choice of habitation that Neckam tells us there was a well-known river in Wales on one side of which the song of this nightingale was often heard, but nobody ever heard it on the other; the Swallow, singular for the form of its nest and for the locality which it selected for building it; the Nuthatch; the Ibis of Egypt; the Dove; and several birds less known, as described by Neckam, are chiefly worthy of notice on account of the singular moralisings and symbolical interpretations which are given to them. The

Sparrow, according to Neckam (long anticipating Sterne), is a libidinous bird, light, restless, "injurious to the fruits of man's labour," too 'cute for the birdcatcher, and subject to epilepsy. The Raven is, by its colour and by its habits, emblematical of the clergy; it is easily domesticated. A Crow foretells rain by its clamorousness.

Neckam has also something to say about the Lark and the Magpie, and something more about the Parrot, "the jongleur of the birds;" but he says of the Cuckoo that it does nothing but repeat the words "*affer, affer*," *i.e.* "give, give,"—and on that account it was the type of avarice, and "sang the old song of those who have not yet divested themselves of the old man." Surely, however, Neckam's ear was at fault in this description, or the Cuckoos of Cirencester sang a very different[Pg 268] song, with a different moral too, from the cuckoos on the banks of Avon in the dayspring of Shakspeare. But it is a novel fact to learn that the saliva of the Cuckoo produced Grasshoppers; yet this was, no doubt, a popular explanation of the well-known cuckoo-spit of our fields. The Pelican of those days killed her own young, after which, in self-remorse, she tore her own body to shed her blood upon them, by means of which they revived. The Cock was symbolical of the Christian preacher or doctor of the Church; and Neckam gives a rather curious physical explanation of the question why it announces the hour of the day by its crowing, and why it has a comb. The Wren was remarkable for its fertility, and for another rather singular quality. When killed and put on the spit before the fire to roast, it wanted no turning, but turned itself with the utmost regularity. Though the smallest of birds, it claimed to be their king, and hence the Latin name of *Regulus*. Did it not, when the birds assembled to choose a king, conceal itself beneath the Eagle's wing, when it was agreed that the throne should be given to the bird which mounted highest towards heaven; and when the Eagle, having soared the highest, made its claim to the prize, did it not start from its hiding-place, jump on the Eagle's back, and claim to be highest of all, and therefore the winner?[62]

VI. Historic Sketches.

[Pg 269]

THE STORY OF FAIR ROSAMUND.

n the noble Park of Blenheim they show you two sycamore-trees on the spot where the ancient Palace of Woodstock was built; and near the Bridge is a spring called Rosamund's Well. Hard by was the celebrated Bower, erected by Henry II., and the scene of Addison's poetical opera of *Rosamund*, in excellent verse, which, wedded to the music of Dr. Arne, proved very successful. Several passages long retained their popularity, and were daily sung, during the latter part of George the Second's reign, at all the harpsichords in England.

Drayton, in the reign of Elizabeth, described "Rosamund's Labyrinth, whose ruins, together with her *Well*, being paved with square stones in the bottom, and also her Tower, from which the Labyrinth did run, are yet remaining, being vaults arched and walled with stone and brick, almost inextricably wound within one another, by which, if at any time her lodging were laid about by the Queen, she might easily avoid peril imminent, and, if need be, by secret issues, take the air abroad, many furlongs about Woodstock, in Oxfordshire."

Nor are these the only memorials of the frail Rosamund, whose history is one of the most interesting in our stock of legendary lore. About two[Pg 270] miles north of Oxford, near the river Isis, there are some remains of the famous Nunnery of Godstow, from which, we are told, "there is a subterranean passage to Woodstock." It was about the end of the reign of Henry I., that this Nunnery was founded, at the instigation of Editha, a pious lady of Winchester. Assisted by benefactions, Editha finished a convent for Benedictine Nuns, in 1138; and King Stephen and his Queen were present at the consecration. Editha was Abbess here; and the lands given were confirmed by grants of Stephen and Richard I. When Prince Henry arrived in England, in 1149, to dispute his title to the crown with Stephen, he happened to visit the Nunnery of Godstow, where he saw Rosamund, the daughter of Lord Clifford; she was not a nun, but boarded in the convent.

Fair Rosamund—*Rosa Mundi*, the Rose of the World—was the second daughter of Walter de Clifford, the son of Richard and grandson of Ponz. Richard is mentioned in the Domesday Survey as holding lands in the counties of Oxford, Gloucester, Wilts, Worcester, and Hereford. Walter de Clifford, by his wife Margaret, had four children:—Lucy, first married to Hugh de Say, and subsequently to Bartholomew de Mortimer; Rosamund, Walter, and Richard. Of Rosamund's early life we have no particulars. Local tradition affirms that Canyngton, about three miles from Bridgewater, was the place of her birth, and that within the walls of its priory she received such education as the age afforded. That, as the daughter of a powerful lord, she was entrusted to the care of some religious sisterhood for nurture, both of mind and body, we have no doubt, though the old chroniclers are silent on the subject. The art of embroidery would appear to have been one of her accomplishments, for the[Pg 271] venerable Abbey of Buildwas long possessed among its treasures a magnificent cope, which bore witness to the taste and skill of its fair embellisher. Of her first acquaintance with Henry II., and the mode and place of her introduction to him, no details have been preserved. Probably she was known to him from her earliest years. Nor have we any reason to suppose that, according to some modern versions of the sad story, a broken vow added its shadow to a life whose record is sufficiently gloomy without this additional darkening of woe. Not a hint of her having been a nun do the chroniclers give us; and, had such been the fact, full use would have been made of such an aggravation of her offence. Her royal lover was one of the most unscrupulous of mankind, and for his many enormities he was notorious. His affection for Rosamund, however, such as it was, was constant. In order to protect her from the vengeance of the Queen, he removed her successively to various places of greater or less security. But the most famous of all, and with which her name is more than with all others associated, was her retreat at Woodstock. It was here that Henry built a chamber, which Brompton describes as of wondrous architecture—resembling the work of Dædalus; in other words, a labyrinth or maze. A manuscript of Robert of Gloucester, in the Heralds' Office, says that—

"Att Wodestoke for hure he made a toure,
That is called Rosemounde's boure,"

the special intent of which was to conceal her from her royal rival. The internal decorations of this abode were as much attended to as its means of escaping external notice. The Abbot of Jorevall describes a cabinet[Pg 272] of marvellous workmanship, which was one of its ornaments. It was nearly two feet in length, and on it the assault of champions, the action of cattle, the flight of birds, and the leaping of fishes were so naturally represented, that the figures appeared to move.

Rosamund did not long occupy the retreat that royal though guilty love had created for her. She died in 1177, while yet without a rival in the King's affections, and, as it would appear, of some natural disease. In after times the injured Queen Eleanor had the credit of discovering her place of concealment, by means of a clue of silk which the King had incautiously left behind him; and which enabled her to thread the intricacies of the path, and of gratifying her revenge by obliging her rival to drink from her hand a cup of poison. That the Queen discovered the abode of Rosamund is possible; and it may have been that the shock of the meeting, and the unmeasured language which her Majesty is said to have employed, were too much for the poor victim of her womanly and natural displeasure. It is only fair, however, to say that the

Queen's part in the entire transaction is not alluded to in the older writers, and is probably the fiction of more modern times.

Rosamund was buried in the first instance before the high altar in the Church of Godstow Nunnery, which was probably selected from its neighbourhood to Woodstock, and which henceforward enjoyed a goodly number of benefactions in memory of her and for the health of her soul. The body was wrapped in leather, and then placed in a coffin of lead. Over the whole Henry built a magnificent tomb, which was covered with a pall of silk, and surrounded by tapers constantly burning. This occurred[Pg 273] in the lifetime of her father, for he gave to the nuns of Godstow, in pure and perpetual alms, for the health of the souls of Margaret his wife and of Rosamund his daughter, his mill at Franton, with all appurtenances, a meadow adjacent to the same called Lechtun, and a saltpit in Wiche. Walter, his son, confirmed the gift. Osbert Fitzhugh added to this the grant of a saltpit in Wiche, called the Cow, pertaining to his manor of Wichebalt.

Indeed, Walsingham goes so far as to say, though incorrectly, that the Nunnery of Godstow was actually founded by King John for the soul of Rosamund. It is not unlikely that a chantry was founded by that king for the object stated, but the foundation of the house was beyond question the work of a much earlier period.

Rosamund's remains, however, were not allowed to occupy their sepulchre in peace. Fourteen years after their solemn commission to this sacred place of interment, Hugh, Bishop of Lincoln, in a visitation of his diocese, came to Godstow. After he had entered the church, and performed his devotions, he observed the tomb occupying its conspicuous position before the high altar, adorned as already described, and forthwith asked whose it was. On being informed that it was the grave of Rosamund, whom Henry, the late king, had so dearly loved, and for whose sake he had greatly enriched this hitherto small and indigent house, and had given lands for the sustentation of the tomb and the maintenance of the lights, he imperatively commanded the nuns to take her out of the church, and to bury her with other common people, as the connexion between her and the King had been base; and to the end that the Christian religion might not be vilified, but that other women might[Pg 274] thus be deterred from similar evil ways.

In obedience to the bishop's mandate the tomb was removed from the church, and erected in the chapter-house. It bore the following epitaph, containing the obvious play upon the lady's name, and declaratory of the unhappy contrast which death had effected:—

"Hic jacet in tumba Rosa mundi, non Rosa munda;
Non redolet, sed olet, quæ redolere solet."

This tomb remained, an object of interest and respect, until the dissolution of the house. It was then destroyed, and a stone was discovered within it, bearing the simple inscription, "TUMBA ROSAMUNDÆ." The bones were found undecayed, and on the opening of the leaden coffin which contained them, "there was a very swete smell came out of it." Another eye-witness described it as having "enterchangeable weavings drawn out and decked with roses red and green, and the picture of the cup out of which she drank the poyson given her by the Queen, carved in stone." A stone coffin, said to be that of Rosamund, was still to be seen at Godstow when Hearne wrote his "Account of some Antiquities in and about Oxford," but this was regarded by him as a "fiction of the vulgar."[63]

In the "French Chronicle of London," 1259-1343, one of our earliest records compiled in illustration of the History of the City of London, under 1262, we read another version of this legend: "In this year the Queen was shamefully hooted and reviled at London Bridge, as she was desiring to go from the Tower to Westminster; and this, because she had[Pg 275]caused a gentle damsel to be put to death, the most beauteous that was known, and imputed to her that she was the King's concubine. For which reason the Queen had her stripped, and caused a bath to be prepared, and then made the beauteous damsel enter therein; and made a wicked old hag beat her upon both arms, with a staff; and when the blood gushed forth, there came another execrable sorceress, who applied two 'frightful toads' to her breasts, which they sucked until all the blood that was in her body had run out, two other old hags holding her arms stretched out. The Queen, laughing the while, mocked her, and had great joy in her heart, in being thus revenged upon Rosamonde. And when she was dead, the Queen had the body taken and buried in a filthy ditch, and with the body the toads.

"But when the King had heard the news, how the Queen had acted towards the most beauteous damsel whom he so greatly loved, and whom he held so dear in his heart, he felt great sorrow, and made great lamentation thereat:—'Alas! for my grief; what shall I do for the most beauteous Rosamonde? For never was her peer found for beauty, disposition, and courtliness.' He then desired to know what became of her body. He caused one of the wicked sorceresses to be seized, and had her put into great streights, that she might tell all the truth as to what they had done with the gentle damsel.

"Then the old hag related to the King how the Queen had wrought upon the most beauteous body of the gentle damsel, and where they would find it. In the meantime, the Queen had the body taken up, and carried to a house of religion which had 'Godstowe' for name, near Oxenforde; and had the body of Rosamond there buried, to colour her evil deeds And then King[Pg 276] Henry began to ride towards Wodestoke, where Rosamond, whom he loved so much at heart, was so treacherously murdered by the Queen. And as the King was riding towards Wodestoke, he met the body of Rosamond, strongly enclosed within a chest, that was well and stoutly bound with iron. And the King forthwith demanded whose corpse it was, and what was the name of the person whose dead body they bore. They made answer to him, that it was the corpse of the most beauteous Rosamond. And when King Henry heard this, he instantly ordered them to open the chest, that he might behold the body that had been so vilely martyred. Immediately thereon, they did the King's command, and showed him the corpse of Rosamond, who was so hideously put to death. And when King Henry saw the whole truth thereof, through great grief, he fell fainting to the ground, and lay there in a swoon for a long time before any one could have converse with him.

"And when the King awoke from his swoon he spoke, and swore a great oath, that he would take full vengeance for the most horrid felony which, for great spite, had upon the gentle damsel been committed. Then began the King to lament and to give way to great sorrow for the most beauteous Rosamond, whom he loved so much at heart. 'Alas! for my grief,' said he, 'sweet Rosamonde, never was thy peer, never so sweet nor beauteous a creature to be found: may then the sweet God who abides in Trinity, on the soul of sweet Rosamond have mercy, and may He pardon her all her misdeeds: very God Almighty, Thou who art the end and the beginning, suffer not now that this soul shall in horrible torment come to perish, and grant unto her true remission for all her sins, for Thy great mercy's sake.'

"And when he had thus prayed he commanded them forthwith to ride[Pg 277] straight to Godstowe with the body of the lady, and there had her burial celebrated in that religious house of nuns, and there did he appoint thirteen chaplains to sing for the soul of the said Rosamond, so long as the world shall last. In this religious house of Godstowe," says the Chronicler, "I tell you for truth, lieth fair Rosamond buried. May very God Almighty of her soul have mercy. Amen."[64]

The history of this unhappy lady, of whom the reader now possesses all that can be gathered from olden sources, and more, perhaps, than can be accepted as true, was a favourite subject of Mediæval romance; and all kinds of embellishments were imported into the story in order to impress a salutary caution against any imitation of the heroine. The story of her being poisoned by Queen Eleanor is of comparatively modern invention. A long ballad of forty-eight verses has been founded upon this piece of strange history.

[Pg 278]

CARDINAL WOLSEY AT ESHER PLACE.

n one of the loveliest and most picturesque vales of the county of Surrey, there exists, to this day, a fragment of Esher, or, as it is termed in old records, Asher Place, the last place of retreat where Wolsey fell,—

"Like a bright exhalation in the evening."

Here,—

"In the lovely vale
Of Esher, where the Mole glides lingering; loth
To leave such scenes of sweet simplicity,"—

was anciently a palace of the prelates of Winchester, built by William Wayneflete, who held the see from 1447 to 1486. It was a stately brick mansion, on the bank of the Mole, within the park of Esher.

The Bishops of Winchester occasionally resided at this palace. Cardinal Wolsey, who was appointed to the see on the death of Bishop Fox, in 1528, gave directions for the repair and partial rebuilding of this house at Esher, purposing to have made it one of his usual residences, after he had bereft himself of the palace which he had erected at Hampton Court, and which he had found it prudent to surrender to his jealous master. Many interesting circumstances relating to this last retirement of Wolsey to Esher, on the decline of his favour with the[Pg 279] King, are related by his biographers.

On the 18th of October, 1529, when the Cardinal was at York House, Westminster (where now stands Whitehall), King Henry sent to him the Dukes of Suffolk and Norfolk, to demand the Great Seal, Wolsey being lord chancellor; and he was ordered, at the same time, to retire to Esher. The order being unaccompanied by any voucher of authority, the chancellor refused to obey it; but the King's messenger returning with his written commands on the following day, the devoted minister submitted. He then went to Putney by water, and having landed, rode to Esher.

Wolsey now took up his residence at Esher, where he continued, with a numerous family of servants and retainers, "the space of three or four weeks, without either beds, sheets, table-cloths, dishes to eat their meat in, or wherewithal to buy any: howbeit, there was good provision of all kind of victual, and of beer and wine, whereof there was sufficient and plenty enough: but my lord was compelled of necessity to borrow of Martin Arundell and the Bishop of Carlisle, plate and dishes, both to drink in, and eat his meat in. Thus, my lord, with his family, continued in this strange estate until after Hallownetide."—(*Stow.*) He then dismissed a considerable part of his attendants; and Thomas Cromwell, afterwards Earl of Essex, who was in his service, went to London, professedly to take care of his interest at court; and having obtained a seat in the House of Commons, where a bill, of articles of impeachment against the Cardinal for treason, was brought forward, "Master Cromwell inveighed against it so discreetly, with such witty persuasions and deep reasons, that the same could take no effect."

Although the charge of treason was for the present abandoned, Wolsey was[Pg 280] indicted for a *præmunire*, the result of which was, to place him at the King's mercy as to all his goods and possessions. Whilst his enemies were thus steadily pursuing their schemes for his destruction, the King betrayed occasional symptoms of returning favour, sending him gracious messages, first by Sir John Russell, and then by the Duke of Norfolk; but it may be questionable whether these demonstrations were not merely meant to cajole him; for, during the time that he was entertaining the Duke, Sir John Shelly, one of the judges, arrived at Esher, for the express purpose of obtaining from Wolsey a formal cession of York House, the town mansion of the Archbishops. The cardinal hesitated at making such an assignment of the property of his see, but at length yielded, yet not without a spirited remonstrance against the conduct of his despoilers. The acts of insult and oppression to which he was subjected, at length brought on severe illness, and he was confined to his bed. Dr. Butts, the court physician, having visited him, informed the King that his life was in danger; and Henry, as if in a moment of conscientious regret, sent him "a comfortable message," with a valuable ring, as a token of regard. Cavendish, in his *Life of Wolsey*, has thus related the circumstances under which the Royal message was delivered:—

"At Christmas, he [Wolsey] fell sore sick, that he was likely to die, whereof the King being advertised, was very sorry therefore, and sent Doctor Buttes, his grace's physician, unto him, to see in what state he was. Dr. Buttes came unto him, and finding him very sick lying in his bed, and perceiving the danger he was in, repaired again unto the King. Of whom the King demanded, saying, 'How doth yonder man; have you seen him?' 'Yea, sir,' quoth he, 'if you will have him dead, I warrant your Grace, he will be dead within these four days, if he receive no comfort from you shortly[Pg 281] and Mistress Anne.' 'Marry,' quoth the King, 'God forbid that he should die. I pray you, good Master Buttes, go again unto him, and do your cure upon him, for I would not lose him for twenty thousand pounds.' 'Then must your Grace,' quoth Master Buttes, 'send him first some comfortable message as shortly as possible.' 'Even so will I,' quoth the King, 'by you. And therefore make speed to him again, and ye shall deliver him from me this ring for a token of our good-will and favour towards him; (on which ring was engraved the King's image within a ruby, as lively counterfeit as was possible to be devised.) This ring he knoweth very well; for he gave me the same; and tell him that I am not offended with him in my heart nothing at all, and that shall he perceive, and God send him life, very shortly. Therefore, bid him be of good cheer, and pluck up his heart, and take no despair. And I charge you come not from him until ye have brought him out of all danger of death.' And then spake he to Mistress Anne, saying, 'Good sweetheart, I pray you at this my instance, to send the Cardinal a token with comfortable words; and in so doing it shall do us a loving pleasure.' She being not minded to disobey the King's earnest request,*whatever she intended in her heart towards the Cardinal*, took incontinent her tablet of gold hanging at her girdle, and delivered it to Master Buttes, with very gentle and comfortable words and commendations to the Cardinal."

The invalid *was* comforted by the seeming kindness of his tyrannical master, and recovered. In his last letter from Esher, which was addressed to Stephen Gardiner, one of his secretaries, he prays him to help him and relieve him in his miserable condition, and remove him from this moist and corrupt air: dropsy had overtaken him, with loss of appetite, and sleep; "wherfor," says the letter, "of necessyte I must be removyd to some other dryer ayer and place, where I may have comodyte of physcyans," &c. Wolsey subsequently obtained permission to remove from Esher to Richmond, where he remained until his journey into Yorkshire, a few months previous to his death, which took place at Leicester Abbey, on the 29th of November, 1530.

When Henry VIII. had resolved to constitute Hampton Court an honour, and[Pg 282] make a chace around it, he purchased several neighbouring estates, and, among them, Esher. A survey of the manor, early in the reign of Edward VI., shows there to have been here a mansion-house, sumptuously built, with divers offices, and an orchard and garden; and also a park adjoining, three miles in circuit, stocked with deer.

We shall not trace the future possessors of Esher Place. The natural undulations of the ground would seem to have required but little improvement from the conceptions of Art. Yet Kent, the landscape-gardener, "the inventor of an art that realizes painting," was employed by the Right Hon. Henry Pelham, a leading statesman in the reign of George II., possessor of the estate; and the artist and patron have thus been inseparably connected with

"Esher's peaceful grove,
Where Kent and Nature vie for Pelham's love."

Noble fir and beech plantations cover the swelling heights of Esher; and there are fine oaks and elms, together with a remarkable holly-tree, the girth of which is between eight and nine feet. There are also several small ornamental buildings in the park; but the principal one in picturesqueness and historic interest, is the old brick tower, which formed part of "Asher Palace," when this estate belonged to the see of Winchester. It also constituted the central division of the mansion of the Pelhams, but was judiciously left standing, when the modern additions, by Kent, were pulled down by

Mr. Spicer, who purchased the estate in 1805, and erected a new mansion upon a more elevated site. In[Pg 283] Mr. Pelham's time, the mansion consisted of little more than the Tower, or Gate-house, to that in which Wolsey had resided, and to which Kent's additions were much inferior, proving, as Walpole remarks, "how little Kent conceived either the principles or graces of Gothic architecture."

The erection of this Tower has been attributed to Wolsey, whose name is associated with several architectural works; but there is inferential evidence to show that he did not erect the Tower at Esher. Although nominated to the bishopric of Winchester in the autumn of 1528, he was not installed until April in the following year (and that by proxy), at which season he was too deeply engaged in the affair of the King's divorce, to have time for extensive building. The only *distinct* notice which has appeared to connect Wolsey's name with any architectural works at Asher Palace, is where Cavendish speaks of the removal to Westminster (Whitehall), of "the new gallery which my lord had late before his fall newly set up at Asher;" and "the taking away thereof," he continues, "was to him corrosive—the which discouraged him very sore to stay there any longer,—for he was weary of that house at Asher, for with continual use it waxed unsavoury."

In the form and character of the Tower itself are also indications of an earlier period than that of Wolsey; and this well-built structure may be assigned to the days of Bishop Wayneflete, who preceded the Cardinal in his possession of the see by about eighty years, and is known to have erected "a stately brick mansion" and "gate-house" in Esher Park. The Tower is luxuriantly mantled with ivy, which was planted by a son of Mr. Spicer, whilst yet a boy. The interior comprises three storeys; but the apartments are small and much dilapidated. There is, however, within one[Pg 284] of the octagonal turrets, a very skilfully-wrought *newel*, or geometrical staircase, of brick, in excellent preservation; and in the roofing of which the principles of the construction of the oblique arch, (a supposed invention of modern times) are practically exhibited.[65]

There is, on the Esher estate, another structure, which is popularly associated with Wolsey's name. This is a small building, of flints and rude stones, with a central recess and stone seat; and at the foot a refreshing spring, called *Wolsey's Well*. It is most probable that this little edifice was raised by Mr. Pelham, as the *buckle*, a part of his family arms, is sculptured upon a stone over the middle arch, and also the initials, H. P. The seat is more properly named "the Travellers' Rest." Wolsey spent some weeks at Esher, a prey to his fears and mortified ambition. As might be expected, the world, that had paid him such abject court in his prosperity, deserted him in this fatal reverse of his fortunes. Wolsey was not himself prepared for what he conceived to be base ingratitude: it surprised and deceived him; and the same pride, unsupported by true dignity of character, which made him be vainly elated with his recent grandeur, made him now doubly sensitive to the humiliations of adversity. Under any circumstances he would be unfit for solitude: the glory and the gaze of the multitude being the breath of his nostrils, the calm contentment of private life was to him a sound[Pg 285] of no meaning. What, then, must have been his feelings in this first hour of his misery? Baffled in all the schemes of his ambition, disgraced before his rivals, abandoned by the world, and forsaken by his royal master, his heart was not yet sufficiently chastened by affliction to seek for consolation in its only true source—religion; but still clung, with the despair of a lover, to the hope of the royal mercy. His letters to Gardiner, whom he had the merit of bringing forward from obscurity, and who, excepting his other secretary, Cromwell, of all his followers, alone retained grateful respect for their benefactor in his fallen fortunes, bespeak the agony of his feelings. They are severally subscribed, "With a rude hand, and sorrowful heart, T. Card[lis] Ebor. *miserrimus*," and are scarcely legible, from the excitement under which they seem to have been written.

In chastening verse has our great moralist thus portrayed the proud Churchman:—

"In full-blown dignity see Wolsey stand,
Law in his voice, and fortune in his hand:
To him the Church, the realm, their pow'rs consign;
Through him, the rays of regal bounty shine:
Turn'd by his nod, the stream of honour flows;
His smile at once security bestows.
Still to new heights his restless wishes soar;
Claim leads to claim, and pow'r advances pow'r;
Till conquest unresisted ceased to please;
And rights submitted, left him none to seize!
At length, his Sov'reign frowns—the train of state
Mark the keen glance, and watch the sign to hate;
Where'er he turns, he meets a stranger's eye;
His suppliants scorn him, and his followers fly.
Now drops at once the pride of awful state,
The golden canopy, the glittering plate,
The regal palace, the luxurious board,
[Pg 286]The liveried servants, and the menial lord!
With age, with cares, with maladies oppress'd,
He seeks the refuge of monastic rest.
Grief aids disease, remember'd folly stings,
And his last sighs reproach the faith of Kings."—JOHNSON.

Whatever appertains to the record of his appalling fall is treasurable as an addition to the narrative in our popular histories. A few points of novelty and interest as regards Wolsey have been derived from a State manuscript of the reign of Henry VIII., now in the possession of Sir Walter C. Trevelyan, Bart. F.S.A. a junior member of whose family was one of the chaplains to Henry VIII.; and through him it may have found its way to the venerable seat of Nettlecombe, in the county of Somerset, where this MS. relating to domestic expenses and payments has for some centuries been deposited.

In this manuscript Wolsey is spoken of by his double title of Cardinal of York and Bishop of Winchester, in connexion with a payment to him of one thousand marks, out of the revenues of Winchester. By the above entry, confirmed by a subsequent passage in Cavendish, it is clear that this was a pension of 1,000 marks; and that in consideration of the necessities of the Cardinal, it was to be allowed him beforehand. After all his pomp and prosperity, after all his vast accumulation of wealth, after all his piles of plate and heaps of cloth-of-gold, and costly apparel, Wolsey, in March 1530 (judging only from this entry), was reduced to the necessity of obtaining a loan of a thousand marks. This, too, to carry him to his exile at York, whither his enemies had by this date induced the fickle, selfish, and luxurious King to banish his great favourite.

[Pg 287]

Of Wolsey's subsequent residence at Cawood, we find in this MS. an item to David Vincent, of the considerable sum of 35*l*. 6*s*. 8*d*. (more than 200*l*.), whence we may infer this messenger to have made some stay there, watching the progress of Wolsey's illness, and sending intelligence to the King, who was more anxious for the death than for the life of his victim, in order that he might seize upon the remainder of his moveables. It is quite evident that the Cardinal was not at this period so destitute as many have supposed, and that he had carried with him a very large quantity of plate, of which the King possessed himself the moment the breath was out of the body of its owner. Among the payments for January, 22 Henry VIII., we read in the Trevelyan MS. that two persons were employed for three entire days in London "weighing the plate that came from Cawood, late the Cardinalles." Such are the unceremonious terms used in the original memorandum, communicating a striking fact, of which we now hear for the first time.

It is a curious and novel circumstance which the Trevelyan manuscript has brought to light, that exactly three months before the death of Wolsey, the Dean and Canons of Cardinal's (now Christchurch) College, Oxford, had so completely separated themselves from Wolsey, and from all interest he had taken in their establishment, that, instead of rewriting to him for the comparatively small sum of 184*l*. for the purpose of carrying on their works, they applied to the King for the loan of the money; the entry of which loan is made in this State manuscript, "upon an obligation to be repaid agayne," "on this side of Cristinmas next cumming;" so that even this trifling advance could not be made out of[Pg 288] the royal purse, filled to repletion by the sacrifice of Wolsey, without an express stipulation that the money was to be returned before Christmas.

To the credit of Wolsey it must be told, that in the midst of his troubles his anxiety for his new college was unabated, and it is upon record, that, among his last petitions to the King, was an urgent request that "His Majesty would suffer his college at Oxford to go on."[66]

Everything in Wolsey—his vices and his virtues—was great. He seemed incapable of mediocrity in anything: voluptuous and profuse, rapacious and of insatiable ambition, too magnanimous to be either cruel or revengeful, he was an excellent master and patron, and a fair and open enemy. If we despise the abjectness which he exhibited in his first fall, let it be remembered from and to what he fell, from a degree of wealth and grandeur which no subject on earth now enjoys, to instantaneous and utter destitution. He wanted at Esher the comfort which even a prison would have afforded, the very bed on which he slept having been taken from him. We are also to take into account the abject submission which he had long been taught to exercise towards the tyrant,

"Whose smile was transport, and whose frown was fate."

There are certain circumstances connected with Wolsey's death and interment which are noteworthy. "He foretold to Cavendish that at eight o'clock he would lose his master.... Towards the conclusion, his accents began to falter; at the end his eyes became motionless, and his sight[Pg 289] failed. The abbot was summoned to administer the extreme unction, and the yeomen of the guard were called in to see him die. As the clock struck eight he expired."

Cavendish and the bystanders thought Wolsey must have had a revelation of the time of his death; and from the way in which the fact had taken possession of his mind, it is supposed that he relied on astrological prediction.

Mr. Payne Collier observes:[67] "It is unnecessary, as well as uncharitable, to suppose what there is no proof of—that Wolsey died of poison, either administered by himself or others. The obvious and proximate cause of his death was affliction. A great heart, oppressed with indignities and beset with dangers, at length gave way, and Wolsey received the two last charities of a death-bed and a grave, with many circumstances affectingly told by Cavendish, in the Abbey of Leicester."

Wolsey's remains were privately interred in one of the chapels of the Abbey at Leicester, which has long been reduced to a mass of shapeless ruins. The Cardinal had, however, designed a sumptuous receptacle for his remains. Adjoining the east end of St. George's Chapel at Windsor is a stone edifice, built by King Henry VII., as a burial-place for himself and his successors; but this Prince afterwards altering his purpose, began the more noble structure at Westminster, and the Windsor fabric remained neglected until Wolsey obtained a grant of it from Henry VIII. The Cardinal, with a profusion of expense unknown to former ages, designed and began here a most sumptuous monument for himself, from whence this building obtained the name of *Wolsey's Tomb-house*. This[Pg 290] monument was magnificently built; and at the time of the Cardinal's disgrace 4,250 ducats had been paid to a statuary of Florence for the work already done; and 380*l*. 18*s*. sterling had been paid for gilding only the half of this costly monument. It thus remained unfinished; in 1646 it was plundered by the rebels of its statues and figures of gilt-copper. The Tomb-house is now in process of decoration as a memorial to the late Prince Consort.

Wolsey had also executed for him at Rome a beautiful marble sarcophagus, but which did not arrive in time for the burial of the Cardinal: it lay neglected for two centuries and three-quarters, when it was removed to the crypt of St. Paul's Cathedral, and in it were placed Nelson's remains.

It is scarcely possible to leave the Tower at Esher without saddening thoughts that "lie too deep for tears." Here, amidst "the sweetest solitude" of wood and grove, stands the memorial of the ambitious minister, the powerful favourite, the selfish ecclesiastic, and the victim to tyranny,—yet a tyranny that he had himself assisted both to form and exercise. How troubled were the times which the sight of this structure recals! How painful is the contrast with the scene of peaceful nature around it!—with the refreshing quiet of the wood and glade, and the repose of the water, whereon the nothingness of human glory may be shown in one simple but sublime lesson—the circle that expands into nought. How painful, we repeat, is the contemplation of such contrasts; yet, how fraught with lessons for our happiness! We weep over the fallen fortunes of men, and their abuse of the means entrusted to them for the welfare of their fellow-men; yet what a rebuke do we receive in the[Pg 291] reflection that Nature surrounds us with the means of endless enjoyments, while Art, by its subtlety, perverts and corrupts, thus weaning the affections from the beautiful and the pure.

Yet, if "Asher Place" had its vicissitudes in past ages, so too has Claremont—a portion of the same manor—in our own times. Here, in the mansion built for the great Lord Clive, Leopold, Prince of Saxe-Cobourg, half a century since, brought his bride, the fair-haired daughter of England, and lived for a short and blissful period, in all the happiness of conjugal and domestic union, when premature death struck down the Princess and her infant offspring. Here Louis Philippe and his Queen found an asylum, in the year of Revolutions, 1848; and have since gone to their earthly home a few miles distant. Leopold, too, has descended to the tomb, full of years and kingly honours, having received in marriage, in succession, a daughter of the King of England, and a daughter of the King of France.

[*The Life of Wolsey*, by Cavendish, (quoted in the preceding pages,) is one of the most interesting and valuable specimens of biography in the English language. Its first merit is originality in the strictest sense of the word. The writer, one of Wolsey's gentlemen, and much in his confidence, was not merely a spectator, but an agent, and in some degree, a sufferer in the scenes which he describes. In the next place, though he writes from the heart, there is an air of impartiality in some parts of the work, which gives them the clear stamp of veracity. Of the hauteur and insolence of the Cardinal during his elevation, he sometimes allows himself to speak with asperity. The tender compassion which rendered him the faithful companion of his fallen fortunes, gives an amiable and pleasing colour to the latter part of his narrative. Besides, the cumbrous magnificence of the reign of Henry VIII., under the great change of manners which two centuries and a half have produced, is become in its representation to us, extremely picturesque; and for this part of his undertaking Cavendish was eminently qualified. He was not one of those[Pg 292] unobserving men, who seem never to apprehend that what is familiar to themselves will become curious to posterity. He saw with an exact and discriminating eye, and what he beheld he was able to describe. In no other work, perhaps, is to be found so minute and faithful a detail of what the palaces of kings and prelates, and the houses of the great nobility then were; their loads of plate, their hangings of arras, the ponderous plenty of their tables, and the useless accumulation, as we should conceive, of cloth, linen, &c., which were sometimes exhibited in their great galleries as in so many warehouses. Add to this, the innumerable links then subsisting in the great chain of dependence, the haughty distance of the superior to his immediate inferior, the obsequiousness of the immediate inferior in return; the young nobility serving in the houses of the greater prelates like menial servants, and these prelates themselves as often, perhaps, on the knee to their king as to their God. All these particulars, acquired from the life by the writer before us, form so many vivid pictures presented to the mind's eye, so that ideas become images, and we seem to behold what we only read of.—See Dr. Wordsworth's *Ecclesiastical Biography*.]

TRADITIONS OF BATTLE-FIELDS.

[Pg 293]

t has been frequently remarked that the general decay of local traditions, or the difficulty of obtaining particulars of events, or the sites of the most remembered passages of history, is, year by year, becoming more evident. It might be expected that in the vicinity of great transactions, among a rude and ignorant peasantry, we should find more frequent vestiges of the one memorable action which made their locality famous; yet, it is astonishing to find how often these are completely obliterated.

Much of this falling-off in tradition may be referred to the more rigid test to which it is subjected by means of the printing-press; as well as to the new class of materials for history. For a century or so, the habit had prevailed of receiving implicitly the traditions and records of past times, assuming them to have been substantiated at the date of their publication. This mode of constructing history consisted merely of breaking up and re-arranging the old materials, which have been compared to stereotype blocks. The worthlessness of this mode of proceeding has become apparent; and now the opposite error has come strongly into vogue—that of going back to neglected documents of the same date as the transaction, and, on their evidence, revoking the settled deliberate verdict of past centuries. The vast accession of materials of this kind[Pg 294] obtained of late years, is truly surprising. There is likewise another means of verifying the dates, places, and names, of great events: we mean in the visits of archæologists to the sites, and the comparison of the actual localities with recorded details; proceedings of the most pleasurable and intellectual kind.

Nevertheless, the old traditional stock is not yet entirely exhausted. There are no families in the British Islands more ancient than many of those which are yet to be found among our yeomanry and peasantry. Every now and then some proof comes to light of an antiquity of tenure on the part of such families, far exceeding that of the Stanleys or Howards. The Duke of York, for example, ejected from a farm at Chertsey a certain Mr. Wapshott, who claimed lineal and accredited descent from Reginald Wapshott, the armour-bearer of Alfred, who is said to have established Reginald in this very farm. This personage was an example of the tenacity with which tradition might be thus preserved, for his family version of their origin derived them from Wapshott, the warrener, and not the armour-bearer of Alfred.[68]

Again, we have recovered of late a series of instances, which show how few individuals not uncommonly intervene between ourselves and the eye-witnesses of remarkable men or actions. King William IV. had spoken to a butcher at Windsor, who had conversed with Charles II. What is still more remarkable, a person living in 1847, aged then about sixty-one, was frequently assured by his father that, in 1786, he repeatedly saw one Peter Garden, who died in that year at the age of 127 years; and who, when a boy, heard Henry Jenkins give evidence in a court[Pg 295] of justice at York, to the effect that, when a boy, he was employed in carrying arrows up the hill before the battle of Flodden Field.

In this year, 1856, Mr. Sidney Gibson, F.S.A. showed, as above, that a person living in 1786, conversed with a man that fought at Flodden Field.

We now proceed to narrate a few instances in which the details of early battles have been most successfully investigated and identified.

There is not much myth about the BATTLE OF HASTINGS. On that undulating upland, and in that steep morass, raged on Saturday, October 14th, A.D. 1060, from nine till three, when its tide first turned, as fierce a battle, as real a stand-up fight between the army of England and the great Norman host, as any which has ever decided the destinies of countries. There is no important battle, the details of which have been so carefully handed down to us. How the Conqueror's left foot slipped on landing—the ill omen—and how his right foot "stacked in the sand"—the good omen of "seisin;"— how the ships were pierced, so that his host[Pg 296] might fight its way to glory without retreat; and how he merrily extracted an omen for good even while putting on his hauberk the wrong side foremost; how brother Gurth with the tender conscience counselled brother Harold with the seared conscience to stay away from the fray, lest his broken oath to William should overtake him; and how, as they reconnoitred the vast Norman host, the elder brother's heart had failed him, had not the younger one called him scoundrel for his meditated flight; the prayerful eve in the one camp and the carousing eve in the other, "with wassails and drinkhails;" the exploits of valiant knight Taillifer between the lines; how the Normans shot high in air to blind the enemy; and the dreadful *mêlée* in the "blind ditch Malfosse shadowed with reed and sedge;" and the Conqueror's hearty after-battle meal, when he was chaired among the dying and the dead; and that exquisitely pathetic touch of story which tells how Edith, the swan-necked,—for the love she bore to Harold,—when all others failed to recognise him, was brought to discover his mutilated corse among the slain; and the Conqueror's vow, so literally redeemed, to fix the high altar of the "Abbey of the Battaile" where the Saxon *gonfanon* fell—all these, and a thousand other minute circumstances of the memorable day, stand out in as clear relief at this distance of time as the last charge of Waterloo, or the closing scene at Trafalgar.

Sussex has little occasion to feel humbled by having been the scene of this well-contested field. Whatever the inhabitants of the British isles have since been able to effect for their own greatness and for the happiness of the human race, is attributable in no small degree to the issue of that fight. Thenceforth the Saxon was guided and elevated by the high spirit and far-reaching enterprise of the Norman, and the[Pg 297] elements of the national character were complete.[69]

Among the memorials of the conquered must not be forgotten the roll of the companions of the Conqueror, which was installed with great festivity in August, 1862, at Dives, a small town on the seacoast, in the department of Calvados, in Normandy. It was near this town, at the mouth of the Dives, that William and his companions in arms met previous to their embarkation for the subjugation of England.

The very spot was already marked by a column erected in 1861, by M. de Caumont, the eminent Norman savant and archæologist; and the fête in August, 1862, was held under the auspices of the same learned gentleman. The commemoration was intended to be international, and a public invitation was given to the English residents in the locality; but, from some unexplained cause or other, no English person attended. Sir Bernard Burke attributes this absence to the announcement being imperfectly made; "for what," he asks, "could more come home to the better and more educated classes of English people than the inauguration of a roll which contains the greatest names amongst us; a roll to which the proudest feel prouder still to belong, and which may be said to form the very household words of our glory—the roll, in fact, of what has since been the best and bravest aristocracy in the universe?"

The fête commenced by a meeting in the Market-hall of Dives, which was characteristically decorated; one of the objects being a large picture of the construction and embarkation of William's fleet, painted from the Bayeux Tapestry. The Dives Roll is deposited within the church, over the principal entrance. It differs from the Battle Abbey Roll in this[Pg 298] respect, that the latter is the roll of those who actually fought at Hastings, and the former is the roll of those who assembled for the expedition, and were otherwise engaged in furthering the conquest of England. The roll is printed in the *Bulletin de la Societé des Antiquaires de Normandie*, and in the *Vicissitudes of Families*, third series.

Next are three battles of the fifteenth century: Towton, Tewkesbury, and Bosworth. TOWTON FIELD, supposed to be the most fierce and bloody battle that ever happened in any domestic war, was fought between the Houses of York and Lancaster in 1461. On the 29th of March, the armies met at Towton: the Lancastrians were totally routed, and Edward left unquestionably king. The carnage of this terrible field is appalling. Proclamations forbidding quarter were issued before the engagement. Like Leipsic, it reached over the night; but, unlike Leipsic, even the hours of darkness brought no rest. They fought from four o'clock in the afternoon, throughout the whole night, on to noon the next day. Like Waterloo, it was fought on a Sunday. And the accounts of contemporary writers state, in words very like the letters from Mont St. Jean, that, for weeks afterwards the blood stood in puddles, and stagnated in gutters, and that the water of the wells was red. No inaccuracy is more frequent in ancient authors than that of numbers, and generally on the side of exaggeration. But on this occasion we can form a more correct estimate of the carnage by the concurrence of unusually reputable testimonies; and, perhaps, in these times it will give the best idea of it, to say that the number of Englishmen slain exceeded the *sum* of those who fell at Vimiera, Talavera, Albuera, Salamanca, Vittoria, and Waterloo.[70]

[Pg 299]

TEWKESBURY FIELD has been minutely explored. Mr. Richard Brooke, F.S.A., after narrating, from Holinshed, the circumstances which preceded this memorable battle—

from the arrival of Queen Margaret at Weymouth, to the termination of the conflict, and the murder of Prince Edward—points out the field of battle as close to the first mile-stone on the high road leading from Tewkesbury through Tredington to Cheltenham and Gloucester. On the western side of the town of Tewkesbury is the Home-ground, or Home-hill, where once a castle stood; a part of this elevated ground is a field, called "the Gastons," which extends to the first mile-stone, just opposite which, on the eastern side of the road, is a field which has been immemorially called "Margaret's Camp." The battle was, according to tradition, fought on that place, and in the adjacent fields on the southward, as also in those a little eastward of it. In "Margaret's Camp," in the centre is a small circular inclosure, surrounded by a ditch, without hedge or bank, but having some large elm trees growing round its inner edge. This is too insignificant to have been a military entrenchment; but it may have been the place of interment of some of the slain; or is thought to have been formed in comparatively modern times to commemorate the spot where the Lancastrian army was posted. In the field, called "Gup's Hill," Mr. Brooke was told by elderly persons, bones had formerly been discovered.

The old annalists and chroniclers, Mr. Brooke says, have left us much in the dark as to the exact spot near the camp of the Lancastrians where Edward's forces passed the night prior to the battle; but on the morning of the battle, and immediately before it commenced, his army, according both to tradition and probability, took up a position upon some elevated[Pg 300] ground adjoining the turnpike-road, and to the southward of and opposite the Lancastrian army. From that position a tract of ground (now fields and closes) slopes downwards, so as to form a depression between it and the spot occupied by the Lancastrians. This tract of ground was formerly called the "Red Piece," and it is now intersected by the turnpike-road, and forms two fields, one on each side of the road, one of which is called the Near Red Close, and the other the Further Red Close. This tract of ground extends to the field called "Margaret's Camp," and it appears almost certain that it was on the southward side of the latter that Edward's forces made their attack.

A meadow in the rear of the Lancastrian position, and lying on the westward side of the turnpike-road, half a mile from Tewkesbury, and within a few hundred yards of the Tewkesbury Union Workhouse, is called the "Bloody Meadow:" an idea is generally entertained that it derives its name from the slaughter of many of the fugitives, who fled from the battle towards the meadow, in hope of getting over the Severn, as there is a ferry not far from it. Fourteen or fifteen years ago, was found in the Bloody Meadow a long piece of iron, which appeared to have been part of a sword-blade.

BOSWORTH FIELD is a still more memorable site. On August 22, 1485, was fought the famous battle of Bosworth, the precise spot being pointed out by the following passage contained in a proclamation sent by Henry VII., almost immediately after his victory, to the municipality of York: "Moreover, the King ascertaineth you that Richard, Duke of Gloucester, lately called King Richard, was slain at a place called Sandeford, in[Pg 301] the county of Leicester, and brought dead off the field," &c.

The field of battle lies about three miles south of Market Bosworth; and it is clear from direct historical testimony, which is in this instance fully corroborated by local traditions, that the principal encounter between the forces of Richard and Richmond took place on "Ambien Hill," on the southern slope of which rises the spring, "Richard's Well," from which the King is traditionally reported to have drank during the engagement. The plain of Redmoor was also partly comprehended in the movements of the two armies, and across which there cannot be a doubt the flight of the vanquished royalists was afterwards directed towards Dadlington, Stoke Golding, and Crown Hill, besides the strong position of Ambien Hill, on the south and west. It is, therefore, evident that the place where the King fell must be looked for in the immediate vicinity of these two well-ascertained sites of conflict. Now *Sandeford*, or *Sandford*, named in the proclamation of Henry VII., is not known to have existed as a hamlet or village in the county of Leicester, from the date of Domesday-book; hence Sandford is taken to imply an ancient road or passage over some fordable stream or water-course. It has been found that the old road from Leicester to Atherstone, through the villages of Peckleton and Kirkby Mallory, and along which road Richard advanced, when on his march from Leicester upon Sunday, August 21, to meet his antagonist, used formerly, after skirting and partially traversing the field of battle, to cross a *ford*, remembered by the present generation, and situated at but a short distance from the south-western slope of Ambien Hill. And part of the comparatively modern highway which now passes over the site of the same[Pg 302] ford, is called the *Sandroad* at the present time. The stream which once flooded the highway, is now carried through a vaulted tunnel beneath it. The ford has consequently disappeared; but any visitor to Bosworth Field, who inquires for the *Water Gate*, may yet stand on the ground pointed out as the scene of the death of Richard III. by the words of his rival Henry VII. It should be added that Mr. J. F. Hollings, of Leicester, who has communicated the above details to *Notes and Queries*, 2nd S., No. 150, has shown also that the Ordnance Map is not altogether to be relied upon as a guide to the various localities connected with the battle of Bosworth.

Mr. Syer Cuming, F.S.A., in a paper read to the British Archæological Association, in 1862, has grouped these interesting Memorials of Richard III. On this occasion, the archæologists proceeded from Leicester to the battle-field; and a considerable accession to the number being received at Bosworth, the procession extended upwards of half-a-mile in length. On arriving at the field, large numbers of people had preceded the procession and congregated round the platform, and altogether there could not have been fewer than a thousand persons present. The platform was decorated with banners. A facsimile of the crown of Richard III. was shown on a cushion in front of Major Wollaston, who presided on the occasion. A flag marked the place where King Richard died, near a small pond, and a white flag pointed out the position of Richmond's army.

Richard Plantagenet was born about the year 1450, of Lady Cecilia, wife of Richard, Duke of York, in the ancient castle of Fotheringhay, Northamptonshire; but his natal abode was swept away by order of our[Pg 303] first James, and we have perhaps no earlier relic of the Prince than his official seal as Admiral of England the date of which is fixed by Mr. Pettigrew between the years 1471 and 1475. It bears on it a large vessel, the mainsail blazoned with the arms of France and England, crossed by a label of three points; similar charges appearing on a flag held by a greyhound at the aft-castle. The verge represents a collar of roses, and within it is a legend setting forth that it is the seal of Richard, Duke of Gloucester, Admiral of England, for the counties of Dorset and Somerset—*S' Rici: Dvc' Glovc': Admiralli: Angl: I: Com: Dors' et Soms.*

[When Dr. Dibdin was on his "Northern Tour," published in 1838, at Whiburn, in the neighbourhood of Tynemouth, he had the good fortune to be introduced to Sir Hedworth Williamson's old trunk of family seals, in red and white wax, among which he found a warrant of Richard III., then Duke of Gloucester, dated 20th of February, in the thirteenth year of Edward IV., with the Autograph of the Duke, and part of the Seal appended; both of which are of most rare occurrence.]

If tradition is to be believed, King John and Queen Elizabeth must have had as many palaces as there are counties in England; and though the name of Richard III. is less frequently connected with old mansions, there are still plenty of antiquated houses which are said to have been his abiding-places for more or less lengthy periods. Among others may be mentioned the Black Boy Inn, Chelmsford, where were formerly to be seen two carved bosses on the ceiling of its great room: one being painted with a blue boar on a deep red field, surrounded by a collar of seven stars or mullets; the other, with a full-blown rose, once entirely[Pg 304] white, but subsequently white and red, indicative of the union of the Houses of York and Lancaster. Both these bosses were communicated to the *Gentleman's Magazine* (May, 1840), by John Adey Repton; but the editor of that serial contended that the boar is the insignia of Vere, Earl of Oxford, and that the tradition regarding Richard must therefore be rejected, forgetful of the fact that after the attainder of the Earl for high treason, his vast possessions in Essex and other counties were given to the Duke of Gloucester, so that the Black Boy Inn may, after all, have served as a hunting-lodge of the Plantagenet. Of Richard's two London residences one has altogether vanished, and the other has lost much of its antique aspect, but Shakspeare has given a world-wide and lasting fame to both. Baynard's Castle stood on the northern bank of the Thames, and was destroyed in the Great Fire of 1666. It was in the court of this fortress that

Stafford, Duke of Buckingham, offered the crown to the Duke of Gloucester, and where the dramatist makes the latter say:—

"Since you will buckle fortune on my back,
To bear her burden, whe'r I will or no,
I must have patience to endure the load."
Richard III. ii. 7.

The other dwelling alluded to is Crosby Place, Bishopsgate, built by Sir John Crosby about the year 1467; and, in spite of alterations and renovations, this is still one of the finest examples of Early Domestic architecture in England. Hither Shakspeare makes Gloucester invite the Lady Anne; and bid the murderers repair after the assassination of Clarence and the young princes in the Tower.

The old building in Leicester, which was properly called "King Richard's[Pg 305] House," was known to be part of the Old Blue Boar: at the commencement of the last century, it was used as an inn, and known by that sign, though originally it bore the name of the "White Boar," the cognizance of King Richard III.; but, after his defeat, this sign was torn down by the infuriated populace, and the owner or landlord compelled to change the title. Popular tradition has always identified the building with the ill-fated monarch, and the inquiries of our local antiquaries confirm the tradition. It was taken down in the month of March, 1836; but, fortunately, before its destruction, a drawing was made of the front; and that has been frequently engraved. In this house Richard took up his quarters, and slept on a bedstead, the remains of which are believed to be in existence. It had a false bottom, in which a large sum of money could be concealed, and did duty as a military chest. Engravings of the house and bedstead are given in Hutton's *Battle of Bosworth Field*, 2d edition, by J. Nichols, F.S.A.

Richard is reported to have been peculiarly subject to the influence of omens. "During his abode at Exeter," says Holinshed, "he went about the citie, and viewed the seat of the same, and at length he came to the castle; and when he understood that it was called Rugemont, suddenlie he fell into a dumpe, and (as one astonied) said, 'Well, I see my dayes be not long.' He spake this of a prophecy told him, that when he once came to Richmond, he should not long live after." He had more rational cause for alarm when Jockey of Norfolk produced the doggrel warning found in his tent, for it clearly indicated the desertion and treachery that were about to prove fatal to him.

On the night before the battle, going the rounds, Richard found a[Pg 306] sentinel asleep, and stabbed him, with the remark, "I found him asleep, and have left him as I found him."

The vanguard of Richard's army was commanded by the Duke of Norfolk; the centre and main body by the King himself, who rode at their head, mounted on his celebrated milk-white steed, White Surrey, and arrayed in the splendid suit of armour which he had worn at Tewkesbury. Like Henry V. at Agincourt, Richard wore a golden crown, not as a man would wear a hat or cap, but by way of crest over his helmet. Richmond, too, bore himself gallantly, and rode through the ranks, marshalling and encouraging his men, arrayed in complete armour, but unhelmeted. His vanguard, commanded by the Earl of Oxford, began the battle by crossing the low ground towards the elevated position where Richard prudently waited the attack. "The trumpets blew, and the soldiers shouted, and the King's archers courageously let fly their arrows. The Earl's bowmen stood not still, but paid them home again; and the terrible shot once passed, the armies joined, and came to hand-strokes."[71]

The leaders of those days deemed it a point of honour to fight hand to hand, if possible, and Oxford and Norfolk managed to engage in a personal encounter. After shivering their spears on each other's shields or breastplates, they fell to with their swords. Oxford, wounded in the arm by a blow which glanced from his crest, returned it by one which hewed off the vizor of Norfolk's helmet, leaving the face bare; and then, disdaining to follow up the advantage, drew back, when an arrow[Pg 307] from an unknown hand pierced the Duke's brain. Surrey, hurrying up to assist or avenge his father, was surrounded and overpowered by Sir Gilbert Talbot and Sir John Savage, who commanded on the right and left for Richmond:—

"Young Howard single with an army fights;
When, moved with pity, two renownèd knights,
Strong Clarendon and valiant Conyers, try
To rescue him, in which attempt they die.
Now Surrey, fainting, scarce his sword can hold,
Which made a common soldier grow so bold,
To lay rude hands upon that noble flower,
Which he disdaining—anger gives him power,—
Erects his weapon with a nimble round,
And sends the peasant's arm to kiss the ground."—
Bosworth Field, by Sir John Beaumont, Bart.

If we may credit tradition or the chroniclers, all this was literally true. When completely exhausted, Surrey presented the hilt of his sword to Talbot, whom he requested to take his life, and save him from dying by an ignoble hand. He lived to be the Surrey of Flodden Field, and the worthy transmitter of "all the blood of all the Howards."

When Richard was about to make that renowned charge, which historians describe as the last effort of despair, he was bringing up his main body, and intelligence reached him that Richmond was posted behind the hill with a slender attendance. His plan was formed on the instant; nor, although fiery courage or burning hate might have suggested it, was it ill-judged or reckless. Three-fourths of the combatants, if we include the Stanleys, were ready to side with the strongest. Richmond's army, without

Richmond, was a rope of sand. His fall would be the signal for a general scattering, or a feigned renewal of hollow allegiance to the[Pg 308] conqueror. Neither did the execution of the proposed *coup de main* betoken a sudden impulse inconsiderately acted upon. Richard rode out at the right flank of his army, and ascended a rising ground to get a view of his enemy, with whose person he was not acquainted. He summoned to his side a chosen body of knights, all of whom, with the exception of Lord Lovell, perished with him; and he paused to drink at a spring, which still goes by his name. That Richard's horse was slain is very doubtful; and, for aught we *know*, it was White Surrey that bore him, like a thunderbolt, against the bosom of his foe; and it was spear in rest that he dashed against Richmond's surprised and fluttered bodyguard.

The personal prowess of the pair who were contending for a kingdom, is thus estimated by Hutton: "Richard was better versed in arms, Henry was better served. Richard was brave, Henry was a coward. Richard was about five feet four, rather runted, but only made crooked by his enemies; and wanted six weeks of thirty-three. Henry was twenty-seven, slender, and near five feet nine, with a saturnine countenance, yellow hair, and grey eyes." According to Grafton, Richard, so soon as he descried Richmond, "put spurs to his horse, and, like a hungry lion, ran with spear in rest towards him." He unhorsed Sir John Cheney, a strong and brave knight,[72] and rushing on Sir William Brandon, Henry's standard-bearer, cleft his skull, tore the standard from his grasp, and[Pg 309] flung it on the ground. "He was now," says Hume, "within reach of Richmond himself, who declined not the combat." Others say that Richmond drew back, as a braver man might have done in his place—

"No craven he, and yet he shuns the blow,
So much confusion magnifies the foe."

Fortunately for him, Sir William Stanley came up at the very nick of time, "with three thousand tall men," and overpowered Richard, who died, fighting furiously, and murmuring with his last breath, *Treason! Treason! Treason!* So nicely timed was Stanley's aid, that Henry afterwards justified the ungrateful return he made for it, by saying: "He came time enough to save my life, but he stayed long enough to endanger it." Richard received wounds enough to let out a hundred lives; his crown had been struck off at the beginning of the onset; and his armour was so broken, and his features were so defaced, that he was hardly to be recognised when dragged from beneath a heap of slain.

And can that stripped and mutilated corpse be the crowned monarch who at morning's rise led a gallant army to an assured victory, who had recently been described by Philip de Commines as holding the proudest position held by any King of England for a hundred years? Nothing places in a stronger light the depth of moral degradation and insensibility, fast verging towards barbarism, to which men's minds had been sunk by the multiplied butcheries of these terrible conflicts, than the[Pg 310] indignities heaped upon the dead King, with the sanction, if not by the express orders, of his successor. The body, perfectly naked, with a rope round the neck, was flung across a horse, like the carcase of a calf, behind a pursuivant-at-arms, and was thus carried in triumph to Leicester. It was exposed two days in the Town-hall, and then buried without ceremony in the Gray Friars' Church. At the destruction of the religious houses, the remains were thrown out, and the coffin, which was of stone, was converted into a watering-trough at the White Horse Inn. The best intelligence that Mr. Hutton, who made a journey on purpose in 1758, could collect concerning it, was that it was broken up about the latter end of the reign of George I., and that some of the pieces had been placed as steps in the cellar of the inn. "To what base uses may we return!" The sign of the White Boar at Leicester, at which Richard slept, was forthwith converted into the Blue Boar; and the name of the street called after it has been corrupted into Blubber-lane.

Leicester and Richard III. are associated in traditional history, which the Corporation have handed down, with a newly-built bridge, in two inscriptions:—1. "This bridge was erected by the Corporation of Leicester, in the mayoralty of S. Viccars, Esq., A.D. 1862, on the site of the ancient Bow Bridge, over which King Richard III. passed, at the head of his army, to the battle of Bosworth Field, August, 1485. Joseph Whetstone, Chairman of Highway Committee; S. Stone, Town Clerk; E. S. Stephens, Borough Surveyor." The plate on the opposite side bears the legend in verse, according to Speed's *History of Great Britain*:—

"Upon this bridge [as tradition hath
[Pg 311]Delivered] stood a stone of some height,
Against which King Richard, as he passed
Towards Bosworth, by chance struck his spur,
And against the same stone, as he was brought
Back, hanging by the horse's side, his head
Was dashed and broken, as a wise woman
[Forsooth] had *foretold*, who, before Richard's
Going to battle, being asked as to his success,
Said that where his spur struck, his head
Should be broken."

This is legendary evidence of Richard's belief in omens, in addition to that recorded at page **305**.

Richard had a habit of gnawing his under lip, and a trick of playing with his dagger, which, although misconstrued into signs of an evil disposition, were, probably, mere outward manifestations of restlessness. Polydore Virgil speaks of his "horrible vigilance and celerity." It was the old story of the sword wearing out the scabbard; and the chances are, that he would not long have survived Bosworth Field had he come off unscathed and the conqueror.

"In the dreadful wars of York and Lancaster," writes Mr. Brooke,[73] "it is said that more than 10,000 Englishmen lost their lives; but that is merely the number believed to have been slain in battle; and, however repulsive it may be to our feelings, it must be admitted that it cannot include the numbers who must have perished during that disastrous period, in unimportant skirmishes, in marauding parties, in private warfare, by assassination, by the axe or by the halter, in pursuance of or under the colour of judicial sentences, or by open and undisguised murder. Besides this horrible sacrifice of human life, during this[Pg 312] distracted period it is shocking to think what sufferings unprotected and helpless persons must have been exposed to, from the lawless partisans of the rival parties, when they passed through or were located near any district, which they chose to consider as favouring their antagonists. Pillage, cruelty, violence to women, incendiarism, and contempt of the laws and of religion, were the natural attendants upon a civil war, carried on with feelings of bitter hatred by each party; and it is certain that the examples of cruelty and wickedness which were openly set by the nobles and leaders of both factions would readily be copied by their followers. One of our ancient historical writers correctly states, that 'this conflict was in maner unnaturall, for in it the sonne fought against the father, the brother against the brother, the nephew against the uncle, the tenant against his lord.'"

It is well known that the Wars of the Roses had weakened to the last degree the great nobles—destroying many of the houses, and impoverishing all to such an extent that when Henry assumed the Crown he found himself in possession of nearly absolute power. Under his Plantagenet predecessors the great nobles had so much authority that at times they could defy the Crown, and an influential earl might be regarded as almost the rival of the Sovereign. The English barons were now reduced to comparative insignificance, and the descendants of men who in the bygone time might have aspired to the throne, and actually ruled as independent princes in their ample domains, were content to appear at Court and to swell the train of their Sovereign liege. The Wars of the Roses had in reality precipitated in England a change which was gradually approaching—the destruction of the feudal, and the rise[Pg 313] of the municipal system. But the decay of the feudal system and the rise of the municipal produced consequences which are very important for their social and political bearings.[74]

Sad are the memories of these devastating wars, which are intertwined with many a legendary tale and fitful romance. Not the least curious of these records is the story that in a beautiful district of England, whilst the wars raged, there was discovered in the garden of Longleat Priory, in Wiltshire, a French rose-tree, covered on one side with *white* roses, and on the opposite with *red*; which, being known, attracted crowds of persons, who believed it to portend the speedy return of peace to their country, by the union of the rival powers. According to the same tradition, a short time afterwards, the tree bore roses of mixed petals, and there immediately followed the marriage of

Henry VII. and Elizabeth, thus fulfilling the floral prediction by the friendship and union of the contending parties. The rose is thought to have been an early specimen of our "York and Lancaster;" a red-white—the colours of the two houses—hence its name; and although the account is probably but a fable, it has, like many others, found its way into history.

The tendency to embalm falsehoods is a part of the question of the worth of traditions, which is really worthy of a philosophical inquiry. The rib of the Dun cow and Guy's porridge-pot are still shown at Warwick Castle, though the one is the bone of a fossil elephant, and the other a military cooking vessel of the time of Charles I. Sir Samuel Meyrick scientifically classified and arranged the collection of armour in the[Pg 314] Tower, but the Beefeaters stick to the old stories still. Richard the Third's bed in the neighbourhood of Bosworth, turns out to be Elizabethan;[75] Queen Mary's, at Holyrood, to be of the last century. Only the other day they sold off at Berkeley the bed of the murdered Edward as an undoubted anachronism and admitted imposture. Old chairs are as little to be trusted. Some persons have even doubted the famous Glastonbury specimen, but these are unduly cautious and sceptical. St. Crispin's chair in Linlithgow Cathedral is of excellent mahogany,—a wood which he could only have obtained by miracle previous to the discovery of America. Princes of Wales are not more fortunate in their traditions than the Popes themselves, for the Tower of Carnarvon, in which it is said that the first of them was born, was almost certainly built after he came into existence. The printing press will dispose of these false traditions in time, as it has already extinguished so many others, whether false or true.[76]

[Pg 315]

CURIOSITIES OF HATFIELD.

his noble seat has been incidentally noticed in the preceding pages.[77] Although the Princess Elizabeth was kept a prisoner at Hatfield, she occasionally went to London to pay her court to Queen Mary; and in 1556 she was invited to court, and proceeded thither with great parade. Elizabeth, however, preferred the quiet and pleasant scenery of Hatfield. The hall of the old palace now accommodates about thirty horses. The combination of old trees, the rich-coloured brickwork, and the curiously-wrought ironwork of the flower-garden gate, independent of its historical associations, forms a pleasing scene.

The noble park is eleven miles in circuit: here the new house, finished, in 1611, by Cecil, Earl of Salisbury, comes boldly to view. The river Lea passes through the park. Nor far from the house are a racket-court and riding-school, both large buildings: near here is an ancient oak of extraordinary size, called the "Lion oak," a venerable tree, which, although deprived of many branches, is still crowned by large masses of green foliage and numerous acorns, is upwards of thirty feet in circumference, and reputed a thousand years old.

A long and noble avenue of trees, with sunlight glistening on the grey mossy trunks and boughs, leads to the kitchen-garden. Here is an old oak, now much stunted, under which the Princess Elizabeth was sitting when the messengers brought to her the news of Queen Mary's death, and[Pg 316] saluted her as Queen. With pomp, and amid great rejoicing, Queen Elizabeth progressed to London—a journey accomplished with much greater trouble three hundred years since than at present. Decayed parts of this historical oak, the "Lion oak," and some others, have been, from time to time, covered with *cement*; and this has not only had the effect of stopping the progress of destruction, but also been the means of producing both new wood and vegetation.

At the further end of the avenue just mentioned is a building of two or three centuries old, but which has been much disguised by alterations: it is now used as the gardener's lodge. Through this we reach the vineyard,—a curious example of the trim gardening of former days. From a terrace a bank descends by a deep gradient to the river Lea. On the upper portion of the terrace are yew-trees planted at intervals, and dressed into singular shapes; in other parts the yew-trees are so cut, that up to a considerable height they seem as straight and solid as a wall: openings are left here and there which lead to dark avenues, cunningly formed by the arching of the branches. From the centre a broad flight of steps, covered with turf, leads to the Lea. On the opposite side of the river, an opening has been made in the trees, which shows a picture that stretches away in long perspective. Descending the steps, and looking upward, the view is very striking, and we perceive that the design is intended to imitate a fortress, with its towers of defence, loopholes, and battlements,—in fact, vegetation is made to assume an architectural form, which has an extraordinary effect. The vineyard is admirably kept.[78]

Of the many fine ancestral mansions in England, Hatfield, the seat of[Pg 317] the Marquis of Salisbury, is, perhaps, the most interesting for its historical documents, and other illustrations of English history. Here are preserved the forty-two articles of Edward VI., with the superscription of that pious Monarch; the first Council Book of Queen Mary; Cardinal Wolsey's Instructions to the Ambassador sent to the Pope by

Henry VIII., with that eminent churchman's autograph; the original draft of the Proclamation Secretary Cecil used at the Accession of James I.; and a very amusing Pedigree of Queen Elizabeth, emblazoned (dated 1559), by which the ancestry of that Sovereign is exhibited as traced to Adam. Here also are several manuscript letters of Elizabeth, and the celebrated Cecil Papers; the cradle of Elizabeth, of oak, ornamented with carving, decidedly Elizabethan; also James I.'s purse, and the first pair of silk stockings introduced into England, worn by Queen Elizabeth.

In the long gallery of the mansion is a state chair, said to have been used by Queen Elizabeth; and in a black cabinet is preserved a hat with a broad circular brim, which, we are told, was worn by the Princess Elizabeth, when seated under the oak in the park just mentioned. This historical tree is inclosed by a dwarf fence. When Queen Victoria and Prince Albert visited Hatfield, in 1846, Her Majesty was much interested with this memorial oak; and, as a memento of her visit, had a small branch lopped from the tree.

In each bedchamber of the mansion are wardrobes and closets carved in the style of the reign of James I.; the carved mantelpieces are very large; some supported by massive pillars entwined with flowers, others[Pg 318] supported by caryatides and figures. The bedsteads and much of the furniture are of the same date as the other fittings. King James's bed-room has the fittings, it is said, exactly as when the king last used them: the hangings, of deep crimson, are profusely ornamented with tassel-work and fringe; the quilted coverlid has wrought flowers in the centre, and at the top of the bed are a royal crown, and other ornaments. It should be mentioned that many of the rooms throughout Hatfield House are fitted with woods of different kinds, and are named, in consequence, "the Oak-room," "the Rose-room," "the Walnut-room," "the Elm-room," &c. The chapel and a suite of ten rooms completed by the present Marquis of Salisbury in the old baronial style, have panelling of various woods, some being of oak, walnut, ash, sycamore, &c.

Among the historical pictures at Hatfield is Zucchero's famous portrait of Queen Elizabeth:—She wears a robe embroidered with eyes and ears, a favourite device of hers to express her ubiquitous and sleepless intelligence; and not satisfied with the symbolic eyes and ears, she grasps a rainbow, with the motto, "*Non sine sole Iris.*"

In the recent exhibition of National Portraits at South Kensington were nineteen portraits of Queen Elizabeth, wonderful examples of her fantastic and execrable taste. "It was a bad time for the arts of portraiture. The costume, in which the Queen led the taste of both sexes, and was a keen critic of it after her fashion, was over-laden, stiff, and unbecoming. The monstrous ruffs, high-shouldered leg-of-mutton sleeves, long-pointed stomachers, and broad-hipped Spanish fardingales of the women are not redeemed from deformity by all their wealth of lace, embroidery, pearls, and jewels; while the round hats of the men—their long-waisted doublets, their hose, wide-swelling at the thigh, and tight to the knee, would defy even a Titian to make them picturesque, in spite of silk and satin and velvet, lace and slashes, ropes of pearl,[Pg 319] rich pendants, jewelled belts, and hatbands of goldsmiths' work. There never was a time when foppery ran so rampant, and the Queen was the worst of all in the bad taste and extravagance of her attire. Melville, the Scottish Ambassador, tells us how she had weeds of all countries, and would appear in a different one at every audience—how she talked to him of millinery and dress-making, hair and head tires, and seemed more anxious for his opinion on such matters than on affairs of State. We have her wardrobe books when she was 68, and find among her stores of finery, exclusive of 99 State dresses, Coronation, mourning, Parliament, and Garter robes, French gowns 102, round ditto 67, loose ditto 100, kirtles 126, foreparts 136, petticoats 125, cloaks 96, safeguards 13, jupes 43, doublets 85, lap mantles 18, fans 27, pantofles 9. And we may see among her 19 pictures here wonderful examples of her fantastic and execrable taste. The Hatfield Zucchero looks true, but, after all, it is to the Hampton Court picture of her at 16 that we turn with pleasure when she was still King Edward's 'sweet sister Temperance,' and the docile pupil of Roger Ascham in the pleasant shades of Ashridge, or Hatfield, and not that withered, gray old woman, her mind heavy with black and bloody memories, who sat on the cushions for ten days and nights, and for the last 24 hours silent, staring on the ground, with set tearless eyes, and her finger in her mouth."—*Times* journal.

In the collection at South Kensington, too, was the portrait of the man who brought the news of Mary's death to Elizabeth at Hatfield, one of her commanders in Scotland in 1547, and one of the many who supped once too often with my Lord of Leicester, and died in 1570, after eating figs at that table, where the wariest guests were careful only to taste the same dishes as my lord ate of.

Among the pictures, which are hung through the house, are the portraits of the great Lord Burghley, and his two sons; various portraits of Queen Elizabeth and Queen Mary of England; and Queen Mary of Scotland, at the age of sixteen. Here are the Earl of Leicester of Elizabeth's reign; James I. and Charles I.; Philip of Spain: Van Tromp; the famous Charles[Pg 320] of Sweden, and Peter the Great of Russia; various members of the Salisbury family; and the curious picture of Horselydown Fair, described at pp. **254-258**. In the Great Hall, which has a minstrels' gallery, ornamented with carvings of figures and animals, heraldry, &c. are a picture, life-size, of the white horse on which Queen Elizabeth rode at Tilbury Fort: and ten large paintings of Adam and Eve.

The Lady Elizabeth kept her state at Hatfield with no small cost and splendour. At a subsequent period, after her imprisonment at Woodstock, her Highness obtained permission to reside once more at Hatfield, under the guardianship of Sir Thomas Pope, who not only extended to her the kindest care and most respectful attention, but devised, at his own cost, sports and pastimes for her amusement. "The fetters in which he held her," says Agnes Strickland, "were more like flowery wreaths flung lightly around her, to attract her to a bower of royal pleasaunce, than aught which might remind her of the stern restraint by which she was surrounded during her incarceration in the Tower, and subsequent sojourn at Woodstock." Thus, we read of maskings in the Great Hall at Hatfield, banquets, and "the play of Holophernes," which Queen Mary misliked.

When Queen Mary visited her sister at Hatfield, Elizabeth adorned her great state chamber for Her Majesty's reception, with a sumptuous suite of tapestry, representing the Siege of Antioch, and had a play performed after supper, by the choir-boys of St. Paul's; at the conclusion of which one of the children sang, and was accompanied on the virginals by the Princess herself.

Hatfield, during Elizabeth's reign, remained vested in the crown. At her[Pg 321] decease, however, her successor, King James, exchanged it with Sir Robert Cecil for the palace of Theobalds, and thenceforward Hatfield has continued uninterruptedly in the possession of the noble family of Salisbury. Sir Robert Cecil was styled by his royal mistress, Elizabeth, "the staff of her declining age," and was so highly esteemed by King James, that his Majesty created him successively Baron Cecil, Viscount Cranbourne, and Earl of Salisbury; conferred on him the blue riband of the Garter, and finally appointed him Lord High Treasurer of England. About this period, his lordship laid the foundations of the present mansion of Hatfield, which he finished in 1611, in a style of equal splendour with that of Burghley, which his father had erected in the preceding reign. The year after the completion of Hatfield, worn out by the cares of state the Earl of Salisbury died at Marlborough, in Wiltshire, on his way to London: he was interred in Hatfield Church, under a stately monument. How striking an example does the closing year of his life present! In his last illness, he was heard to say to Sir William Cope: "Ease and pleasure quake to hear of death; but my life, full of care and miseries, desireth to be dissolved."

He had some years previously (1603) addressed a letter to Sir James Harrington, the poet, in nearly the same querulous tone: "Good Knight," saith the minister, "rest content, and give heed to one that hath sorrowed in the bright lustre of a court, and gone heavily on even the best seeming fair ground. 'Tis a great task to prove one's honesty, and yet not mar one's fortune: you have tasted a little thereof in our blessed Queen's time, who was more than a woman, and, in truth, sometimes less than a woman. I wish I waited now in your[Pg 322]presence-chamber, with ease at my food, and rest in my bed. I am pushed from the share of comfort, and know not where the winds and waves of a court will bear me. I know it bringeth little comfort on earth; and he is, I reckon, no wise man that looketh this way to heaven."

Hatfield is a very interesting seat, not only for its association with the past, but for its presenting, at this moment, a picture of the baronial life of two centuries and a half since. The Hall of the ancient Palace remains; the historic Oak is preserved; the vineyard was in existence when Charles I. was conveyed here a prisoner to the army, and its famous yew walk is left; and the deer are still numerous. The mansion has been restored to its pristine magnificence; the landscape gardening is fine. The noble owner of Hatfield has devoted a portion of his domains to the pastimes of the people; and on every occasion, whether it be the reception of royalty, or the entertainment of the toilers of the country, it is carried out in the generous spirit of olden English hospitality. And this princely place lies within a score of miles of the metropolis and its three million of people, who are brought almost to the park gates within an hour's railway journey.

THE GRAND REMONSTRANCE.

he most memorable sitting in Parliament, in the fourth year of King Charles the First, was that of the House of Commons, on March 2d, 1629, which was pronounced by Sir Simonds D'Ewes as "*the most gloomy, sad, and dismal day for England that had happened for five hundred years.*"

The incidents of this day will be recollected by every one. Sir John Eliot is said, according to all accounts, to have made an indignant attack upon Lord Weston, the new Treasurer, and to have concluded by moving the adoption of a Remonstrance. The Speaker, Sir John Finch, declined to put the Remonstrance to the vote, and announced that he had received the King's command to adjourn the House until the 10th of March. The House paid little attention to the royal message, contending, first, that it was not the office of the Speaker to deliver any such command; and, secondly, that the power of adjournment belonged to the House, and not to the Crown. Regardless of these arguments, the Speaker prepared to obey the royal mandate. He rose and quitted the chair, when two members, Denzil Holles, son of the Earl of Clare, on the one side, and Benjamin Valentine, on the other side, stepped forward, and forced him back into his official seat. He appealed to the House with abundance of tears. Selden argued and remonstrated with him. Sir Peter Hayman disavowed him, we are told, "as a kinsman," and denounced him as a disgrace to a noble family. Again he endeavoured to quit the chair. Sir Thomas Edmondes, who was old enough to have been ambassador from Queen Elizabeth to Henry IV. of France—a man of small stature, but of great courage—with other privy councillors, pressed forward to the Speaker's help; but Holles violently held him in his chair, and swore, by what is termed Queen Elizabeth's oath, "God's wounds!" that he should sit still until it should please the House to rise.

In the midst of this uproar, Coriton and Winterton, two of the members, are said to have fallen to blows, numbers of the more timid fled out of the House, and the King, hearing of the tumult, sent to Edward Grimstone, the Serjeant-at-Arms, who was then within the House in attendance upon the Speaker, to bring away the mace, without which it was supposed that no legal meeting could be held. To defeat this object, the key of the door was taken from the Serjeant-at-Arms, and delivered to Sir Miles Hobart. Sir Miles stopped the egress of the Serjeant-at-Arms, and having taken from him the mace, quietly put him out of the House and locked the door. The mace was then replaced upon the table, and Holles, standing by the side of the Speaker, put to the House three resolutions, which were deemed to be voted by acclamation. The King is said to have sent, in the meantime, Mr. Maxwell, the Usher of the Black Rod, to summon the House to attend in the House of Lords, but Maxwell could gain neither hearing nor admission. Grown now, as is stated in Lord Verulam's manuscript, "into much rage and passion," the King sent for "the Captain of the Pensioners and Guard to force the door." Ere this officer could muster his stately band, the House had done its work. The resolutions had been passed, the Speaker had been[Pg 325] released from the strong grasp of Denzil Holles, Sir Miles Hobart had unlocked the door, the excited members had been set free; and, *for a period of eleven years, parliamentary discussion in England had come to an end.*

Such is the narrative which was read by Mr. Bruce to the Society of Antiquaries, in 1859, upon his reading also a "True Relation" of the scene, in the handwriting of Lord Verulam, now in the manuscript collection at Gorhambury. Other MSS. of the proceedings of this Session are not uncommon, and many variations occur. Mr. Bruce has, in his paper, printed that portion of Lord Verulam's MS. which relates to the sitting of the 2d of March. Mr. Bruce, who has narrated the leading points according to Lord Verulam's MS., instead of Hayman's word, "kinsman," gives these words: "he was sorry he was a Kentish man, and that he was a disgrace to his country, and a blot to a noble family." Lord Verulam, too, gives Mr. Stroud's speech, not in other MSS.: he "tould the Speaker that he was the instrument to cutt off the libertie of the subject by the roote, and that if he would not be perswaded to put the same to question, they must all retorne as scattered sheepe, and a scorne put upon them as it was last session." This is important, since it explains more precisely than had hitherto been known, why he (Stroud) was prosecuted for his share in that day's transactions. On the other hand, Lord Verulam's MS. does not mention the Resolutions that were put to the House by Holles standing by the Speaker's chair. The concurrent testimony of a variety of authorities, however, forbids us to doubt that those Resolutions were really passed in the way described, and that in this respect Lord Verulam's MS. is defective.

CAVALIERS AND ROUNDHEADS.

he word *Cavalier* was not at first necessarily a term of reproach. Shakspeare does not so employ it when he speaks of the gay and gallant English eager for French invasion—

"For who is he ... that will not follow
These cull'd and choice-drawn Cavaliers to France?"

But it was most unquestionably used in a reproachful sense on the occasion of the tumult in the reign of Charles I., probably to connect its French origin with the un-English character of the defenders of the Queen and her French papist adherents, to whom it was chiefly applied; it was likewise bandied about in declarations alternately issued on the eve of the war by the Parliament and the King, the latter speaking of it more than once as a word much in disfavour. Charles, when the battle of Edgehill had been fought, elaborately accuses his antagonists—"pretenders to peace and charity"—of a hateful attempt "to render all persons of honour, courage, and reputation, odious to the common people under the style of *Cavaliers*, insomuch as the highways and villages have not been safe for gentlemen to pass through without violence or affront." Even in the very earliest popular songs on the King's side, the word has not the place it afterwards assumed, and one meets with Royalist poets of a comparatively sober vein,—

"Who neither love for fashion nor for fear,
As far from Roundhead as from Cavalier."

D'Ewes's earliest uses of the word, in his MS. journal, occur under 10th January, and March 4th, 1641-2, and 3d June, 1642. In the first he is speaking of parties who had been suspiciously entering the Tower; in the second, of the Cavaliers at Whitehall who wounded the citizens; and in the last of the King's party in Yorkshire.

Of the word *Roundhead*, on the other hand, and the mixed fear and hatred it represented and provoked, decidedly the most characteristic example is furnished by the ever quaint and entertaining Bishop Hacket, who tells a story of a certain worthy and honest Vicar of Hampshire who always (in such a manner as to evade the notice of one section of his hearers while he secretly pleased the other) changed one verse in the last verse of the Te Deum—"O Lord, in thee have I trusted, *let me never be a Roundhead*!" William Lilly, however (*Monarchy or no Monarchy in England*, edit. 1651), referring to tumults of which he was an eye-witness, describes Puritans to have received the nickname as follows: "In the general, they were very honest men and well-meaning: some particular fools, or others, perhaps, now and then got in amongst them, greatly to the disadvantage of the more sober. They were modest in their apparel, but not in their language; they had the hair of their heads very few of them longer than their ears; whereupon, it came to pass that those who usually with their cries attended at Westminster (Whitehall), were by a nickname called *Roundheads*. The Courtiers[Pg 328] again, having long hair and locks, and always swordes, at last were called by these men *Cavaliers*: and so, so few of the vulgar knowing the sense of the word Cavalier."—Notes to Forster's *Arrest of the Five Members*.

Swift, regarding Cavalier in the reproachful sense, says: "Each party grows proud of that appellation which their adversaries at first intended as a reproach: of this sort were the Guelfs, and Ghibelines, Huguenots, and Cavaliers."

Nevertheless, Cavalier was formerly an ordinary English term for a horse-soldier. Kersey gives it as "a Sword-gentleman, a brave Warrior."

Nares gives it: "Cavalero, or Cavalier. Literally a Knight; but, as the persons of chief fashion and gaiety were knights, any gallant was so distinguished. Hence it became a term for the officers of the Court party, in Charles I.'s wars, the gaiety of whose appearance was strikingly opposed to the austerity and sourness of the opposite order." *Glossary*, New Edit. 1859.

In the Roundhead accounts of the period are details of the contests and assaults that were continually made between the years 1648 and 1658 upon the Roundheads *abroad*, for *at home* the Cavaliers were too weak to indulge frequently in such manifestations of party feelings.

[Pg 329]

THE EVELYNS AT WOTTON.

It has been well observed of the Evelyn family, that "rarely do we read of people who so admirably combined a love of rural life with literature." Studious retirement, not isolation, was what John Evelyn sought; and nowhere did he so delightfully enjoy his tastes as at Wotton House or Place in Surrey. This "great Virtuoso," as Aubrey called him, has left us the following account of his family, and of their first settlement at Wotton:—"We have not been at Wotton (purchased of one Owen, a great rich man) above 160 years. My great grandfather came from Long Ditton (the seat now of Sir Edward Eveylin), where we had been long before; and to Long Ditton from Harrow-on-the-Hill; and many years before that, from Evelyn, near Tower Castle, Shropshire. There are of our name in France and Italy, written *Ivelyn*, *Avelin*: and in old deeds I find *Avelyn*, alias *Evelyn*. One of our name was taken prisoner at the battle of Agincourt. When the Duchess of Orleans came to Dover to see the King [Charles II.], one of our name (whose family derives itself from Lusignan, king of Cyprus) claimed relation to us. We have in our family a tradition of a great sum of money, that had been given for the ransom of a French lord, with which a great estate was purchased; but these things are all mystical."

Wotton House, placed in a valley south-west of Dorking, though really[Pg 330] upon a part of Leith Hill, was first erected in the reign of Queen Elizabeth. Here, on October 31, 1620, was born John Evelyn, "*Sylva* Evelyn," as he was called from the title of his valuable work on Forest-trees. When four years old, he was taught at the porch of Wotton Church. He then learnt Latin in a school at Lewes; whence his father proposed to send him to Eton, but he was terrified at the reported severity of the discipline there, and he was again sent to Lewes, which he "afterwards a thousand times deplored." In 1636 he was admitted to the Middle Temple; whence he removed to Balliol College, Oxford. He returned to London in 1640; but on the death of his father he relinquished all thoughts of legal practice.

Mr. Evelyn, thus become his own master, purposed a life of studious seclusion, and actually commenced making a kind of hermitage at Wotton, at that period the seat of his eldest brother. The park is watered by a winding stream, and is backed by a magnificent range of beech-woods: the goodly oaks were cut down by John Evelyn's grandfather, and birch has taken the place of beech in many cases; but we trace to this day Evelyn's hollies, "a *viretum* all the year round;" and the noble planting of the author of *Sylva*, who describes the house as "large and ancient, suitable to those hospitable times, and so sweetly environed with delicious streams and venerable woods. It has rising grounds, meadows, woods, and water in abundance.... I should speak much of the gardens, fountains, and groves that adorne it, were they not generally known to be amongst the most natural (until this later and universal luxury of the whole nation, since abounding in such expenses), the most magnificent that England afforded, and which, indeed, gave one of the[Pg 331] first examples of that elegancy since so much in vogue, and followed in the managing of their waters, and other ornaments of that nature."

Evelyn, by whom, in his brother's lifetime, the chief improvements in these grounds were directed, thus speaks of their origin in his *Diary*, under the date 1643, after the disastrous contest had commenced between the King and the Parliament:—"Resolving to possess myself in some quiet, if it might be, in a time of so great jealousy, I built, by my brother's permission, a *study*, made a *fish-pond*, and an *island*, and some other solitudes and retirements at Wotton; which gave the first occasion to those water-works and gardens which afterwards succeeded them."

Further alterations were made in 1652, and are thus described:—"I went with my brother Evelyn to Wotton to give him what directions I was able about his garden, which he was now desirous to put into some forme; but for which he was to remove a mountaine overgrowne with huge trees and thicket, with a moate within ten yards of the house. This my brother immediately attempted, and that without greate coste; for more than a hundred yards south, by digging down the mountaine, and flinging it into a rapid streame, it not only carried away the sand, &c., but filled up the moate, and levelled that noble area, where now the garden and fountaine is."

In 1641, Evelyn, tired of this seclusion, made a tour in France and the Netherlands, in which he appears to have gathered from observation such knowledge of Gardening as led him into its systematic study. He describes the Tuileries as rarely contrived for privacy, shade, or company; and he specially describes a labyrinth of cypress, with an artificial echo, "redoubling the words distinctly, and never without[Pg 332] some fair nymph singing to it." "Standing at one of the focuses, which is under a tree, or little cabinet of hedges, the voice seems to descend from the clouds; at another, as if it was underground." He tells us, too, of the curious garden of the Archbishop of Paris, at St. Cloud, with a Mount Parnassus, and a grotto, or "shell-house," on the top of the hill, the walls painted with the Muses, many statues placed about it, and within, "divers water-works, and contrivances to wet the spectators," reminding one of the famous copper-tube willow-tree at Chatsworth. Evelyn speaks of the Luxembourg Gardens as a paradise, where the Duke of Orleans kept tortoises in great numbers. The young traveller was charmed with the gardens of Italy; and at Padua he bought, for winter provision, three thousand weight of grapes, and pressed his own wine, which proved excellent.

Faithful to the Crown, Mr. Evelyn (who had become a volunteer in an English regiment serving in Flanders) joined the King's army at Brentford; but that he had not the temperament of a hero we may judge from the fact that, on the day before the battle of Edgehill was fought, after seeing Portsmouth delivered up to Sir William Waller, "he was able to make a careful archæological survey of the city of Winchester, calmly noting its castle, church, school, and King Arthur's Round Table." Knowing this characteristic trait, we are not surprised that he left his distracted country for the pleasures of foreign travel. On returning from Italy he visited Paris, and at the English Embassy met his future wife, the daughter of the Ambassador, Sir Richard Browne. He married her when she was little more than fourteen, and some months afterwards left her, as he admits, "still very young," under the appropriate care[Pg 333] of her mother, whilst he transacted business in England. The Prince de Condé besieged Paris, and a year and a half elapsed before Evelyn rejoined his wife.

Upon their return to England, they took up their abode at Sayes Court, the property of Sir Richard Browne, whose estate had been considerably curtailed during the Commonwealth. It was wholly unadorned. Here, from a field of one hundred acres in pasture, Evelyn formed a garden, which was an exemplar of his *Sylva*, with a hedge of holly, 400 feet long, 9 feet high, and 5 feet thick. He began immediately to set out an oval garden, which was "the beginning of all the succeeding gardens, walks, groves, enclosures, and plantations there;" and he planted an orchard, "new moon, wind west." Evelyn next planned a royal garden to comprehend "knots, trayle-work, parterres, compartments, borders, banks, and embossments, labyrinths, dedals, cabinets, cradles, close-walks, galleries, pavilions, porticoes, lanterns, and other relievos of topiary and hortular architecture; fountains, cascades, piscines, rocks, grotts, cryptæ, mounts, precipices, and ventiducts; gazon-theatres, artificial echoes, automate and hydraulic music."

When Evelyn left Sayes to pass the remainder of his days at Wotton, he let the former estate, first to Admiral Benbow, and next to the Czar Peter, to be near the King's dockyard, (through the wall of which a doorway was broken), that he might learn shipbuilding, but the Czar and his retinue damaged the house and gardens to the extent of 150*l*. in three weeks. A portion of the Victualling-yard now occupies the place of Evelyn's shady walks and trim hedges; on the site of the manor-house stands the parish workhouse of Dieptford and Stroud; and an adjoining[Pg 334] thoroughfare is named Evelyn-street.

Evelyn may have been misled in ornamental gardening by the taste of his age, but there was nothing to mislead him in that useful branch of the art which supplies the table with its luxuries, and which in his time received considerable improvement. Here we may mention that in 1664 Evelyn published the first Gardeners' Almanack, containing directions for the employment of each month. This was dedicated to Cowley, and drew from him, in acknowledgment, one of his best pieces, entitled *The Garden*; in the prefix to which he says:—"I never had any other desire so strong, and so like to covetousness, as that one which I have had always, that I might be master at last of a small house and large garden, with very moderate conveniences joined to them, and there dedicate the remainder of my life only to the culture of them, and the study of nature."

In 1694, Mr. Evelyn went to Wotton, with his brother George. In 1696-7, he says:—"I am planting an evergreen grove here to an old house ready to drop." In the great storm of 1703, above 2,000 goodly oaks were blown down. The woods of Wotton have since suffered greatly from high winds, particularly in November 1837, when many hundred trees were laid low during a violent storm.

In his *Sylva*, Evelyn thus deplores the former devastation: "Methinks that I still hear, sure I am that I feel, the *dismal groans* of our forests, when that late dreadful Hurricane, happening on the 26th of November, 1703, subverted as many thousands of goodly Oaks, prostrating the trees, laying them in ghastly postures, like whole regiments fallen in battle by the sword of the conqueror, and crushing all that grew beneath them. Myself had 2,000 blown down; several of which, torn up by[Pg 335] their fall, raised mounds of earth, near 20 feet high, with great stones intangled among the roots and rubbish, and this almost within sight of my dwelling;—now no more Wotton [Wood-town], stripped and naked, and almost ashamed to own its name."

In the *Diary*, the same calamity is thus noticed: "The effects of the Hurricane and tempest of wind, rain, and lightning thro' all the nation, especially London, were very dismal. Many houses demolished, and people killed. As to my own losses, the submersion of woods and timber, both ornamental and valuable, through my whole estate, and about my house, the woods crowning the garden mount, and growing along the Park meadow, the damage to my own dwelling, farms, and outhouses, is almost tragical, not to be parallel'd with anything happening in our age. I am not able to describe it, but submit to the pleasure of Almighty God."

Notwithstanding these losses, Evelyn's brother would not depart from the œconomy and hospitality of the old house, but, "*more veterum*, kept a Christmas in which they had not fewer than 300 bumpkins every holiday."

We find recorded among the Curiosities of the place, an oaken plank "of prodigious amplitude," cut out of a tree which grew on this estate, and was felled by Evelyn's grandfather's orders. Its dimensions, when "made a pastry-board" at Wotton, were more than five feet in breadth, nine feet and a half in length, and six inches in thickness; and it had been "abated by one foot," to suit it to the size of the room wherein it was placed.

Upon the death of his brother, in 1699, without any surviving male[Pg 336] issue, John Evelyn became possessor of the paternal estates. Wotton House, built of fine red brick, has been enlarged by various members of the Evelyn family. Hence the absence of uniformity in the plan of the house, and within our recollection it has parted with many of its olden features. The apartments are, however, convenient, and realize the comforts of an English gentleman's proper house and home. An etching by John Evelyn shows the mansion in 1653.

Through the valley at Wotton winds a rivulet which was formerly of much importance. Evelyn, in a letter to Aubrey, dated 8th of February, 1675, says that "on the stream near his house formerly stood many powder-mills, erected by his ancestors, who were the very first that brought that invention into England; before which we had all our powder from Flanders." He gives an account of one of these mills blowing up, which broke a beam, fifteen inches in diameter, at Wotton Place; and states that one standing lower down towards Sheire, on blowing up, "shot a piece of timber through a cottage, which took off a poor woman's head, as she was spinning." Besides these mills, were brass, fulling, and hammering mills.

The Evelyns possess much land in the adjoining parish of Abinger; and the seat of the Scarletts, Abinger Hall, gave the title to Lord Chief Baron Scarlett. Originally, it was a small dwelling at the foot of the Downs, belonging to the Dibble family, of whom it was purchased in the reign of George II. by Catherine Forbes, Countess of Donegal, who was the daughter of Arthur, Earl of Granard, and had the honour of being complimented by Dean Swift, in the following lines:—[Pg 337]

"Unerring Heaven, with bounteous hand,
Has form'd a Model for your Land,
Whom Love bestow'd, with every grace,
The glory of the Granard race;
Now destined by the powers Divine
The blessing of another Line.
Then, would you paint a matchless Dame,
Whom you'd consign to endless fame,
Invoke not Cytherea's aid,
Nor borrow from the Blue-eyed Maid,
Nor need you on the Graces call;
Take qualities from DONEGAL."

Abinger Church is of considerable antiquity, and has a higher site than any other church in the county: indeed, Aubrey conjectures the parish to be named from *Abin*, an eminence, or rising ground. The church was carefully restored in 1857. The west end is of the Norman period; the nave Early English; the altar has sedilia, and formerly had a piscina; and on the north side is a chancel belonging to the Wotton estate, and restored at the expense of Mr. Evelyn: here is a small organ. The altar-window of three lights has been filled with painted glass by O'Connor, a very meritorious work. In the churchyard in a vault are interred Lord Chief Baron Abinger, and his first wife: to the latter there is a marble monument on the inner wall of the chancel. His Lordship married secondly the widow of the Rev. Henry John Ridley, a descendant of Bishop Ridley, the Protestant martyr; and among the relics of that devout churchman which descended to Lady Abinger, was the chair in which the Bishop used to study.

On the east side of the churchyard is a small green, on which are stocks and a whipping-post; but these, to the honour of the parish, are believed never to have been used.

There was a Mill at Abinger at the time of the Domesday Survey; and it[Pg 338] is not improbable that the present corn and flour mill, at a short distance from the road, may occupy the same site. To return to Wotton House.

The interior of the old place, with its oddly-planned rooms, its quaint carvings, its pictures, more especially the portraits of the Evelyn family, is a most enjoyable nook. The author of *Sylva*, by Kneller, will be recognised as the original of the engraved frontispiece to Evelyn's *Diary*, by economy of printing now become a household book. Among the Wotton relics, of special historic interest, are the Prayer-book used by Charles I. on the scaffold; a pinch of the powder laid by Guido Fawkes and his fellow-conspirators to blow up the Parliament; a curious account, in John Evelyn's hand, of the mode in which the Chancellor Clarendon transacted business with his royal master; several letters of John Evelyn, and his account (recently found) of the expense of his building Milton House, which occupied four years: the house remains to this day. The library of printed books and pamphlets is curious and extensive. Evelyn was a most laborious annotator, never employing an amanuensis: among his MSS. is a Bible in three volumes, the margins filled with closely-written notes.

John Evelyn died at his house (called *the Head*) in Dover-street, Piccadilly, Feb. 27, 1705-6. His remains were interred in Wotton Church: his lady surviving him until 1708-9; when, dying, in her seventy-fourth year, she was buried near him in the chancel. It was Evelyn's wish to have been interred in the Laurel Grove, planted by him at Wotton: this wish was expressed in his Will: "otherwise," he says, "let my grave be in the Corner of the Dormitory of my Ancestors." This was done; and in[Pg 339] digging the new Vault was found "an entire skeleton, of gigantick stature."

In all the characters of child, wife, mother, and mistress, Mrs. Evelyn, quiet and unassuming as she was, shone forth pre-eminently. Her trials were many and heavy; her heart was torn with the death of child after child, some in infancy, some in ripe age when they had grown to be the pride and stay of their parents. All died, one by one, out of that numerous progeny, till only a daughter, Mrs. Draper, was left, and the bereaved pair were alone in their old age in the wide old mansion at Wotton. Nothing can exceed the touching pathos of those few words in Mrs. Evelyn's will, where, after desiring that her coffin might be placed near to that of her dear husband, whose death preceded hers by three years, she adds:—"Whose love and friendship I was happy in, fifty-eight years nine months; but by God's providence left a desolate widow, the 27th day of February, 1705, in the seventy-first year of my age."

Mrs. Evelyn had acquired the more polished manners of French society without losing her naturally simple tastes. That she cannot have formed a favourable opinion of English refinement we know from the contrast which her husband draws between the two countries in his *Characters of England*, written when they returned from the Continent.

Mrs. Evelyn was an experienced housewife, and had a special eye "to the care of cakes, stilling, and sweetmeats, and such useful things." "The hospitality of Sayes Court, which was accepted by royalty and extended to *savans*, divines, and men of letters, was not withheld from the country neighbours at Deptford." Certainly, her own words depict her[Pg 340]practice, for she considered "the care of children's education, observing a husband's commands, assisting the sick, relieving the poor, and being serviceable to her friends, of sufficient weight to employ the most improved capacities." That Mrs. Evelyn had close insight into character and great nicety of judgment, we learn from her contemporaries, as also that her "great discernment and wit" were never abused. Ever sedate and kindly, she bore a succession of family bereavements with Christian resignation.

At Wotton, many curious memorials remain. Adjacent to the house are the conservatory, flower-garden, the former stored with curious exotic and native plants and flowers, and the latter embellished with a fountain, a temple, or colonnade, and an elevated turfed mount, cut into terraces; and here, enclosed within a brick wall, is all that remains of Evelyn's flower-garden, which was to have formed one of the principal objects in his "Elysium Britannicum." His *Diary* is well known; and his *Sylva* is a beautiful and enduring memorial of his amusements, his occupations, and his studies, his private happiness and his public virtues. Many millions of timber-trees have been propagated and planted at the instigation and by the sole direction of that book—one of the few books in the world which completely effected what it was designed to do. While Britain [says D'Israeli the elder] retains her awful situation among the nations of Europe, the *Sylva* of Evelyn will endure with her triumphant oaks. It was an author in his studious retreat, who, casting a prophetic eye on the age we live in, secured the late victories of our naval sovereignty. Inquire at the Admiralty how the fleets of Nelson have been constructed, and they can tell you that it was with the oaks which the[Pg 341] genius of Evelyn planted.

Persons who are familiar with the picturesque environs of Dorking will remember Milton House, which was built at Evelyn's expense. It is now called Milton Court, and is about a mile west of the town. It is of red brick, and has a grand staircase with massive supports and balusters, a great hall, and many noble rooms. The house was let some years since in tenements to poor families. It has since been restored and furnished in the style of the period. Its history has a literary interest. For nearly a quarter of a century it was the abode of Jeremiah Markland, a model critic "for modesty, candour, literary honesty, and courteousness to other scholars." He will be remembered as one of the eminent Grecians of Christ's Hospital. He lived in bachelorship at Milton Court, among his books; or, as his pupil, Strode, tells us, "In 1752, being grown old, and having, moreover, long and painful fits of the gout, he was glad to find, what his inclination and infirmities, which made him unfit for the world and company, had for a long time led him to—a very private place of retirement, near Dorking, in Surrey." In this sequestered spot Markland saw little company: his walks were almost confined to the garden at the back of the house; and he described himself, in 1755, to be "as much out of the way of hearing as of getting." We have more than once enjoyed the elysium of the old scholar's garden. But troubles came to disturb his peace. Markland had not the rambling old house to himself. His landlady, the widow Rose, got into a lawsuit with her son, when Jeremiah distressed himself to aid the widow in the suit, which she lost; and after that Markland spent his whole fortune in relieving the[Pg 342] distresses of the Rose family. This led him to accept an annuity from his former pupil, Strode. Markland died at Milton Court in 1776, in his eighty-third year; and Strode placed a brass plate in the chancel of Dorking Church in memory of the learning and virtue of Markland. He left his books and papers to Dr. Heberden. The story of old Jeremiah's charity is very naïve:—"Poor as I am," said he, "I would rather have pawned the coat on my back than have left the afflicted good woman and her children to starve,"—an episode of charity and friendship which has its sweet uses.

There are two ancient objects at Milton. The water-mill, adjoining the green, is believed to be that mentioned in the survey of the manor, in Domesday book; and on Milton-heath, upon an elevated spot, is a *Tumulus*, now distinguished by a clump of firs; and near it is *War*-field. The name of the adjoining estate, Bury Hill, makes us, as Miss Hawkins observes, "seek, in our walks, the very footmarks of the Roman soldier."

[Pg 343]

LORD BOLINGBROKE AT BATTERSEA.

his parish and manor, three miles south-west of London, on the Surrey bank of the Thames, appertained, from a very early period, to the Abbey of St. Peter at Westminster; and is conjectured, by Lysons, to have been therefrom named, in the Conqueror's Survey, Patricsey, which, in the Saxon, is Peter's water, or river; since written Battrichsey, Battersey, and Battersea. It passed to the Crown, at the dissolution of religious houses: in 1627 it was granted to the St. John family, in whose possession the property remained till 1763.

Here, in a spacious mansion, eastward of the church, was born, October 1, 1678, Henry St. John, Viscount Bolingbroke, one of the brilliant lights of the Augustan age of literature in England. Here Pope spent most of his time with Bolingbroke, after the return of the latter from his seven years' exile;[79] and his house became also the resort of Swift, Arbuthnot, Thomson, Mallet, and other leading contemporary men of[Pg 344] genius. Lord Marchmont was living with Lord Bolingbroke, at Battersea, when he discovered that Mr. Allen, of Bath, had printed 500 copies of the *Essay on a Patriot King* from the copy which Bolingbroke had presented to Pope—six copies only were printed. Thereupon, Lord Marchmont sent Mr. Gravenkop for the whole cargo, who carried them out in a waggon, and the books were burnt on the lawn in the presence of Lord Bolingbroke. Thenceforth he mostly resided at Battersea from 1742 until his death in 1751. He sunk under the dreadful malady beneath which he had long lingered—a cancer in the face—which he bore with exemplary fortitude; "a fortitude," says Lord Brougham, "drawn from the natural resources of his mind, and, unhappily, not aided by the consolation of any religion; for having early cast off the belief in revelation, he had substituted in its stead a dark and gloomy naturalism, which even rejected those glimmerings of hope as to futurity not untasted by the wiser of the heathens."

Bolingbroke, with his second wife, niece of Madame de Maintenon, lie in the family vault in St. Mary's Church, where there is an elegant monument by Roubiliac, with busts of the great lord and his lady; the epitaphs on both were written by Lord Bolingbroke: that upon himself is still extant, in his own handwriting, in the British Museum: "Here lies Henry St. John, in the reign of Queen Anne Secretary of State, and Viscount Bolingbroke; in the days of King George I. and King George II.,[Pg 345] something more and better."

The greater part of Bolingbroke House was taken down in 1778. In the wing of the mansion, left standing, a parlour of round form, and lined with cedar, was long pointed out as the apartment in which Pope composed his *Essay on Man*; it is said to have been called "Pope's Parlour." The walls may still be seen, but they support a new roof, and can only be distinguished from the rest of the building by their circular form. The mansion was very extensive—forty rooms on a floor.

Upon part of the site was erected a *horizontal mill*, by Captain Hooper, who also built a similar one at Margate. It consisted of a circular wheel, with large boards or vanes fixed parallel to its axis, and arranged at equal distances from each other. Upon these vanes the wind could act, so as to blow the wheel round. But if it were to act upon the vanes at both sides of the wheel at once, it could not, of course, turn it round; hence one side of the wheel must be sheltered, while the other was submitted to the full action of the wind. For this purpose it was enclosed in a large cylindrical framework, with doors or shutters on all sides, to open and admit the wind, or to shut and stop it. If all the shutters on one side were open, whilst all those on the opposite side were closed, the wind acting with undiminished force on the vanes at one side, whilst the opposite vanes are under shelter, turned the mill round; but whenever the wind changed, the disposition of the blinds must be altered, to admit the wind to strike upon the vanes of the wheel in the direction of a tangent to the circle in which they moved.—(Dr. Paris's *Philosophy in Sport*.) This mill resembled a gigantic packing-case, which gave rise to an odd story, that when the Emperor of Russia was in England, in 1814, he took a fancy to Battersea[Pg 346] Church, and determined to carry it off to Russia, and had this large packing-case made for it; but as the inhabitants refused to let the church be carried away, the case remained on the spot where it was deposited.

This horizontal air-mill served as a landmark for many miles round: the proprietor was Mr. Hodgson, a maltster and distiller. It was visited by Sir Richard Phillips in his *Morning's Walk from London to Kew*, in 1813, who says: "The mill, its elevated shaft, its vanes, and weather or wind-boards, curious as they would have been on any other site, lost their interest on premises once the residence of the illustrious Bolingbroke, and the resort of the philosophers of his day. In ascending the winding flights of its tottering galleries, I could not help wondering at the caprice of events which had converted the dwelling of Bolingbroke into a malting-house and a mill. This house, once sacred to philosophy and poetry, long sanctified by the residence of the noblest genius of his age, honoured by the frequent visits of Pope, and the birthplace of the immortal *Essay on Man*, is now appropriated to the lowest uses. The house of Bolingbroke become a windmill! The spot on which the *Essay on Man* was concocted and produced, converted into a distillery of pernicious spirits! Such are the lessons of time! Such are the means by which an eternal agency sets at nought the ephemeral importance of man! But yesterday, this spot was the resort, the hope, and the seat of enjoyment of Bolingbroke, Pope, Swift, Arbuthnot, Monson, Mallet, and all the contemporary genius of England—yet a few whirls of the earth round the sun, the change of a figure in the date of the year, and the group have vanished; while I behold hogs and horses,[Pg 347] malt-bags and barrels, stills and machinery!

"'Alas!' said I to the occupier, 'and have these things become the representatives of more human genius than England may ever witness on one spot again—have you thus satirised the transitory state of humanity—do you thus become a party with the bigoted enemies of that philosophy which was personified in a Bolingbroke or a

Pope?' 'No,' he rejoined, 'I love the name and character of Bolingbroke, and I preserve the house as well as I can with religious veneration: I often smoke my pipe in Mr. Pope's parlour, and think of him with due respect as I walk the part of the terrace opposite his room.' He then conducted me to this interesting parlour, which is of brown polished oak,[80] with a grate and ornaments of the age of George the First; and before its window stood the portion of the terrace upon which the malt-house had not encroached, with the Thames moving majestically under its walls.

"'In this room,' I exclaimed, 'the *Essay on Man* was probably planned, discussed, and written!' Mr. Hodgson assured me this had always been called 'Pope's Room,' and he had no doubt it was the apartment usually occupied by that great poet, in his visits to his friend Bolingbroke. Other parts of the original house remain, and are occupied and kept in good order. He told me, however, that this was but a wing of the mansion, which extended, in Lord Bolingbroke's time, to the churchyard, and is now appropriated to the malting-house and its warehouses."

Sir Richard met with an ancient inhabitant of Battersea, a Mrs.[Pg 348] Gilliard, a pleasant and intelligent woman, who well remembered Lord Bolingbroke; that he used to ride out every day in his chariot, and had a black patch on his cheek, with a large wart over his eyebrow. She was then but a girl, but she was taught to look upon him with veneration as a great man. As, however, he spent little in the place, and gave little away, he was not much regarded by the people of Battersea. Sir Richard mentioned to her the names of several of Lord Bolingbroke's contemporaries, but she recollected none, except that of Mallet, whom she said she had often seen walking about in the village while he was visiting at Bolingbroke House.[81]

In the first volume of the *Diaries and Correspondence of the Right Hon. George Rose*, we find the following entry respecting the treachery of Mallet:—"It appears by a letter of Lord Bolingbroke's, dated in 1740, from Angeville, that he had actually written some Essays dedicated to the Earl of Marchmont, of a very different tendency from his former works. These Essays, on his death, fell into the hands of Mr. Mallet, his executor, who had, at the latter end of his life, acquired a decided influence over him, and they did not appear among his lordship's works published by Mallet;[82] nor have they been seen or heard of since. From whence it must be naturally conjectured, that they were destroyed by the[Pg 349] latter, from what reason cannot now be known; possibly, to conceal from the world the change, such as it was, in his lordship's sentiments in the latter end of his life, to avoid the discredit to his former works. In which respect he might have been influenced either by a regard for the noble Viscount's consistency, or by a desire not to impair the pecuniary advantage he expected from the publication of his lordship's works."

Upon this, the Editor of the *Diaries*, the Rev. Leveson Vernon Harcourt, notes: "The letter to Lord Marchmont here referred to, has a note appended to it by Sir George Rose, the editor of the *Marchmont Papers*, who takes a very different view of its contents from his father. He gravely remarks, that as the posthumous disclosure of Lord Bolingbroke's inveterate hostility to Christianity lays open to the view the bitterness as the extent of it, so the manner of that disclosure precludes any doubt of the earnestness of his desire to give the utmost efficiency and publicity to that hostility, as soon as it could safely be done; that is, as soon as death could shield him against responsibility to man. Sir George saw plainly enough that when he promised in those Essays to vindicate religion against divinity and God against man, he was retracting all that he had occasionally said in favour of Christianity; he was upholding the religion of Theism against the doctrines of the Bible, and the God of nature against the revelation of God to man."

It is painful to reflect upon this prostration of a splendid intellect; and we are but slightly relieved by Lord Chesterfield's statement, in one of his Letters, published by Lord Mahon, in his edition of Chesterfield's *Works* (ii. 450), that "Bolingbroke only doubted, and by no means rejected, a future state." We know that Bolingbroke denied to[Pg 350] Pope his disbelief of the moral attributes of God, of which Pope told his friends with great joy. How ungrateful a return for this "excessive friendliness" was the indignation which Bolingbroke expressed at the priest having attended Pope in his last moments![83]

It is now, we believe, admitted on all hands that Christianity has not found a very formidable opponent in Bolingbroke, and that his objections, for the most part, only betray his own half-learning. Lord Brougham, whose touching remark we have already quoted, concludes his sketch of Lord Bolingbroke with this eloquent summing up: "Such was Bolingbroke, and as such he must be regarded by impartial posterity, after the violence of party has long subsided, and the view is no more intercepted either by the rancour of political enmity, or by the partiality of adherents, or by the fondness of friendship. Such, too, is Bolingbroke when the gloss of trivial accomplishments is worn off by time, and the lustre of genius itself has faded beside the simple, translucent light of virtue. The contemplation is not without its uses. The glare of talents and success is apt to obscure defects, which are incomparably more mischievous than any intellectual powers can be either useful or admirable. Nor can a lasting renown—a renown that alone deserves to be courted of a rational being—ever be built upon any foundations save those which are laid in an honest heart and a firm purpose, both conspiring to work out the good of mankind. That renown will be as imperishable as it is pure."[84]

Among the memorials of the Bolingbrokes, in Battersea Church, is the[Pg 351] altar-window, filled with old stained glass, preserved from the former church, and executed at the expense of the St. Johns. It includes portraits of Henry VII., his grandmother, the Lady Margaret Beauchamp, and Queen Elizabeth; together with numerous shields of arms, showing the alliances of the family.

York House, at Battersea, the mansion of Booth, Archbishop of York, who died in 1480, and bequeathed it to his successors in the See, was mostly taken down some sixty years ago. Archbishop Holgate was one of the few prelates who resided here; he was imprisoned and deprived by Queen Mary for being a married man, and lost much property by illegal seizure. In Strype's *Life of Cranmer*, p. 308, it is stated that the officers who were employed to apprehend the Archbishop rifled his house at Battersea, and took away from thence 300*l.* of gold coin; 1600 ounces of plate; a mitre of fine gold, set with very fine diamonds, sapphires, and balists, other good stones and pearls; some very valuable rings; and the Archbishop's seal and signet.

There was long a tradition at Battersea that some ancient walls remaining there were a portion of the residence of the father of Queen Anne Boleyn. It appears from the monument to Queen Elizabeth, in Battersea Church, that the Boleyns were related to the St. Johns. Upon this Sir Richard Phillips contends that at York House, above named, resided Wolsey, as Archbishop of York. "Here Henry VIII. first saw Anne Boleyn; and here that scene took place which Shakspeare records in his play of Henry VIII.; and which he described truly, because he wrote it for Elizabeth, the daughter of Anne Boleyn, within fifty years of the event, and must himself have known living witnesses of its verity. Hence it becomes more than probable, that Sir Thomas Boleyn actually resided in the vicinity, and that his daughter was accidentally among the guests at that princely entertainment. I know it is contended that this interview took place at York House, Whitehall; but Shakspeare makes the King come by water; and York House, Battersea, was, beyond all doubt, a residence of Wolsey, and is provided with a creek from the Thames, for the evident purpose of facilitating in the course by water. Besides, the owner informed me, that a few years since he had pulled down a superb room, called 'the ball-room,' the panels of which were curiously painted, and the divisions silvered. He also stated that the room had a dome and a richly-ornamented ceiling, and that he once saw an ancient print, representing the first interview of Henry VIII. with Anne Boleyn, in which the room was portrayed exactly like the one that, in modernizing his house, he had found it necessary to destroy."

THE LAST OF EPPING FOREST.

n the twelfth edition of *The Ambulator*, edited nearly half a century ago by that trustworthy topographer, Mr. E. W. Brayley, under "Epping Forest," we read "a plan for the inclosure of the Forest has been recently projected." And this plan has been slowly but surely put into execution; the inclosures having been so numerous that little remains of this charming forest district, with its verdant glades, secluded dells, thickets, majestic oaks, and sinking vistas of enchanting wilderness and cheerful landscape, to gladden the hearts of the toilers in the vast metropolis.

The Forest remains where it was. Brayley describes it as a royal chase, extending from Epping almost to London, anciently a very extensive district; and, under the name of the Forest of Essex, including a great part of the county. It had afterwards the name of Waltham Forest, which it long since yielded to its present appellation. To this Forest, that of Hainault, which lies to the south-east, was once, it is supposed, an appendage: it was formerly styled "the Queen's Forest," and it possesses more beautiful scenery than, perhaps, any other forest in England. The Crown possesses the whole of the rights over Hainault, and the encroachments are not nearly so numerous here as in Epping Forest, where[Pg 354] the Crown has only certain rights—the right of vert and venison. The loss of the picturesque features of wild expanse of woodlands, heath, and mosses; of vast masses of umbrageous tree-tops, and little patches of cultivation—here and there a little town, sending up its fleecy smoke amidst the forest boughs—must excite concern amongst all who take interest in the amusements of the people. How truthfully has the isolated picture of forest life been sung:

"From age to age no tumult did arouse
The peaceful dwellers; there they lived and died,
Passing a dreamy life, diversified
By nought of novelty, save now and then
A horn, resounding through the forest glen,
Woke them as from a trance, and led them out
To catch a brief glimpse of the hunt's wild rout—
The music of the hounds; the tramp and rush
Of steeds and men;—and then a sudden hush
Left round the eager listeners; the deep mood
Of awful, dead, and twilight solitude,
Fallen again upon that forest vast."

The Forest remains where and as it was, save that invasions on the waste, and encroachments, have from time to time greatly restricted its extent; not so the city, for that has advanced, and meets the old liberty at half-way. Now the metropolis reaches to Bow, or nearly to Stratford, where the Forest commences; and there the road divides, one branch leading northward to Chigwell, the other eastward to Romford. In extent it reaches five miles from Ilford on the south, nearly to Abridge on the north, by four miles from Woodford-bridge on the west, to Havering-at-Bower on the east. Were the whole area of this scope one continuous chase, there would be some 12,000 acres; but from the[Pg 355]numberless excisions from, and appropriations of the liberty, the contents of the whole do not at present amount to 4,000 acres.

It appears that an Act of Parliament was passed (the 14th and 15th Vict.) for the disafforesting and inclosure of Hainault Forest; that on the 24th August, 1851, a commission was formed for the purpose: and summary execution was done upon 14,000 oak-trees, which had stood unmolested for centuries. This was preliminary to the utter clearance, parcelling out, and selling off of the whole domain.[85]

The signal advantage of Epping Forest over all other open spaces is that in it alone thousands can at the same time enjoy the country in its natural aspect in that privacy without which the country, as such, is no enjoyment at all. That the inhabitants of London highly appreciate this advantage is shown by the fact that thousands every fine day in the year pass by the Parks that are provided for them near their own doors, and travel weary miles to reach the fragment of the Forest that is left to them.

The case of Epping Forest is matter of dispute. There is an opinion entertained by persons whose opinions command respect that the lords of the several manors included within the precincts of Epping Forest are entitled to call for an inclosure of the portions of the Forest in which they are respectively interested, whenever they please; and that the Crown is not justified, on the ground of public advantage, in setting up its rights as an impediment to such inclosure.

The case as between the lords of the manor, the Crown, and the public appears to be this:—The Forest comprises the wastes of certain manors, over which, from time immemorial, the lords of these manors had the[Pg 356] accustomed rights of pasturage; the Crown had the forestal right of keeping deer in them, and for that purpose of keeping them uninclosed: and the general public had the common right of going upon them as uninclosed land. The lords of the manor are in the actual enjoyment of all the rights of property they ever had in the Forest, but they desire to acquire a species of property in it which has never hitherto belonged to them, and which is inconsistent with other existing rights. The right of the public to go upon the Forest land while it is in its present open condition has become one of transcendent importance; and the real question presented to the Crown is whether it shall cede its rights for the benefit of half-a-dozen persons who desire to acquire a valuable property to which they have no present title, or maintain them for the benefit of the large proportion of the British people who live in London and its vicinity. In short, it appears that the rights of the Crown and the public have not been maintained in Epping Forest, because the Government would not incur the expense of litigation.

To show how persons sometimes defeat the cause which they advocate, it may be mentioned that at a meeting held at the Bald-faced Stag, Buckhurst-hill, upon this Forest question, several speakers expatiated at great length on the injustice of excluding the working classes of the east end of London from the rural enjoyments of the Forest, owing to the inclosures made by the lords of the manor and other parties. It was, however, shown at the meeting that two gentlemen of the Committee had inclosed a very large portion of the Forest, parts that are the most picturesque and that were most resorted to by the London holiday folks;[Pg 357] but, alas! no more Forest remains in the once sylvan neighbourhood of Buckhurst-hill.

The reduction of Epping Forest began in the reign of King John, and was confirmed by Edward IV., when all that part of the Forest which lay to the north of the highway from Stortford to Colchester (very distant from the present boundaries) was disafforested. The Forest was further reduced; but the metes and bounds of it were finally determined in 1640. The office of Chief Forester for Essex was deemed highly honorary, and was generally bestowed on some illustrious person. The stewardship was also usually enjoyed by one of the nobility. It continued in the De Veres, Earls of Oxford, for many generations; but was taken from them by Edward IV., for their adherence to the Lancastrian party. On the accession of Henry VII., it was restored by grant to John, Earl of Oxford. The steward had the power to substitute a lieutenant, one riding-forester, and three yeoman-foresters, in the three bailiwicks of the Forest. He also had many lucrative privileges, and was Keeper of Havering-at-Bower, and of the house and park trees.

We remember, many years since, to have visited the Forest for the sake of inspecting the house known as *Queen Elizabeth's Hunting Lodge*, which stands about a mile west of the main road to Epping; and the most direct road to which, in the heart of the Forest, we found to be from about midway between the Bald-faced Stag Inn and the village of Loughton. The view from this point is of surpassing beauty and extent; whilst it is no wide stretch of conjecture to set down the ancient forest as nearly covering the entire county. The towns, villages, and seats which now stud the district, and the roads which intersect the[Pg 358] woody waste, may have been the work of a few centuries; inns and lodges would be among the earliest buildings for retainers, whose business it was to defend and preserve this royal chase, for the privilege of hunting here was confined to the Sovereign and his favourites. Again, those who flocked thither, with such privilege, would well repay the hospitalities of an inn, and "hosteller," even were we to leave out of the reckoning the boon companionship of foresters, and the debauched habits of marauders, who fattened by the infringement of the royal privilege, in wholesale deer-stealing for the London markets. We were told that in Epping churchyard is the tombstone of a follower, whose business it was to convey venison to the metropolis, but who, in one of his midnight returns, was shot by an unknown hand; the almost headless body being found on the road next morning.

The Lodge stands in the parish of Chingford,[86] about one mile from the village, and thus served the purpose of a manor-house, the courts being held here. Chingford Hall, the actual manor-house, is situated a short distance hence; but Mr. Lysons thinks it probable that the site of the ancient manor-house was that of the present Lodge. The manor was purchased in or about 1666, by Thomas Boothby, Esq., from whose family it descended by marriage to the Heathcotes. The Lodge consists of the[Pg 359] main building, a basement, and two floors,—and a building abutting upon it, chiefly occupied by the spacious staircase. The exterior has little of the air of antiquity comparatively with the interior. The basement is principally the kitchen, where the large projecting chimney, the olden fire-dogs, and cheerful wood fire, reminded us of "the rural life," if they carried us not back to

"Great Eliza's golden time."

The staircase is of surprising solidity: its width is about six feet; it is divided by six landings, with four stairs between each, and each stair or step consists of a solid oak sill. The first floor contains two chambers, one hung with tapestry in fine preservation, and the chimney opening has a flattened arch. The height of the first floor and basement has been sacrificed to the story above, which entirely consists of a large room, or hall, entered from the staircase by a low, wide doorway. The dimensions of the hall we take to be twenty-four feet wide, and forty-two feet high; its height reaches to the open roof, the tiles of which are merely hidden by rough plaster; and the sides of the room consist of massive timbers, filled in with plaster, and originally lit with four windows. The roof-tree, we should add, is supported by timbers which spring into two pointed arches, and render it probable that the original roof was of a different form as well as material from the present one. In this apartment were held the manorial courts; and on the plain plaster walls hung three large-sized whole length portraits of one of the Boothbys (lords of the manor), in infancy, accompanied by his brother, in boyhood, and in manhood. The timbers of the staircase sides and roof are massive, and spring into arched frames; and all the[Pg 360] doorways in the building have flattened arches.

Tradition reports the Lodge to have been a favourite hunting-seat of Queen Elizabeth. It was occupied, at the time of our visit, by the bailiff of the manor, who had lived there twenty years, and his father occupied the Lodge half a century before him. To the tradition was added, that Elizabeth was accustomed to ride upstairs on horseback, and alight at the door of the large room, upon a raised place, which is to this day called *the horse-block*. We confess the story savours of the marvellous; but the width and solidity, and many landings of the staircase, are in its favour; and, not many years previously, a wager of ten pounds was won by a sporting gentleman riding an untrained pony up the assigned route of the chivalrous Queen.

There are circumstances related which render it more than probable that the Lodge was fitted up for the reception of Elizabeth. That the Queen was extremely fond of the chase, and hunted at an advanced age, is a well-established fact. That she hunted in Epping Forest is nearly ascertained; for the Earl of Leicester once owned Nakedhall Hawke, or old Wansted House, in the neighbourhood: it is mentioned in a document of Richard II., and seems to have been the manorial residence. Here, in May 1578, Leicester entertained Queen Elizabeth four or five days, and one of the rooms in the mansion was called *the Queen's*. Again, in this mansion was solemnized Leicester's marriage with the Countess of Essex, Sept. 20, 1578, the Queen being then on a visit to Mr. Stonard, at Loughton, in the Forest; and old Wansted House is introduced in the background of a picture of Queen Elizabeth, in the collection at Welbeck.

Of the Queen's *hunting the hart* in Enfield Chase we have this[Pg 361] circumstantial record. Twelve ladies in white satin attended her on their ambling palfreys, and twenty yeomen clad in green. At the entrance to the forest she was met by fifty archers in scarlet boots and yellow caps, armed with gilded bows; one of whom presented to her a silver-headed arrow winged with peacock's feathers. The splendid show concluded, according to the established laws of the chase, by the offering of the knife to the Princess, as first lady on the field; and her *taking say* of the buck with her own fair and royal hand.

In addition to the Hunting Lodge, we found other memorials of the age of Elizabeth in the neighbourhood. Thus, the hill, or point, when we left the main road to cross the Forest to the Lodge, is to this day remembered as Buckhurst-hill, as may be reasonably supposed, from Sackville, Lord Buckhurst, the accomplished poet, and favoured flower of Elizabeth's court.

In conclusion, the Londoners have lost the Epping Hunt, and the "Common Hunt" no longer goes out; and the old Pumpmaker's Fair, which originated in a wayzgoose of beans and bacon, is no longer held around the oak of Fairlop; but let us not lose the Forest itself; else, of what service is our railway gain?

APPENDIX.

[Pg 362]

ANCIENT BRITISH DWELLINGS.

(*Pages* **1-7**.)

e have, says Sir Richard Colt Hoare, in his *Ancient Wiltshire*, "undoubted proof from history, and from existing remains, that the earliest habitations were pits, or slight excavations in the ground, covered and protected from the inclemency of the weather by boughs of trees or sods of turf." These dwellings usually formed villages, conveniently situated near streams or rivers, the habitations of the lords of the soil before the Roman occupation. Amongst the moorlands and wilds of Yorkshire, in spots where the spade and plough have not been in operation, upwards of forty British villages were described and inspected by Dr. Young, of Whitby. Many early dwellings are likewise to be met with in other parts of England; some sunk in the chalk, where cultivation has not entirely obliterated them, which is the case in the eastern counties. The large tumuli and barrows which remain, pertain to a much later era of our history; generally to the Roman and Saxon periods, when the use of bronze and iron became known.[87]

At a recent meeting of the Norwich Archæological Society, the members[Pg 363] made an excursion to Brandon and neighbourhood, and at Grime's Graves Mr. Manning read a paper on the Graves, in which he maintained that this irregularly-shaped cluster of holes are ancient British dwellings, forming the remains of an ancient town. Each hole was lined with a layer of stones, and, when inhabited, roofed over with boughs or grass. The term "graves" means pits or holes, and the name "Grime's" was probably derived from "Græme," the Saxon for witch, or rather for anything supernatural. Thus the term "Grime's Graves" meant "Witches' Work." After leaving Grime's Graves, the party examined the Devil's Dyke, a long and extensive fosse and bank, supposed to have been made by the Ancient Britons for military purposes.

www.ingramcontent.com/pod-product-compliance
Lightning Source LLC
LaVergne TN
LVHW040053080526
838202LV00045B/3614